Beginning with **Pauline Kael's** first collection of criticism, *I Lost it at the Movies,* in 1965, her books have offered a chronicle of contemporary filmmaking. She is the only movie critic to receive a National Book Award (for *Deeper Into Movies,* 1973). *Movie Love* is her twelfth book.

Also by Pauline Kael

MOVIE *Love*

Complete Reviews 1988–1991

PAULINE KAEL

A WILLIAM ABRAHAMS BOOK

PLUME

PLUME
Published by the Penguin Group
Penguin Books USA, Inc., 375 Hudson Street,
New York, New York 10014, U.S.A.
Penguin Books Ltd, 27 Wrights Lane,
London W8 5TZ, England
Penguin Books Australia Ltd, Ringwood,
Victoria, Australia
Penguin Books Canada Ltd, 2801 John Street,
Markham, Ontario, Canada L3R 1B4
Penguin Books (N.Z.) Ltd, 182–190 Wairau Road,
Auckland 10, New Zealand

Penguin Books Ltd, Registered Offices:
Harmondsworth, Middlesex, England

First published by Plume, an imprint of New American Library,
a division of Penguin Books USA Inc.
Simultaneously published in Dutton hardcover edition.

First Printing, September, 1991.
10 9 8 7 6 5 4 3 2 1

All the reviews in this book originally appeared in *The New Yorker* Magazine from the
years 1988, 1989, 1990 through the present.

All material in the book originally appeared in *The New Yorker*.

 REGISTERED TRADEMARK—MARCA REGISTRADA
LIBRARY OF CONGRESS CATALOGING-IN-PUBLICATION DATA:

Kael, Pauline.
   Movie love/Pauline Kael.
     p.   cm.
   "All material in this book originally appeared in the New Yorker"—
   —T.p. verso.
   "A William Abrahams book."
   ISBN 0-452-26635-1:
   1. Motion pictures—Reviews.   I. Title.
PN1995.K245 1991
791.43'75—dc20   91–8176
                                                                       CIP

Printed in the United States of America
Set in Garamond Light
Designed by Eve L. Kirch

Contents

Author's Note

What thou lovest well remains, the rest is dross
What thou lov'st well shall not be reft from thee
What thou lov'st well is thy true heritage. . . .
                                          Pound, Canto LXXXI

The years covered in this book (1988 to early 1991—the end of my regular reviewing) have not been a time of great moviemaking fervor. There were surprises and, in a few cases, amazements—*Women on the Verge of a Nervous Breakdown*; *Dangerous Liaisons*; *Let's Get Lost*; *Batman*; *Casualties of War*; *My Left Foot*; *The Fabulous Baker Boys*; *Drugstore Cowboy*; *Enemies, A Love Story*; *The Grifters*; *Vincent & Theo*; *Everybody Wins*. Mostly, though, what has been sustaining is that there is so much to love in movies besides great moviemaking. The young writer Chuck Wilson reports that his earliest movie memory is of his mother and his aunt taking him, when he was six, to see *Funny Girl*, and as he recalls, "In the final scene, when Barbra Streisand, as Fanny Brice, sings, 'My Man,' it seems to me that I grew taller, yes, I leaned forward, some part of me rose up to meet the force coming from the screen. . . . I was rising to get close to the woman I saw there. But I also rose to get closer to my self."

An avidity for more is built into the love of movies. Something else is built in: you have to be open to the idea of getting drunk on movies. (Being able to talk about movies with someone—to share the giddy high excitement you feel—is enough for a friendship.)

Our emotions rise to meet the force coming from the screen, and they go on rising throughout our moviegoing lives. When this happens in a popular art form—when it's an art experience that we discover for ourselves—it is sometimes disparaged as fannishness. But there's something there that goes deeper than connoisseurship or taste. It's a fusion of art and love.

I am indebted to movie friends—to Ray Sawhill and Polly Frost, and to John Bennet, Bruce Diones, and Hal Espen at *The New Yorker*. I want to thank William Shawn; William Abrahams, the book editor who has stuck by me from the first volume through this twelfth; my daughter Gina, and that most avid of movie lovers, her son William.

MOVIE
Love

BIRD THOU
NEVER WERT

Bird

The musicians in swing bands wore tails (monkey suits, they were called) or bright-colored uniforms or spangled zoot suits; their leaders flashed their teeth and, if they were black, jiggled and jived. Black or white, they made us feel that entertaining us and keeping us dancing was the highest calling they aspired to—even if they'd played the same arrangements over and over—and that our happiness was their happiness. One of the ways the modern-jazz musicians of the postwar forties let us know that they didn't consider themselves entertainers was by wearing their street clothes on-stage. Though this bebop movement was interracial, its front-runners were black, and men such as Charlie Parker, Dizzy Gillespie, Thelonious Monk, and Bud Powell ushered in a new hipster militancy along with the intricate music that they had developed late at night in Harlem jam sessions—the music they played for themselves. When the boppers began to get engagements, they didn't care if you couldn't dance to their music; they wanted you to listen— or, rather, they let you listen. Bebop never became widely popular; it was a jazz avant-garde movement, and the music, which seemed very demanding at the time, angered many of the older jazz musicians (possibly because bop intellectualized their music, speeded it up, made it abstract, and brought it new shades of emotion).

The boppers didn't try to be ingratiating; they barely acknowledged the audience's existence. The trumpet man Dizzy Gillespie—the cutup of the movement, in his beret and shades and with a little dab of goatee—used his quick, barbed wit on whitey; he became the symbol of the new playful yet hostile cool. The alto saxophonist Charlie Parker—Bird, the master of improvisation, and a man known for his chameleon charm and his cocky arrogance—became the charismatic figure of the artist who nakedly expresses himself in his art. Born in 1920, by 1945 he was part of a liberation with its own emblems and signals. As Grover Sales pointed out in *Jazz* (Prentice Hall, 1984), "Some beboppers refused to straighten or 'conk' their hair in defiance of a rigid convention of black show business. Charlie Parker's close-cropped 'natural' made an early proclamation that 'black is beautiful.' " Parker gave out other messages, in spite of himself. He was drug-addicted from the age of seventeen until his death at thirty-four, and though he said that he played best straight, and warned his admirers about the misery of addiction, he set the potent archetype of the self-destructive jazz artist. Heroin became the "in" drug for boppers.

Bird, starring Forest Whitaker and directed by Clint Eastwood, from a script by Joel Oliansky, has just opened, after being honored at the New York Film Festival. It was hailed as "the first honest jazz movie" by Parker's biographer Gary Giddins in the October *Esquire,* and it's being saluted all over the place. Yet what I saw was a rat's nest of a movie—all flashbacks and rain. Eastwood has been conscientious: he hasn't commercialized the material. But he hasn't presented it, either, and he doesn't draw you into what he does present—not even at the basic level of giving you something to see. The picture looks as if he hadn't paid his Con Ed bill—the black actors are swallowed up in darkness. And, with the film flashing back and forth, you can't get the hang of Parker's life, and you don't come out with much understanding of his achievement or what made him a legend.

Though the movie runs two hours and forty-one minutes, it doesn't indicate what was going on in the postwar period—the resentment that the black boppers felt toward the white musicians who had been ripping them off, along with the agents and record companies and radio stations. (The boppers believed that their "difficult," far-out music would defeat imitators.) And though you're taken inside recreations of the Fifty-second Street clubs and of Birdland on Broadway, you don't get the bop elation, or the heightened awareness of sex which the black and white intermingling brought about, or any hint of the beginnings of the movement among black jazzmen to drop Christianity (as the white man's religion) and take Muslim names.

Forest Whitaker's Bird trudges off to his gigs around the country like a jazz version of Willy Loman; he's always fouling up—boozing and doping and smashing things. When his common-law wife Chan (Diane Venora) tells the doctor who wants to give him electroshock that he's a very special, creative person, it's the jazz equivalent of "Attention must be paid." The script sinks to the level of attempting to explain Parker's addiction as his way of soothing the pain of his ulcer. (He uses heroin instead of Gelusil.) From moment to moment, Whitaker's performance is richly felt; he's always believable, and, with his heavy hunched shoulders, he often looks like the photographs of Charlie Parker (especially in Parker's last years). Leonard Feather, who knew Parker, says in the August *Jazz-Times* that five minutes into the picture he forgot he was watching an actor. Yet Whitaker—maybe it's because of the way he was directed—comes across as just a genial big blob of a fellow who can't get his life together. And since this overgrown kid doesn't suggest Parker's glow you don't understand why so many women find him a turn-on.

Diane Venora brings an experimental, stagy tingle to Chan's scenes—she gets something going. It's almost incidental that she manages to resemble Chan Parker (who appears in *Celebrating Bird,* the 1987 video documentary co-directed by Giddins and Kendrick Simmons). It's her mastering Chan's low voice that's the key to her performance. The voice is very controlled and self-dramatizing and slightly abrasive. (She sounds a little like Ida Lupino doing a good-bad bitch.) And you feel, Of course, this is exactly the kind of passionate and intelligent jazz-struck girl who'd get involved with a suicidal, sponging genius-martyr like Charlie Parker. Some of Whitaker's scenes with Venora have a pricklish originality even when they're loaded with too much meaning. And a few of his scenes with Michael Zelniker as Red Rodney, the white trumpeter who toured the South with Parker, have something comic and unresolved in them—Parker shows a streak of "just kidding" sadism toward him. As actors, Zelniker and Whitaker play off each other in a way that Sam Wright (as Diz) and Whitaker don't. (The dialogue Diz has been given can put you in a dull funk.) In general, the scenes between blacks don't achieve any kind of intimacy. But then some of Parker's scenes with whites are fairly awkward, too, and, except for Chan, the white women who are attracted to him are photographed like blond Nazi vampires.

In a late-night scene near the beginning, Charlie Parker and Chan run into the room when they hear their sick baby crying, and proceed to stand over the crib quarrelling. Neither one tends to the infant; the crying just disappears from the soundtrack. (Ramshackle scenes like this one are part of what the *Times* respectfully refers to as "the Eastwood œuvre.") It's true that Eastwood has taken pains with Charlie Parker's music. Unreleased tapes as well as studio recording were processed by Lennie Niehaus: in some cases, he eliminated the backup men and recorded new arrangements in stereo, retaining Parker's solos. (All this is said to have been necessary because of the poor quality of the originals.) The effect is lovely and pure, but too much like listening to classics; the combos don't really sound like combos. And, the way the numbers are scattered through the movie, the music doesn't build the edgy excitement that drew people to jazz clubs. Why, then, are jazz critics, and most of the movie press, too, praising the movie? I think they're impressed by the care and affection that Eastwood put into producing facsimiles of the bebop people and places and events. And jazz critics like to see jazz solemnized—that confers dignity on *them*. (Of course, stardom is sexy, and they, like the movie press, love having a reason to interview a big men's-action star with an œuvre.) And—maybe the capper—when a man who isn't an artist makes an art film it's just what they expect art to be: earnest and lifeless.

Gorillas in the Mist

As the anthropologist Dian Fossey, in *Gorillas in the Mist,* Sigourney Weaver storms into a large hotel restaurant in central Africa, stalks the length of the room, delivers a strident tongue-lashing to a Dutch zoo broker who's having lunch with his friends, and, cursing loudly, makes her exit— all the while carrying a good-sized baby gorilla in her arms, holding it tenderly, with awe. Weaver's physical strength alone is inspiring in this movie, and there's a new freedom in her acting. She's so vivid that you immediately feel Dian Fossey's will and drive. Weaver's Dian is ecstatic when she steps off the plane in Africa, and she's enraptured when she's perched high up on a mountain, crouched down opposite a giant gorilla, mimicking his language and gestures from the inside—trying to think the way he does. Weaver is something to see. What happens between her and the animals is really happening (or, at least, appears to be), and there's joy in it. It makes everything else—all the acted-out passion and heroism and melodrama of Dian Fossey's eighteen years on her mountain—seem tired.

Partly, the picture is disappointing because it's overscaled at the start. When Dian enters a huge, crowded lecture hall in Louisville, Kentucky, in 1966, where Dr. Louis Leakey (Iain Cuthbertson) is saying that there are two big adventures left—space and who we are and what made us that way—we're prepared for a whopping epic. *Gorillas* doesn't fulfill the promise of that opening: we never see Dian learn much of anything about primates or about our origins. Instead, we see her arrive in Africa, form an emotional attachment to a gorilla family, and cut herself off more and more from people, until she's a fiercely maternal harridan who can't work with anyone. By then, Weaver's jaw juts out stubbornly; in her mania, Dian becomes apelike. Yet when she thinks of happy times with her favorites, her face is transformed. She blooms. Weaver acts the way she's built—she's monumental.

The director, Michael Apted, and the screenwriter, Anna Hamilton Phelan, want us, I think, to see the movie as a triumphant woman-and-gorillas love story. They probably want us to be inspired by Dian Fossey as an activist heroine—a woman who made a difference. (A title at the close tells us that she saved the mountain gorillas from extinction.) But they didn't find a way to fit this inspirational idea into their account of Dian Fossey's becoming convinced that she was the only one who knew how to protect the gorillas, and operating like a half-crazed terrorist. (In her later years, she probably damaged her cause.)

The movie is quite watchable; it's never sluggish or outright stupid. And it has its high romantic moment—the time a tough old silverback gorilla puts his hand in Dian's hand. A photographer (Bryan Brown) sent out by *National Geo-*

graphic, which is also financing her work, gets the pictures. (Shortly afterward, Dian and the photographer make love.) There's an authentic piece of drama, too, even if it's somewhat muffled: The photographer works out a plan whereby he and Dian can spend six months a year at her station in Rwanda and six months in other places—he on assignment, she doing primate research—and she refuses and sends him packing. It isn't research she cares about; it's her gorilla family. After he has left, she huddles among the gorillas, in the rain.

Yet the movie seems to belong to the past of movies rather than to the modern era. When Dian arrives in the Congo, she spends six weeks tracking gorillas, and then, when she and her head tracker, Sembagare (John Omirah Miluwi), see them for the first time, the cinematographer, John Seale, comes up with the glorious gorillas-in-the-mist vision that's called for. But before you can suck in your breath, music is poured on, signifying lyrical exaltation. (The credit reads "Original music by Maurice Jarre." Hah!) When civil war erupts in the Congo, and Dian argues with the soldiers who are telling her to get out of the country, we're given a dose of agitation music. Miluwi, who's actually a climber and part of the Mt. Kenya rescue team, gives an affecting, quiet performance, but he's used as a symbolic dignified, loyal native who knows right from wrong. And when Dian sets up camp on the other side of the border, in Rwanda, there are cuts to the tracker's worried reactions whenever she displays her ruthlessness—terrifying a Batwa Pygmy child to get information from him, or setting fire to the Pygmy poachers' huts. These shots are like inserts that have been recycled from a forties epic. Despite its subject, the movie can't be taken seriously. It's a feminist version of *King Kong*—now it's the gorillas who do the screaming.

Patty Hearst

Paul Schrader lacks a basic instinct for moviemaking: he doesn't reach an audience's emotions. He doesn't make you feel empathy with his characters, and he's short on humor. By temperament, he cools out hot projects. These limitations make it unlikely that his *Patty Hearst* will appeal to a large audience. But on its own terms—as a stylized movie of ideas—this is a lean, impressive piece of work. Nicholas Kazan's script, which is based on Patty Hearst's own account, *Every Secret Thing,* comes across as bilge-free. The film is a distanced presentation of the kidnapping of the nineteen-year-old heiress, in February, 1974, by an eight-member terrorist group that called itself the Symbionese Liberation Army, and of the fifty-seven days she spent blind-folded, in a closet, being alternately lambasted as a bourgeois parasite and raped, and of her subsequent participation in S.L.A. holdups as Tania, the terror she developed of the F.B.I., and her arrest, trial, and conviction. The whole series of events is like a nightmare that's all of a piece—a kid's nightmare that no one's on your side. And it answers the question that people asked before, during, and after the trial: Did she become part of the S.L.A. willingly, out of conviction, or was she simply trying to save her life? The movie shows you that, in the state she was in, there was no difference.

The S.L.A. punished Patty Hearst for being a representative of the rich; so did the jury. The movie errs, I think, in its quick, cursory glimpses of her early life: it doesn't treat her as an individual, either. Her prettiness and her bland manner are used against her, to suggest that she's a nothing, when they could be used as an indication that she was trained to hide her emotions under a polite mask—that her blandness is a form of privacy. And since we're not taken inside her character at the beginning, the movie is flat for a long time. There's some kind of inhuman chic in treating a victimized young girl as if she had no personality, no soul. But, offensive as it is, this attitude ties in with the film's "objective" manner. (The format suggests a staged documentary: we don't find out any more about the S.L.A. members than Patty does.) And since the movie sticks to a step-by-step factual view of what happens to her, it does her justice—cold justice though it is. When her capture by the S.L.A. is followed by her capture by the police, everything you've seen starts to add up, and suddenly the film is overwhelming.

Natasha Richardson, the twenty-five-year-old actress who plays Patty, has been handed a big unwritten role. She feels her way into it, and she fills it by having Patty react meekly yet almost furtively to her indoctrination and to the exchanges among the terrorists. Patty's reticence is much more than a veneer: it's how she deals with the terrorists, whose next moves she can't predict. (She retreats to being a hidden observer; you feel her reminding herself to look eager to please.) Richardson lets us see only a flicker of Patty's feelings toward the men she's forced to have sex with. (It's not until the trial, when she's specifically asked how she felt about one of them, that she lashes out with "I hated him.")

In movies, we are always primed to cheer those who fight back, even when we know that realistically they couldn't. Here's a passive victim—a girl who is raped in mind and body, and no longer knows when it started. (In memory flashes, she sees herself as having been blindfolded when she still lived at home with her family.) The film's Patty has a marvellous confused plaintiveness. Nine weeks after the terrorists bang her on the head and throw her in the trunk of a car, she takes part in a bank holdup, and only a few weeks later (in May) the police surround the S.L.A.'s Southern California bungalow hideout and, after an exchange of thousands of rounds of ammunition, the house goes up in flames and the six S.L.A. people who were there are incinerated. Patty, who's away in a motel with the other two S.L.A. members, Bill and Emily Harris, watches the shootout and the fire on TV. The commentators and the police assume she was inside, and she knows that if she had been she would have burned to death, too. She stares at the TV and says wonderingly, "They didn't even try to take us alive." What the terrorists have been telling her—that now that she's joined up, the police are out to kill her—sinks in; it traumatizes her, and she cowers in fear in the motel john. "They think I'm dead," she says. "I *am* dead." Sixteen months later, in September, 1975, she is arrested and put on trial; when she's asked why she didn't run away from the S.L.A. and she replies "Where would I go?" we feel how alone and paralyzed she was. She buried Patty Hearst out of fear, and Tania didn't have anybody. You can hear that buried child in Richardson's voice—thin and girlish here, like Patty Hearst's. (At one point, though, Richardson hits a contralto tone that evokes her mother, Vanessa Redgrave, whom she often evokes visually.)

Richardson always has something in reserve—you keep waiting for what she may show you next. Hiding out with the Harrises in rural Pennsylvania, she's impressed by the guts that the fugitive radical Wendy (Jodi Long) shows in standing up to the foolish, irrational Bill Harris (William Forsythe). Wendy is spirited, and Patty draws some strength from talking with her. But when she's in police hands she's blocked again: her every attempt to be truthful gets her in worse trouble. At the trial, she grasps how hopeless her case is, and, for the first time, she shows a trace of bitterness. When she's in the Federal Correctional Institute talking to her father, we see her in full face, and she looks luminously beautiful. Her words are perhaps too explicit: she says she has finally figured out what her crime was—"I lived." Her face transcends the statement.

And the film, I think, transcends its flaws. The idea of keeping us blindfolded, along with the dazed Patty, is somewhat deadening: keeping us in the dark with her is too conceptual a notion, and the effect is a little too art-conscious. Yet the hypnotic formality of the film's conception holds it all together. Schrader and Kazan are willing to sacrifice immediate pleasure for the full effect. And they show a dry wit here: Forsythe's performance as the bespectacled white middle-class Bill Harris who keeps trying to become a black revolutionary leader is a comedy turn played close to the vest. (Schrader is making wicked fun of these Che Guevara-style guerrillas, but he's not just putting them down—he enjoys their absurdist craziness and even, to a degree, identifies with it.) Dana Delany's lyrical, sweet profile is so incongruous among the S.L.A. faces that it seems almost loony. Nobody in the group really fits—that's part of what saves its members from looking like the usual movie terrorists. When the group's black General Field Marshal Cinque (Ving Rhames) announces, "I am a prophet," his eyes don't flash with insane ambition, and when he tells Patty to take her clothes off, no cataclysmic music is heard. The percussive score, by Scott Johnson, doesn't wet down the material. Not once.

OCTOBER 17, 1988

WHAT'S WRONG WITH THIS PICTURE?

Another Woman

Not so long ago, Woody Allen movies were awaited with joy; then he began to make tasteful versions of Ingmar Bergman pictures. He has a new one, *Another Woman*, and— Well, I didn't much care for *Wild Strawberries* the first time. (An homage, according to Peter Stone, is a plagiarism that your lawyer tells you is not actionable.) Cast in the Victor Sjöström role, Gena Rowlands is Marion, the cold, cerebral professor looking back over her life and realizing that she missed the boat: a fearful, prudent careerist, she lost out on passion, on motherhood, on life itself. (Does she also lack passion for her work? We're not told, but it's implied.)

The opening music, Satie's "Gymnopédie No. 3," is like the soothing Vangelis arrangements that are used in commercials for Gallo wines—music that's selected because it couldn't upset the most delicate sensibilities. (It has the qualities of a digestif.) The audience laughs, taking the wine-country connection to be a joke. It's a jump ahead of Woody Allen, who must be so secluded from the world of commercials that he didn't anticipate the reaction. He has become so conventional in his tastes that this genteel slumber-party music is his idea of an artistic prelude.

The story has a more intricate design than that of Allen's *Interiors* or *September*. Just turned fifty, the firm-minded Marion, philosophy professor and director of undergraduate studies at "a fine women's college," has taken a year off to write a book and has sublet a second apartment, to work in. But "reality" leaks through: voices invade her sanctuary. They're the voices of an analyst's patients, coming through the air vent from the office next door. And she becomes obsessed with one voice—that of the tearful, distraught, and hugely pregnant Hope (Mia Farrow). Marion spies on her, follows her around Manhattan, and manages to meet her. Hope's confused feelings awaken Marion to all the risk-taking she has put out of her orderly life: as if by magic, she begins to encounter people she used to know and to flash back to scenes from her past.

Woody Allen has become an accomplished craftsman, and he moves around a large group of Marion's intertwined friends and relatives in the past and the present. The cast includes, among many others, Blythe Danner, Sandy Dennis, Martha Plimpton, Gene Hackman, Ian Holm, Harris Yulin, Philip Bosco, Kenneth Welsh, Bruce Jay Friedman, and John Houseman and David Ogden Stiers playing Marion's father in his later years and when she was still a young woman. (Stiers' voice matches up with Houseman's.) Every detail is in place, from Sven Nykvist's pristine, mellow images to Gena Rowlands' designer writing ensembles and her distinguished-woman hairdo—the braided knot on the back of her head looks as if it had been cast in bronze. And Marion's voice-overs keep briefing us. The movie is so lucidly constructed it's like a diagram of all the characters' relations to each other. It's fluid even during Allen's flourishes—when, for example, the older Marion talks across time to

her brother Paul as a young man, or when Marion dreams
that she's at the rehearsal of a play about her life. The basic
units, though, are Bergman scenes: Marion's aged father expresses regret that his wife was not the woman he loved
most deeply, and remorse at how he treated Marion and her
brother; there's speculation about whether Marion's first
husband committed suicide; Marion's second husband's first
wife interrupts a party to denounce him; Marion wants to
know why she and this second husband don't have sex anymore; and so on. And Marion's wet, suffering eyes speak of
her misery over what she now recognizes has been a sterile
existence, in which she has been judgmental about everyone but herself. (She is psychoanalyzed by overhearing the
pregnant woman on the analyst's couch.)

Quiet as it is, this is a soaringly ambitious movie; it's
clearly intended as a celebration of Allen's becoming a father (it's his child that Mia Farrow is carrying) and as an
assertion of a new commitment to life, in all its passionate
messiness. Yet, except for a few scenes where the performers' individuality stirs the surface (Hackman, in tip-top form,
sneaks in a hint of eroticism; Sandy Dennis lets loose with
bursts of smudgy, chaotic anger; Martha Plimpton has her
laconic, easygoing freshness; and Blythe Danner hugs herself, wrapping her long fingers around her skinniness like
an American Maggie Smith), nothing in the movie has the
slightest resonance. Bergman's version had at least a mysterious sensuality and raw, gothic images and great disturbing faces that helped you over the banalities and stayed in
the memory. Woody Allen's picture is meant to be about
emotion, but it has no emotion. It's smooth and high-toned;
it's polished in its nothingness.

When Marion, upset, sits down alone and, in voice-over,
tells us, "I thumbed through my mother's edition of Rilke,"
what universe are we in? (One where this isn't recognized
as a line to hoot at.) Woody Allen may identify with Marion's new desire for release, but he's filming a delusionary
world derived from books, plays, and movies, where stick

figures accuse each other of betrayals, infidelities, lack of courage—and it's all weightless. Marion talks of Rilke's black panther, his symbol of death; and a white mask is displayed—we're told it's from a performance of *La Gioconda*. The pregnant woman is named Hope, which is also the title of a Klimt painting of a pregnant nude exhibited for us; Brecht is referred to, and Kurt Weill is performed in an enervated version. Marion, who has been in love with order but realizes it's death and now finds Hope, belongs to a whole race of cultured zombies.

This is the seventeenth film that Woody Allen (in his early fifties now) has written and directed; it's easy to believe that, like Marion, he has trained himself to be overdisciplined. The evidence is here in this howlingly groomed production, which is intended to represent a movement toward liberation but was made by a man who doesn't even accept his own humor. A viewer of all Woody Allen's movies—the comedies and the vacuous dramas—may conclude that he misstates his problem in *Another Woman*. You can see in his comedies that he associates messy emotions with Jewishness and foolishness and laughter. But he wants to escape all that and be a "serious" dignified artist, so he sets his dramas in an austere Gentile world. And then what is the protagonist's tight-nostrilled anguish about? Being repressed. Being a perfectionist. Not being emotional enough. That was the interior-decorator mother's soul-sickness in *Interiors,* and it's Marion's soul-sickness here. Woody Allen is caught in his own Catch-22: his protagonist's problem is not being Jewish.

Another Woman was made by an upscale control freak. Even the workplace Marion sublets is in impeccable taste. The soundtrack music is Bach and Mahler with popular classics in arrangements that seem modulated to go with the carpeting. The only bright side to all this is that, having reached a peak of self-rejection, Allen shouldn't need to go any further in this direction. If there's a tragic waste in his career, it's that he doesn't place a high enough value on his own talent; he labors to be an artist like Bergman and turns into a pseud. If he could just stop dichotomizing himself between "funny" Allen and "serious" Allen! Maybe even Marion would recognize that life includes cracking a joke now and then, and letting in a little rock 'n' roll. How can you embrace life and leave out all the good vulgar trashiness?

Punchline

Standup comics appear to come from several groups: bright, verbal children who clamor for the attention they didn't get from their families; bright, verbal "born comics," the family pets who made everyone laugh until their indefatigability drove everyone nuts (the pets clamor for more of the attention they did get); and other kids—maybe adolescents, or even adults—who fall in love with comedy. It comes pretty much to the same thing. They all find a way to remain kids forever: they turn their talkativeness and their intense, exaggerated reactions into entertainment. It's the handiest vehicle for their hyper-responsiveness. They turn it into routines because what else can you do with it? Well, David Seltzer, who wrote and directed *Punchline,* found something else he could do with it: turn it into pop-psych moral uplift and sell it.

Seltzer wants us to see the blistering young comic Steven Gold (Tom Hanks) as "troubled." Seltzer points up Steven's hostility, his inability to relate to other people, his not understanding what love is. And everything that Seltzer points up is soggy and only partway believable. (He's the Gail Sheehy of moviemakers.) Some sharp, high-energy comics may have had a tantrummy smartass childhood, but as the kids' childhood experiences became stylized acts they took on a satirical, self-lampooning tone. And if the kids became jazz artists of language and let loose their imaginations we might hear our own kookiest buried thoughts spring out of their mouths. Or maybe even—as with Mel Brooks—hear sprightly thoughts more cockeyed than we'd ever dreamed of. When touched-in-the-head—gifted—comics like Robin Williams or Andrea Martin (or Woody Allen) take flight, they're emancipated from sanity. So why does Seltzer present the gifted Steven Gold as one of the hundred neediest cases? Because pathos serves Seltzer's purposes, and zest doesn't.

Hanks convinces you that Steven *has* to be a comic; he can't be anything else—or, at least, there's nothing else that he wants to be. Somehow, the movie uses this against him. Whiplash-smart and manic, Steven works out at several places each day and night; his home base is the Manhattan club the Gas Station, where he earns fifteen dollars a show plus chits for drinks at the bar. He lives on the money his doctor father sends him for medical school, but—and here's the Seltzer touch—Steven can't go on with his studies, because even though he might make an excellent doctor he's squeamish about blood. He's a tortured fellow—compulsive, restless, derisive. But Lilah (Sally Field) sees the soft, suffering child within. She's a New Jersey housewife and mother of three who hopes to become a comic, and she wears what I guess is meant to be an all-purpose, practical coat. It's plaid, with some frowzy animal around the neck, and it makes her look like a toby jug three feet high. Every time she put on that grotesque coat, I could feel my gut tightening; her coat began to stand for everything that's wrong with the movie.

As Seltzer presents the story, audiences warm to Lilah because she has a wholesome, normal outlook; Lilah incarnates what Steven has been denied, and the movie gives her an insipid radiance while it pulls back from Steven's aggressive twisted smile and his stabbing vocal rhythms. (These

two are Lenny Bruce and Erma Bombeck.) Essentially, the
movie pulls back from its own subject—standup comics.
Sally Field has an almost scary plaintive look in some scenes,
but the movie never gets very far into why Lilah is running
around buying jokes. We're supposed to dislike Steven's
brashness and desperation, and approve of Lilah because
she's decent and only temporarily driven. This is the kind
of movie in which Lilah's husband in Jersey is tender and
wise when he says, "Someday, Lilah . . . you'll remember
that the people in this house loved you whether you were
funny or not."

You can't have much respect for a writer-director who
falls back on the plot device of a contest to be held at the
Gas Station—the winner will get a shot on the Johnny Car-
son show. (Is this a Muppet movie?) And Seltzer employs
tricks that used to jerk tears, like having the cheerful, rau-
cous act that Steven performs for the patients in a hospital—
the one routine where he comes across as a man being funny
and not a wiseguy—end with his slipping away to speak
comfortingly to a dying child. The bedraggled plotting
forces Hanks into maudlin situations. Steven gets up to perform, sees his father and brother at a table, and falls apart:
he talks slowly, fumblingly about his childhood humilia-
tions until he's led offstage. Lilah follows him out, and he
weeps on her shoulder. This is the low point of the movie;
it comes to a halt, and Hanks can't save himself, maybe because the breakdown doesn't have any nuances—it's not
grounded in anything believable. In another scene, Steven
and Lilah are in a diner, and he, euphoric about his feelings
for her, urges her to pack up her children and come to him,
and they'll get married. (He doesn't even have a place for
her to come to; he has been locked out of his apartment.)
She tells him that she loves her husband; anguished, he says
he has nothing to keep him going without her, and he walks
outside into a downpour, la-la-ing the beginning of "Singin'
in the Rain," and dancing and miming a long takeoff of Gene
Kelly's solo, with Kelly's blissfulness converted into self-

dramatizing bitterness and dejection. When his dance is over, he stands in the rain looking back at her for an instant of formal eye contact before he disappears from the frame. Hanks performs this number with such physical grace that he transcends the banality of the idea and outclasses *Punchline*.

Sally Field, Hollywood's queen of vulnerability, is too skillful at what she does; she seems used up, as if she'd hit her limits a long way back. (It's almost inconceivable that she once had the range to play the fractured identities of *Sybil*.) She doesn't find anything to reveal to us, and her plucky darlingness is a blight on this movie. To be more exact, it's the picture that's a blight, because Seltzer's sitcom style of humor is just like Lilah's. When she learns how to perform and does her act, we're supposed to be charmed by the naughty vibrator jokes that pop out of her little head and "embarrass" her. And we're supposed to see what a blooming, healthy, *nice* person she is. The truth of Steven's character is supposed to be the hurt, not the comedy; understanding this, she knows that he needs to win the contest more than she does. This shabby plot even undercuts Steven's final routine, which begins bewilderingly.

Field is lucky to have John Goodman, as Lilah's insurance-salesman husband, to carry her. Goodman's cheeks and chest have become huge, and his role is heavy and domineering at the beginning; but about midway Lilah changes her hairdo from soft, red, and long to a tightly curled brunette bob (is she imitating Steven?), and she's flustered about what she has done, and is on the verge of tears—and then her husband intercepts, sets her at ease, and we see a different side to him. Right there, Goodman takes over. The conception of the insurance man as the rock that Lilah cleaves to is no more than a plot convenience, but Goodman makes him into a grinning, big-souled character with a happy boom of a laugh. His love of her makes her look substantial instead of just cute-as-a-bug, and the gleam in his eyes when she's performing saves the creaking last scenes.

As a network scout who praises Steven but doesn't take the risk of recommending him, Kim Greist (of *Brazil*) has the TV functionary's sexy manner down pat. And Mark Rydell, as the baby-faced owner of the Gas Station, is eager, self-serving, and almost iridescent in his sleaziness. During the contest, when he's onstage as the m.c., you expect to see a diamond in his eyetooth; he's so proud and excited he's like an enraptured gnome.

It's Hanks, stretching his light comedian's skills, who keeps you watching. While Steven the cutting-edge comic may be written to be nothing but the tears behind the laughter, Hanks gets under the material, and darkens it. Steven reaches out to Lilah because she's a mommy; he knows he's a nit to want a mommy—it's his awareness that keeps him racing. When Lilah's husband comes into the club, Steven looks at him with jealousy and anger; this kid knows what turns him on in a sick way—he's a comic, he's on top of what bothers him. And he's so manic he doesn't know how he's going to take his next breath. Steven is most alive when he's spritzing and not quite in control; I'd like to have heard him do a jeering riff on a few targets that were at hand, like the film's perky score and Lilah-the-housewife's kitchen that's lighted like a margarine commercial and the inserts of onscreen audiences beaming at Lilah's wholesome humor, and don't forget the plaid coat.

Madame Sousatzka

Shirley MacLaine is outrageously miscast in John Schlesinger's *Madame Sousatzka*. As a flamboyant, grande-dame piano teacher, of Russian lineage, she glints her eyes and pinches her tiny lips, she tromps around in layers of clothes and ropes of beads, whirling her velvet cloak. MacLaine seems to have entered the Simone Signoret sweepstakes, but she doesn't project Signoret's generosity—she doesn't spill over emotionally. MacLaine has flurries of physical mannerisms, but she's tight and held in; she's a wacky witch with frizzy red hair—she could be Norma Desmond's small-town spinster sister.

The movie accounts for her Americanness by having her raised in New York, where her performing career was wrecked long ago by her dragon of a virtuoso mother; she lives in London now (in an Edwardian house that is to be demolished) and devotes her energies and her hopes to the most prodigious of her students, a fifteen-year-old Indian boy raised in England, Manek Sen (Navin Chowdhry). Autocratic old Sousatzka battles with the boy's beautiful young mother (Shabana Azmi) and tries to take him over completely, and, still traumatized from her own failed début, she refuses to let him perform in public. The movie is about the boy's breaking free of her, though he knows he'll remain in her debt forever. Changing Manek from the Jewish boy of the 1962 novel, by Bernice Rubens, works fine, but Sousatzka seems to belong to an earlier era than that of the poised, often amused Manek. Chowdhry, who has impressive, big features in an intelligent face, gives you the sense of how he feels about his developing powers, and he's fun when he knows to ignore Sousatzka's bullying. It's a likable, well-directed performance. And the beautiful Shabana Azmi, who acts a little broadly, like a Bengali Jane Seymour, makes you understand her near-hysteria when she has to deal with Sousatzka. The best scenes in the movie show how Manek and his mother live, and the perils of their catering business; there's a wonderful image of Hindu women piled together in a tiny room watching daytime TV.

The script, by Ruth Prawer Jhabvala and Schlesinger, is blindingly derivative but thoughtfully worked out. The conflict between teacher and pupil takes place among Chekhovian intimations of life going on among the tenants of the doomed building: Peggy Ashcroft is Lady Emily, the impoverished landlady; Geoffrey Bayldon is an elderly homosexual osteopath; and Twiggy, who gives an appealingly understated performance, is an aspiring pop singer who isn't getting anywhere, except into the beds of artists' reps and record producers. (Manek, who adores her, pleads with her to take him into her bed.)

The movie has excerpts from musical classics, and a tense scene where the boy makes his début playing the Schumann Piano Concerto and we're alerted that he won't get through it unscathed. The musical community may regard the picture as a treasure. Schlesinger is a professional at mounting a production; it's handsome and textured and reasonably dynamic, and for some people it may serve as the *Red Shoes* of the keyboard. But the core performance is missing. You'd think that, with all those past lives to draw on, MacLaine could come up with a crazily noble, dedicated music lover—an inspiring tyrant—rather than this rouged and tarted-up hollow old crank. MacLaine's Sousatzka has no Old World charm and no New World charm, either. And, without a big, maddening personality to irradiate it, the movie is like a prestige best-seller from an earlier era. As a viewing experience, it's laborious—not bad but not enjoyably bad, either. It should be projected on the wall while you have a polite lunch at the Russian Tea Room—the wall behind you.

OCTOBER 31, 1988

UNREAL

Women on the Verge of a Nervous Breakdown

Pedro Almodóvar may be the only first-rank director who sets out to tickle himself and the audience. He doesn't violate his principles to do it; his principles begin with freedom and pleasure. Born in 1951, this Spaniard from hicksville went to Madrid at seventeen, got a job as a clerk at the National Telephone Company in 1970, and, during the more than ten years he worked there, wrote comic strips, articles, and stories for "underground" papers, acted in theatre groups, composed film scores, recorded with a rock band, performed as a singer, and shot films in Super 8 mm. and 16 mm. He absorbed the avant-garde slapstick of the late sixties and the seventies along with Hollywood's frivolous and romantic pop, and all this merged with the legacy of Buñuel and with his own intuitive acceptance of loco impulses. Generalissimo Franco kept the lid on for thirty-six years; he died in 1975, and Pedro Almodóvar is part of what jumped out of the box. The most original pop writer-director of the eighties, he's Godard with a human face—a happy face.

His new *Women on the Verge of a Nervous Breakdown*, his seventh feature (since 1980), is one of the jauntiest of all war-of-the-sexes comedies. Pepa (Carmen Maura), an actress who works in TV and commercials, and does dubbing, turns on her answering machine and learns that she has been jilted. Infuriated at the way her long-time live-in lover, Iván (Fernando Guillén), has evaded direct contact with her—he can lie to the machine without fear of being challenged—she dashes around, on spike heels, in a short, tight skirt, trying to confront him. Angry and impatient, and imagining she doesn't want to be in her apartment without him, she instantly puts it on the market.

Pepa is so wound up about Iván that although her girl friend the lightheaded Candela (María Barranco) keeps phoning and chasing her, asking for help, Pepa, hearing nothing, answers that she doesn't have time. What Candela is trying to tell her is that her own lover has turned out to be a Shiite terrorist who was using her place as a base of operations, and she thinks the police are after her. Without registering Candela's words, Pepa takes her in. Meanwhile, blankly handsome Carlos (Antonio Banderas), who turns out to be Iván's son, comes to see the apartment, and brings his soon to be discarded fiancée, Marisa (Rossy De Palma, who looks startlingly like the double face of Picasso's 1937 portrait of Dora Maar). Iván's earlier lover Lucia (Julieta Serrano)—she's Carlos's mother—arrives in search of Iván; she was over the edge for twenty years and has just recouped her sanity. And when Pepa, on Candela's behalf, consults a feminist lawyer (Kiti Manver), the woman turns out to be Iván's newest lover—and the next candidate for a breakdown. All these women are sleek-legged and chic and made up as if they were painted in acrylics.

The artificial is what sends Almodóvar sky high. The movie has nothing to do with what passes for nature or realism. It starts with titles set against divided-screen fashion and cosmetics layouts that parody the bright, crisp American-movie openings of the fifties. (All that plugging away to be Mondrian-new and striking.) *Women on the Verge* looks as if it had been made by a mad scientist playing with chemical rainbow colors—John Lithgow in his lab in *Buckaroo Banzai.* When you were a kid, you wondered if your crayons would kill you if you ate them. These toxic colors are toxins for the pleasure of it; Almodóvar makes the artificial sexy.

The film's controlling metaphor is right there at the start, in those sharp-edged layouts: Almodóvar is after the phosphorescent glow of cosmetics in women's magazines. (It's dream-candy color. You don't just see it; you consume it, lustfully.) Pepa and the others in their short short skirts have created themselves in the image of hot, desirable women. They function in the world; they do fine. But when it comes to men, that sassy image may be all that's holding them together. The lovely, wacky Candela is always speeding between panic and ardor; she talks about being entrapped by the Shiites, and her earrings—they're little silver espresso-makers—dangle alluringly. Except for Lucia (who suspects the truth about herself), they all know they look great; that's not a small thing. (Lucia can't keep up her morale; her makeup slips and blurs.)

The movie links Carmen Maura's Pepa to the Hollywood goddesses who blew a trumpet to announce that they were entering the house of passion. Their emotional display was morbidly fascinating; Almodóvar and Maura take off on that display and go further into it. Pepa looks great even though she shows some wear and tear. It's in her nature to charge into things bang, head on, and get scuffed up. She doesn't mind; she enjoys flaunting the ravages of love. It's also in her nature to let off steam; she distracts the police, who come looking for Candela, by giving them a stormy account of intimate experiences. Almodóvar revels in her overdramatizing, but it's never held an instant too long; it's quick and buoyant. It's taken for granted. Pepa is both overtly nuts—a coquettish, fluttering wreck—and profoundly sane and practical. After she gets the kiss-off from the answering machine, she's so zonked on pills and misery that she accidentally sets her bed on fire. She stares at it for a few seconds, then flips her cigarette into the flames and puts them out with the hose from the terrace.

Women on the Verge is serenely unbalanced—a hallucinogenic Feydeau play. Mad-again Lucia, in pale pink, rides to the airport on the back of a motorbike, her wig rising and blowing in the wind. She's determined to catch up with Iván, and he's about to board a plane. Inside the terminal, her head, seen gliding by above a moving walkway, is the head of a mythological creature—a wiggy Fate. When the people in the airport hear a shot fired and try to protect themselves by hitting the floor, they stay down until Iván comes over to Pepa, who has raced Lucia there. Then they all get up at once, like the dancer-spectators in a musical version of a gangster picture. The Madrid of the film is a pop utopia; it's also—as the closing song has it—"Puro Teatro."

Almodóvar celebrates women because they run the theatrical gamut. Carmen Maura is his star, his muse, his comedienne because she's all histrionics; she doesn't make a move that isn't stylized. Yet she's snappy. And it won't take her Pepa twenty years to see through Iván. Gray-haired, vain, and elegant, he's the film's MacGuffin—a shell of a man, and perhaps an archetypal Spanish roué. A dubber by profession, he's a voice pouring out inanities. It pleases him to flatter virtually every woman he sees; he's complimenting himself on his aplomb, his powers of seduction. When he has something to say that might provoke an emotional response, he'd rather talk into a machine. He's a sly fellow: while dodging Pepa, he keeps leaving messages accusing her of avoiding him. (He tells her to pack up his clothes and leave the suitcase with the concierge.) Iván is right to communicate by machine: as a disembodied voice, he gives the illusion of masculine strength. In person, he's just a pretty illusion, like his son, Carlos, and the police officers and the men from the phone company who invade Pepa's apartment.

The script began with Cocteau's *The Human Voice*—the famous telephone monologue in which a woman tries to win back the lover who is leaving her. Almodóvar had already done a turn on the play in his last film, the 1987 *Law of Desire;* this time, the monologue grew into a comic revenge on his old employer the phone company. Pepa grabs her phone and throws it out the window, and she throws out its offspring, the answering machine, too. She's paying them back for the long waits for men to call and the lies listened to.

This high comedy is the most visually assured of the five Almodóvar movies that have opened here. *Law of Desire* and the 1986 *Matador* were more sultry and erotic; this one is fizzier, sexier. Earlier, you could see him trusting his intuitions and taking leaps; now you don't see the risk-taking—he's just up in the air flying. The movie is all coincidences, and each new one adds to the crazy brio. What seem to be incidental jokes turn out to be essential parts of one big joke. This is a movie where after a while you can't tell sexy from funny.

Things Change

Things Change is a modernist version of a sentimental fable. David Mamet, who directed and was the co-writer (with Shel Silverstein), gives you the blueprint but not the feeling. The story is essentially a heart-warmer: Sicilian-born Gino (Don Ameche), a dignified old Chicago shoeshine man who gets mixed up with mobsters and is mistaken for a Mafia don, emerges unscathed because of his simple goodness—his humanity. But it has been directed at a deliberate and unvarying pace. The result is like a Frank Capra–Damon Runyon movie of the thirties in slow motion.

This is the bare bones of the plot: The mob offers the impoverished Gino a deal. If he'll confess to a killing that a man he resembles has been arrested for, he'll serve only three to five years, and when he comes out he'll be able to retire to Sicily and buy the fishing boat he has always wanted. He agrees, and is put in the hands of Jerry (Joe Mantegna), a "probationary," blundering mafioso assigned to lowly tasks, who is supposed to spend the weekend holed up with Gino, coaching him in his story. Gino asks Jerry if he can go for a walk on the beach; the restless, grandiose Jerry decides to give the old gent a break, and takes him, by plane, to Lake Tahoe. That's where Gino is mistaken for a bigwig, and where he and Jerry become buddies.

Mamet piles on improbabilities in a matter-of-fact style, and with a minimum of emotion. Most of what a viewer sees is just Ameche being a straight-backed peasant—a man of his word—and Mantegna being a confused hoodlum. There's nothing to look at except their rather mummified skits. But Mamet cons the audience. He brings it into a hip complicity with him. He gives people the impression that in making them wise to the actors' games he's making them wise to how the world works—that he's letting them in on life's dirty secrets. And flatness of performance seems to be part of the point. Mamet's minimalism suggests a knowingness, a disdain for elaboration or development. (This was also his strategy in the first film he directed, the 1987 *House of Games*.) People can feel one up on the action, the way they can when they're watching the David Letterman show.

Or they may feel that Mamet over-controls the actors and the other elements of moviemaking, and that his approach takes the fun out of hokum. In Capra's 1933 comic fairy tale, *Lady for a Day* (in 1961, he remade it, mawkishly, as *Pocketful of Miracles*), Apple Annie, a Times Square peddler, passes herself off as a society matron, with the assistance of a gang of Broadway racketeers, who are saying, in essence, "We're as hardboiled as they come, but we have big, soft hearts." (They also have a colorful lingo.) And in Hal Ashby's 1974 *The Last Detail,* where Jack Nicholson, escorting Randy Quaid to naval prison, decides to give him a fling, the tension is between the Nicholson character's generous, paternal impulses and his mean, blowhard cowardliness. (Robert Towne provided rowdy, lewd dialogue.) Mamet appears to draw from these films (and when Gino's remarks about the best methods of shoeshining are taken to be parables, to be drawing a little from the Ashby–Jerzy Kosinski *Being There*), but the language is blandly arch, and there's no dramatic tension, just a stiff unease. No one seems to take a breath on his own.

You expect the trip to Tahoe to be a realization of Gino's dreams, but Mamet can't give himself over to the fable—he keeps his hardboiled distance—and so there's no inkling of what Tahoe might mean to Gino, or of what being treated as a Mafia don might mean to him. The movie is an extended, undernourished anecdote. Ameche starts repeating himself early on; Mantegna, a practiced slicker who's all wrong for fraidy-cat buffoonery, doesn't seem sure whether he's playing a dumb mug or just coming across as one. Mamet's talent is for lowlifers' rancorous scrapping, not for comic gangsters and buddy love.

You half expect the actual killer—the guy that Gino is supposed to resemble—to turn up; you wait for the plot to be more clever than it is. That's the only suspense the movie has. Mamet set up a story with a buried theme: the yearning for a day when men kept their word. And then—it's no surprise—he couldn't deliver the third act. Gino has a Mafia lucky coin that keeps saving him, but by the end this device rings like a lead quarter.

NOVEMBER 14, 1988

TRIALS

A Cry in the Dark

If *A Cry in the Dark* had been called "A Dingo Ate My Baby!" that would tell moviegoers what it's about—it would be a Cry from the Heart, and they might line up around the block. But *A Cry in the Dark,* directed by Fred Schepisi and starring Meryl Streep, isn't the kind of movie they would expect to see. Schepisi uses the case of Lindy Chamberlain, who was tried for murder and convicted, to ask why the press and the public jeered at her account of seeing a dingo (the Australian wild dog) slink off from the tent the baby was in. The film asks why Australians were so eager to believe that Lindy, the wife of a Seventh Day Adventist minister and the devoted mother of two little boys, had killed her nine-week-old baby girl, while the family was camping near Ayers Rock, in the Outback, in 1980.

To begin with, there's a lurid, *National Enquirer* ring to her story. And it met with the derision of a rough, cynical people and jangled their national pride. Dingoes are an Australian mascot, and they're not very large (they resemble coyotes), and Ayers Rock, the great monolith in the desert which has been a sacred site for the aborigines for over ten thousand years, is a chief tourist attraction. Australians like to say it's the biggest rock in the world. And, as Seventh

30

Day Adventists (and so vegetarians), Lindy (Streep) and her husband (Sam Neill) were "different," and before long were rumored to be members of a cult with blood rituals. Perhaps the most damning thing, the thing that made the penniless and once again pregnant Lindy the most hated woman in Australia, was that her stoic, matter-of-fact manner was not what the public expected. TV had accustomed people to grieving mothers who showed their frailty and their naked pathos, and here was Lindy on TV—distanced, impersonal, and bluntly impatient at the endless dumb questions.

It's this that makes the role work so well for Meryl Streep. She's a perfectionist who works at her roles from the out-side in, mastering the details of movement, voice, and facial expression, and this thinking-it-all-out approach gives her an aloofness. Of course, she's got the accent; at least, to Amer-ican ears she's got it—the flatness, the low pitch, and the combative swing of the phrasing. It seems more fully ab-sorbed than her meticulous accents generally do. And she's devised a plain, inelegant walk for this woman who has no time for self-consciousness, and no thought of it, either. The walk may be overdone: the actual Lindy Chamberlain, when she appeared on "60 Minutes," didn't move this heavily, as if she'd just put down a washboard. And Streep definitely overdoes the coiffure—witchy black hair with the bowl cut you sometimes see on little boys. But Streep's Lindy has a consistency—she's practical and unrefined, with no phony aspirations. And what gives the performance power is that Streep can use her own aloofness and make it work in the character. (Even her lack of spontaneity works for her here, though sometimes she does seem overcontrolled.) Streep has psyched out Lindy Chamberlain and seen that her hard-ness (unconsciously, perhaps) serves a purpose: it saves a part of her from the quizzing and prying of journalists and lawyers. Lindy, who's scrappy and reacts to fools with comic disbelief, needs her impersonal manner to keep her-self intact. (Maybe the professionally gracious and intelligent Streep has learned this from her own sessions with reporters

and TV interviewers.) From time to time, Streep suggests
the strong emotions that Lindy hides in public, and we feel
a bond with her—we feel joined to her privacy.

Schepisi, who worked on the script with Robert Caswell
(it's based on John Bryson's study of the case, *Evil Angels*),
may have got too many things going. He's a superb moviemaker, but in his attempt to do an epic dissection of how
superstitions can spread, and how false the public perception (based on the media) can be, he put together more elements than he could develop. There are wonderful scenes:
early on, at the campsite, a dingo snaps up a mouse so fast
it's like the whirring of the wind; at dusk, right after Lindy
screams that her baby has been taken, the people in the
camp, in panic and confusion, hunt for the infant in the
darkness; and then there's a gigantic, organized search, with
men and women carrying torches seen from a distance, lined
up across the wide screen. (The image has an awesome horror.) Schepisi introduces the Aussies' casual cruelty to the
aborigines. (Their dogs are ordered shot, though they're
nothing like dingoes.) And when public opinion has shifted,
and the self-contained Lindy is thought to be an icy, tough
customer, he gives us vignettes in homes and bars and
glimpses of the workings of the yellow press. (These are
perhaps the weakest scenes: too many uncouth, boisterous
shouts, too much hubbub, and we're not told enough.) He
provides a quick rundown on the forensic scientist far away
in London who has never seen a dingo but concludes that
one wasn't involved. And he keeps briefing us on the Cham-
berlains. When the trial starts, Lindy is seven months pregnant, and she keeps letting out her dress; by then, her
husband is rattled and almost incoherent. He's losing his
faith and doesn't want to be a pastor anymore. Sitting in the
courtroom, he digs his fingernails into his scalp and blood-
ies them. The two try to hide from the hostile public, and
press helicopters fly overhead, spying on them, the wind
blast buffeting them. You can see why she tells off the lawyer who advises her to be demure on the stand.

A Cry is never less than gripping, and toward the end, when new evidence is found, the picture is powerfully affecting. That's a surprise, because the steadiness of tone and the couple's religious fatalism don't lead you to expect this wave of pure emotion. But *A Cry* is scaled to be a masterwork, and it isn't that. It's more like an expanded, beautifully made TV Movie of the Week. And partly this is because Streep, remarkable as she is (she does some of her finest screen acting), seems to be playing a person in a documentary. This is also true of the very accomplished Sam Neill. Everything that Schepisi does shows integrity, but he doesn't seem to go down deep enough. The picture doesn't have the ambiguities or the revelations of drama; basically, you don't learn much more than you did from the "60 Minutes" segment. And *A Cry* doesn't show the kind of affection for the Australian people that would give it a documentary meaning. You come out moved—even shaken—yet not quite certain what you've been watching.

The Good Mother

In *The Good Mother,* Anna (Diane Keaton), the diffident young divorced mother of a six-year-old girl, remains on amicable terms with the lawyer husband who never aroused her physically. But when she discovers sexual pleasure with an Irish sculptor (Liam Neeson) and begins to live a more bohemian existence, her ex-husband sues for the child's custody on the ground that Anna has allowed sexual irregularities and is an unfit mother. (Once, when she was away, the child touched the lover's penis.) In court Anna's life is spread out and subjected to scrutiny, and she's forced into the humiliating position of claiming that her attempt to raise her daughter without repressive modesty and concealments has been wrong, a mistake. Fearful of losing the child, she buckles under to the court's morality, even offering to give up her lover.

The movie almost gets at something urgent and unsettling that's just below the surface of the material: if we go to court, we may be held to the rules and values we no longer live by. The movie almost goads us into considering what our own lives might look like if they were exposed to legalistic examination. Would they seem as uncentered and weightless as Anna's life? And if we nervously tried to justify the way we live would we sound like amoral weaklings? But the movie, directed by Leonard Nimoy, from Michael Bortman's adaptation of the 1986 Sue Miller novel, sticks to a more specifically feminist view. Nimoy and Bortman ask us to see Anna as a victim of generations of patriarchal domination. The (pre-Keaton) prologue, which starts with Anna's childhood summers in Maine—her grandfather (Ralph Bellamy) bullying her sweet grandmother (Teresa Wright) and crushing her defiant red-haired aunt (Tracy Griffith)—sings a wan, stale tune. The family pattern of men mistreating women seems to be laid out for us so we'll understand why Anna is inhibited and frigid, but when Diane Keaton appears, it's clear that we didn't need all that apparatus just to read Anna's character. Keaton reveals Anna's repression in a few abject glances; the apparatus has been set up to prepare us for the plot.

Keaton goes right to Anna's dissatisfaction with herself. Anna admires women who are passionate—that's what she has always wanted to be. But, despite her vibrancy, she has a school-girl look, and she feels mousy, apprehensive, a hopeless case. She feels ridiculous. Anna, who lives in Cambridge, has no real commitment to her work as a piano teacher, and her part-time job (she washes test tubes in a lab) is strictly drudgery. Her only real pride is in being a good mother. Her daughter has been her joy, her art work; her maternal passion has been her only passion.

Keaton goes through changes here the way Bette Davis did in *Now, Voyager*. Anna comes into her own when she abandons herself to the Irishman. She's reborn as part of a family—man, woman, child—in which all three love each other. She looks sensational, and she's recklessly happy; carnality is everything she hoped for, and more. Then, when the turnaround comes and she has to go to court, she's stunned, cowed. Knowing what she means to her daughter, she's scared of what a separation could do to the child. Her new confidence dissolves: facing the judge, she's flushed and self-distrustful. She doesn't know what the right words are. And in the next phase she's a hysterical wreck until she dims her own light. For the sake of her child, she accepts the limited role in her daughter's future which the court grants her. She learns to live with her loss.

That's where *The Good Mother* loses a sizable chunk of the audience. As moviegoers, we're conditioned to want Anna to shred the thinking behind the court proceedings, to become impassioned and denounce it, and to walk out victorious, with her child and her lover. We know that this sort of heart-swelling triumph is "only a movie," but seeing the protagonist put up a heroic fight against injustice lifts our spirits; we come out feeling high, as if *we'd* won. And if a heroine loses the first round we expect her to keep on fighting, or, at least, to recognize how she's been had. What's the point of presenting melodramatically conceived characters like the stick of an ex-husband (James Naughton) if we're given none of the satisfactions of melodrama—if we're asked to accept a "realistic" ending? Anna just goes limp on us; she rolls with the punches. And though this is what her character has been rigged to do from the start, it's a disturbing letdown for the audience—especially, perhaps, for feminists, who may see it as a betrayal. The movie wants to be about the way the patriarchal system can batter women to a pulp. It does show that conventional-minded men who are trying to be fair can still believe that it's wrong for a mother to be sexually active. But since this is the story of

Anna's defeat—and, even harder to take, her meek, uncomprehending acceptance of defeat and her effort to make the best of it—women can feel it's saying, "That's how it is, folks. Resign yourselves."

The standard Hollywood triumph would all too obviously be a fantasy finish. But so, in a different way, is the ending we're given, which turns the whole movie into a victimization fantasy: losing her child is the price a woman pays for an orgasm. The big clinker in the movie—and this goes back to the novel—is that it's a few decades too late. The message that men will punish women for violating the old codes still applies, but not everywhere. The movie doesn't seem to recognize that, with half the children in America being raised by single parents, the society and the courts are in flux; of course, this means that it's easier for men to win custody than it used to be, but it also makes Anna's resignation appear Old World and arbitrary. You sit in the audience thinking that a different judge would have made all the difference, or that the case might have been won by an attorney less hidebound than the fogey she hires—Jason Robards, in a gloomy brown office that seems to say "All hope abandon." (Why didn't she go to a woman lawyer?) And so the whole structure seems shaky. Those earlier generations with their symbolic characters are piled on to prefigure Anna's being punished for her sexuality; they provide an inevitability that we can't accept.

A movie in which a woman shuts out the man she loves and gives all her emotional resources to the days that she is allowed to spend with her child has to be either worse than this one (so we can enjoy hooting at it) or a whole lot better (so we can empathize with her in her new, constricted life, and not notice all the dubious points being racked up). What *The Good Mother* does have is the central performances. Liam Neeson takes a new cliché—the artist as ideal, sensual man—and plays it with such rhythmic ease that you hardly question it. He's mellow-voiced and exuberant in the early sex scenes, and then, as the relationship with Anna deepens, he has a graceful male-animal presence—silent, erotic. He's even stronger in the courtroom scenes, where he's cruelly served up as the scapegoat: in a series of quiet reaction shots, his face shows the hurt. And Asia Vieira, who plays Anna's unfearful, inquiring-minded daughter, embodies the freedom that Anna wanted her to have; her crooked grin matches up with Keaton's bright smile. Nimoy can be proud of his work with these three performers (though his judgment went to hell in the scenes involving Ralph Bellamy and Teresa Wright).

Diane Keaton is a delight in the "fulfilled" section. Her daring is in her spontaneity. She keeps her performance almost alarmingly fresh—the bloom is on it. That's what makes her so likable. And it's tied in with her gift for making even closed-in characters transparent to our eyes. We watch as Anna withdraws further and further, and becomes nothing but a (bland, guilt-ridden) good mother—she won't imperil what remains of her relationship with her child, no matter what the cost. And, as Keaton plays her, you can't say Anna is wrong. She's true to her feelings; she loves her daughter more than anything else. But you resent the movie (and, to some degree, the novel) for framing the issues this way—for making it appear that women are now and have been forever characters in tearjerkers. Even if you credit Nimoy and Bortman with the best of intentions, they diminish women. The movie has a sickly passivity: Anna caves in and she still can't win anything except what used to be called "peace of mind." The kitschy worst of it is that there are postfeminist young women who will warm to her martyrdom and, responding to the oozing, sad music, clutch their Kleenex.

NOVEMBER 28, 1988

GHOSTS

Scrooged

Dickens' *A Christmas Carol* seems like ideal screen material, and it has been filmed over and over again, starting in 1901, and with versions in 1908, 1910, 1913, 1914, 1916, and so on. Yet as far back as box-office figures go it has never really been a hit—maybe because it's about a wasted life. (The spectacle of a miserly old man getting his comeuppance is not particularly enticing.) And maybe the story's familiarity has worked against it; whatever the latest version was, people could feel that it held few surprises. If *Scrooged,* starring Bill Murray, breaks the jinx (as I assume it will*), the reasons aren't hard to find. Murray plays the character as roughly his own age (thirty-seven), and the script, by Mitch Glazer and Michael O'Donoghue, who teamed up when they were on the writing staff of "Saturday Night Live," plays off against the bewhiskered triteness of the tale; for example, we don't have to be reminded which of the original characters the new ones are based on. The best reason is that *Scrooged* is a striking, outsize entertainment. Murray's Frank Cross, a yuppie egomaniac who's the youngest network president in history, is the meanest

*It didn't.

man in television. (That's the same as meanest man in the world.)

The picture is no more than a blown-up series of skits, but they come together, and what they're getting at is "TV has scrooged us, even the kids among us—especially the kids. It manipulates us and makes us cynical. It debauches us." Frank Cross is the living essence of TV. Dickens' Scrooge is a deviation from the norm, but Frank Cross, given his business environment, is only a crazily heightened version of the norm—and not just in his careerism but in his hip knowingness. He's casually contemptuous of the people who work at the network headquarters and of anybody he encounters outside. He's indifferent to anything but ratings—i.e., his own career. His "personal" pet project for the holidays is a live telecast of *A Christmas Carol,* with Buddy Hackett as a leprechaun Scrooge; it has Christmas-card "authenticity" with Vegas razzle. But TV itself has taken us beyond the point where the three ghosts could appeal to a network president's intellect or emotions: Frank Cross has an answer to everything—he has been delivering heartfelt messages about the network's obligations for so long that responsibility and morality are just blah blah to him. It's as if some Zen therapy was needed to shake him up. So the three ghosts start beating up on him, and the movie turns into a comic revenge fantasy.

When the Ghost of Christmas Present—Carol Kane as a Sugar Plum Fairy out of the *Nutcracker*—abuses Frank (kick, slap, wham, pinch), she's a sadistic whirligig. She revels in punishing him. Carol Kane is a weirdly dainty comedienne, as she demonstrated as Mrs. Latka Gravas, on "Taxi," and opposite Billy Crystal in *The Princess Bride;* here she's a giggly Pre-Raphaelite angel-witch with gossamer wings and with glittering stars in her golden curls. Her madness is infectious. (I had a flash of how different *Wings of Desire* might have been if she'd played the speechifying winged aerialist—maybe with her Gravas accent.) The film transports Frank from one place to another by an ingenious device: pretty Sugar Plum bops him so hard he blacks out, and then he comes to at his brother's or his secretary's or wherever he can undergo a jolt of recognition.

The structure actually stays quite close to Dickens; it's the tones that are different. Frank is such a sleazeball son of a bitch that his self-centeredness keeps us laughing. And the movie itself is a Christmas cornucopia: it keeps popping surprises. Bobcat Goldthwait is the mild little executive whom Frank fires on Christmas Eve, never expecting him to return with a double-barrelled shotgun. John Forsythe, with his resonant moneyed voice, is the phantom of Frank's old boss, the network chief who died seven years earlier on the golf course and wears the moldy remnants of a rakish golf outfit. (An occasional golf ball emerges from his skull.) Robert Mitchum is the genteel, polite chairman of the board, who's even more of a maniacal burnout than Frank. David Johansen (also known as the lounge singer Buster Poindexter) is an actor of absolute confidence as the grinning cabbie whose identification card reads "Ghost of Christmas Past." And the peerlessly wicked John Glover, who may have the highest, sharpest cheekbones in the acting trade, is the new executive who's bucking to replace Frank; he sports a collegiate "Tennis, anyone?" haircut. Famous faces keep turning up— Alfre Woodard, Nicholas Phillips, John Houseman, Mabel King, and there are glimpses of Susan Isaacs and Mary Lou Retton. When four street musicians play "We Three Kings of Orient Are," they're Miles Davis, Larry Carlton, David Sanborn, and Paul Shaffer. TV contains multitudes; even the people behind the box and in the box do time in front of it.

This satirical extravaganza has a visual advantage over most big comedies: it's set in a stylized, made-up universe with deep blues and black backgrounds—suave and velvety. Its vision of New York is the lacquered city in the sky that artists used to dream about. The Seagram Building, which serves as the exterior of the network headquarters, is a seductive emblem of power—especially when the movie has you looking down the steep face of it. Vertigo is part of the skyscraper's seduction. So is its awesome coldness. And the modified Deco of the elevators and offices says "Come play here." The production designer, J. Michael Riva, and the cinematographer, Michael Chapman, must have shared a lust to prove that style can undercut the danger of sentimentality. The heartlessness of the film's beauty is exciting: you're looking at life in an executive's dark mirror.

Every now and then an image takes over. Michael J. Pollard plays a homeless man whom Frank refuses to help; Frank sees him next sitting up in an alley with icicles hanging from him, his eyes still shining with love of life. Frank meets the Ghost of Christmas Future in an elevator, pulls away the clothes covering the Ghost's chest, and sees what's inside: a collection of lost souls screaming and gnashing their teeth. (It's like a wild, stray thought.) Somehow, Frank's hallucinations manage to be satiric and funny—they're never just macabre. Though the director, Richard Donner, can't be said to have a great comic touch, he knows how to scale the scenes, and he does hit the gags on the button. The editors take it from there and keep the movie leaping. Even the dead spots—when, for instance, Karen Allen, as Frank's onetime girlfriend, grins her Woodstock free-spirit grin and the camera is transfixed—move fast.

Scrooged uses the Dickens framework for an allegory of a yuppie rediscovering the sixties spirit (whereas TV, as a selling medium, has been celebrating the yuppie revolt against the sixties spirit). As the picture goes on, and Frank the powermonger begins to crack, his slicked-down hair gets freer, messier, and curlier; he begins to suggest a long-haired kid of the sixties. That's easy. What isn't easy is his attempt to express his new feelings. When Frank interrupts his telecast and speaks, you hear Murray pleading with the movie audience, asking people to accept the unhip message of love, so that "the miracle of Christmas can happen every day." He's saying, "This isn't so offensive, is it? I know I seem like an ass up here, but it really would help if people treated each other with more consideration—you know it as well as I do.'' I felt that Murray believed every word—that this was what the movie was leading up to. It goes against the grain of the Murray you've come to know, but you're forced to recognize that he's trying to find an equilibrium between hip and unhip. He's trying to take the kinks out of his soul—or, at least, out of Bill Murray the hipster character's soul.

Since the film's sixties spirit merges with moral uplift, you may feel your back stiffening. Murray is asking you to believe in the maudlin crap that TV hands you—it's the old Sunday-school/Capraesque number. (Very likely the moviemakers have no other idea of what the alternative to TV's zapping the soul out of you could be.) But when you hear the sentiments you can also hear the intentions behind them—Murray is trying to push past the ''Saturday Night Live'' put-ons. The whole movie breathes his desire to make direct contact. He's saying hipness isn't all, and the proof is in the amazing performance he gives. It's a triumphant parody of yuppie callousness. And it's much more: Murray's freewheeling, screwy generosity is what makes this huge contraption of a movie work.

High Spirits

In *High Spirits,* a busload of American tourists arrive at a castle that's advertised as the most haunted place in Ireland. The producers may have been hoping for something on the order of National Lampoon's Irish Vacation with a jigger of *Ghostbusters.* But even though they whacked away at the film, it's still clear that what the writer-director, Neil Jordan (best known for his 1986 *Mona Lisa),* was trying for was an Irish phantasmagoria—a *Midsummer Night's Dream,* with

love swaps and ghostly transformations. The producers put
the film through a series of American previews, then recut
it, removing between fifteen and twenty-five per cent of the
footage, in the hope, it appears, of making it less complex
and less delicate—easier for audiences to understand. All
they succeeded in doing was messing up Jordan's film—
now it's neither one thing nor the other. It has lovely
ephemera, though, and once you're past the first fifteen
minutes or so (which are clumsily antic) the moody texture
can take hold of your imagination. At its best, the film is a
soft Irish kiss.

There may never have been a movie ghost who was as
sexy and ethereal a love object as Daryl Hannah is here.
With her flower-stem neck tilted and her long legs sheathed
in a lacy, diaphanous gown, she's the bride who was murdered by her husband (Liam Neeson) on their wedding night
and has been doomed to reënact the death scene each night
for two centuries. Now one of the Americans (Steve Guttenberg, unfortunately) intercedes. There's paranormal grace
in the way Hannah and Neeson pass through stone walls,
and when Hannah puts her hands through the wall and over
Guttenberg's eyes it's like being teased in a dream. When
she makes love to him by passing her body through his, it's
perfect poetic sex.

Peter O'Toole is the gentleman souse Peter Plunkett,
who's trying to save the labyrinthine Castle Plunkett from
foreclosure and keep the villagers in the jobs that are their
only means of support; he's busily—and ineptly—staging
apparitions for the tourists when the real ghosts come out
of the crumbling walls. (The exteriors were shot at the medieval Dromore Castle, which was once the county seat of
the earls of Limerick and is said to have been a model for
Ludwig's rococo castle in Bavaria, which, in turn, was a
model for the castle at Disneyland.) O'Toole's Plunkett has
a comic heartbreaker of a scene when the ghost of his father
(played by Ray McAnally) appears and the dissolute son becomes plaintive and young-boyish as he chides his daddy

for leaving him without warning or preparation. The keen-
ing melancholy in O'Toole's voice hovers in the air long
after Daddy apologizes. (O'Toole's voice is his spirit.)

Beverly D'Angelo does some risky comedy as Guttenberg's rich, unsatisfied wife, who stretches her mouth
wide yowling at him and then, encountering the ghostly
Liam Neeson, melts. D'Angelo doesn't have Daryl Hannah's
heaven-kissing height or the sweet irony that Hannah brings
to her scenes, but she has her own walloping gorgeousness.
She's like a more brass-lunged version of the young Joan
Blondell. Batting her big eyes and swinging her hips, D'Angelo knows how to be the tough city girl and yet make you
understand this girl's yearnings. The character she's playing
is American but she's also Irish; D'Angelo holds the picture
together. Jennifer Tilly is nifty as the flirtatious Miranda, who
has sworn off men (temporarily), and Peter Gallagher is the
doubt-ridden Brother Tony, who is just about to take his
final vows; they have a scene together in a revolving bed
that spins faster and faster. Liz Smith (of *A Private Function*)
is Plunkett's wonderfully pie-eyed mother; normally it's disturbing when a widow talks of her long-dead husband as if
he were still around—here it's natural. Donal McCann (of
The Dead) is the skunk-drunk tour guide; Martin Ferrero (of
"Miami Vice") is a skeptical parapsychologist; and Mary
Coughlan, who plays one of the villagers, sings an Irish song
in a low, almost conversational voice—its plainness can get
to you. Guttenberg isn't actually bad as an amiable, love-
struck ninny; he shows a tender side, and he's blandly silly-
funny when he recites lyrics by The Big Bopper. But the
role might have more tingle if it were filled by an actor who
could suggest that he was shifting from one love to another,
and that this meant changing realms.

The picture has special effects by Meddings Magic Camera
Company, which are in an altogether different style from
the usual ones, by Industrial Light & Magic. They're less
industrial and more like storybook illustrations. Sprites with
comet tails flit through the air. A white horse speaks in a

thick brogue. The nuns who gather accusingly around the tempted Brother have scarily stiff wimples and pinpoint eyes; they're domesticated demons—something you could whip up for Halloween. Stones fly out of a wall as if by command (while O'Toole at his most cadenced expresses stupefaction). And when the tour bus, which has sunk in a misty bog, rises and flies you're not sure for a second or two what's going on. The cinematographer, Alex Thomson, wants you to stare a little. Nothing looks newly processed; the magic here feels like magic—it's dark and cobwebby, and even a little musty. And when an effect doesn't quite work—like the small boy who turns into a cardboard cut-out—you're bothered by its not working, because the conception is promising and you wanted to feel the mystery. The tattered *High Spirits* can't be called a good movie, but I'd call it an inspired one. The repeated reënactments of the two-hundred-year-old murder are spooky, beautiful, and passionate; they're a poet's distillation of the mechanical nature of movies.

The Dressmaker

Joan Plowright as Nellie, the prudish unmarried dress-maker, and Billie Whitelaw as Margo, the widow with a roving eye who works in a munitions factory, are sisters in *The Dressmaker*. They head a cast that includes Jane Horrocks, as Rita, the seventeen-year-old niece who has lived with the two since her mother's death, and Peter Postlethwaite, as her butcher father. The setting is Liverpool in 1944, and the plot centers on what happens when the sallow, skinny Rita falls in love with Wesley (Tim Ransom), a Yank from Mississippi. She's frightened of his hands on her and keeps slapping him away. There is certainly a tinge of comedy in the situation, but there is also a tinge of queasy horror. As you watch poor Rita in the throes of romance, you perceive that the movie is about morbid respectability. Plump and placid in her corset, Nellie, the head of the family, is raging inside; she would like to kill.

The script, by John McGrath, is a model of fullness and concision; he has adapted the 1973 Beryl Bainbridge novel (published here in 1974 as *The Secret Glass)* so that the movie develops a cumulative force. Directing his first feature, Jim O'Brien—a major presence in British TV (he co-directed *The Jewel in the Crown)*—makes it possible for the actors to create a maze of claustrophobic subtexts.

The Dressmaker is airless. (It's not a director's movie; it's an actors' movie.) But this isn't a defect. The airlessness is part of the tension. You avidly watch every detail: the gloating smiles of a neighbor (Rosemary Martin) whose bosomy daughter (Pippa Hinchley) gets herself engaged; the lumpy-faced butcher's squeamishness, and his misery when he observes his daughter's unhappiness.

And, of course, you see Plowright's Nellie, with her bright, beady brown eyes, and her containment; her clothes armor her like a tank. And you see Whitelaw's Margo, in her skimpy dresses, frilly at the bodice and tight at the bum. Maybe it's all the years Whitelaw has given to acting Beckett's plays—her blue eyes stab you. She seems to have become the nakedest of performers. In the novel, Nellie recalls how Margo looked after she'd been persuaded not to marry again: "Her face, the look in her eyes for all to see—there was something indecent in the explicitness of her expression." That's exactly what we see. I doubt if either Plowright or Whitelaw has ever before been this scarily effective onscreen. Nellie's sureness seems rooted in her flesh. Margo, the good-time girl, the pushover, feels the force of Nellie's contempt, and does her bidding.

Beryl Bainbridge is very readable, but you don't feel a strong necessity in her writing. This almost-really-good aspect of her novels may be liberating to moviemakers. Bainbridge was an actress before she became a novelist, and possibly the mixed tones of her writing give actors elements to fuse. Her *The Bottle Factory Outing* was filmed in Toronto, in 1982, as *Heartaches,* and the actors (especially Margot Kidder and Annie Potts) surpassed themselves. Here the whole cast seems to rise to the occasion. Jane Horrocks' comic and forlorn Rita hangs on to her idea that Wesley, the Mississippian, is her boyfriend even when he stands her up, week after week. Rita's defeated, slumping, eyes-cast-down posture stays in your mind. So does Billie Whitelaw's blinding sky-blue gaze—it feels as if it will stay in your mind forever.

DECEMBER 12, 1988

LOVE / HATE

Tequila Sunrise

Michelle Pfeiffer tells Mel Gibson how sorry she is that she hurt his feelings. He replies, "C'mon, it didn't hurt that bad," pauses, and adds, "Just lookin' at you hurts more." If a moviegoer didn't already know that *Tequila Sunrise* was the work of a master romantic tantalizer, Gibson's line should clinch it. That's the kind of ritualized confession of love that gave a picture like *To Have and Have Not* its place in moviegoers' affections. What makes the line go ping is that Mel Gibson's blue eyes are wide with yearning as he says it, and Michelle Pfeiffer is so crystalline in her beauty that he seems to be speaking the simple truth. (If she weren't a vision, the picture would crash.) It's a line that Gary Cooper might have spoken to Marlene Dietrich in *Morocco*; it requires youth and innocence in the man and flowerlike perfection in the woman.

You have to be able to enjoy trashy shamelessness to enjoy old Hollywood and to enjoy *Tequila Sunrise*. Robert Towne, who wrote and directed, is soaked in the perfume of thirties and forties Hollywood romanticism. Chances are that while you're watching the triangular shuffle of Gibson and Pfeiffer and Kurt Russell, as Gibson's friend who also gets involved with Pfeiffer, you'll know you're being had

48

but you'll love it. This old shell game can make you feel
alert and happy—at least, it can when it's brought up to date
with the seductive panache of a Robert Towne.

Tequila Sunrise is about flirtation; it's about Towne's
wanting to give pleasure. Set in San Pedro and the other
beach communities in and around L.A., it has a golden, stud-
ied casualness; the cinematographer, Conrad Hall, feasts on
the stars' faces, the three sets of blue eyes, the beachfront,
the water washing through the scenes, the waves crashing
over lovers. All this beauty—and it's about cops and rob-
bers! And not even about that, exactly. Towne has the ef-
frontery to offer us the wizened plot device of the two
friends from school days—one (Gibson) has become a
crook, the other (Russell) a cop—who are in love with the
same girl. But the movie is much too derivative and vague
to be a successful crime melodrama; it doesn't have the
compression of a thriller. There's an emptiness at its center—a feeling of hurt and loneliness, a lesion of vitality.

Gibson's McKussic, a former drug dealer who's desperately trying to succeed in the irrigation business, is driven
to make manic fun of how hard it has been to get out of the
drug trade. He tells Pfeiffer's Jo Ann, "Nobody wants me to
quit. The cops wanna *bust* me, the Colombians want my
connections, my wife she wants my *money,* her lawyer
agrees, and mine likes getting paid to argue with them. . . .
I haven't even mentioned my customers. You *know* they
don't want me to quit." This special pleading for McKussic's
purity is right at the heart of the movie (and it gives Mel
Gibson a warmer character than he has played before). Mac
is like the Bogart heroes who have finer feelings than people
understand, and his love for Jo Ann is a truer, deeper love
than Russell's Nick Frescia offers. (Mac is also a prodigious
cocksman.) It doesn't take long for a viewer to grasp that
Mac is the writer-director's simplified and idealized version
of himself. Besides, Towne has said that his legal troubles—
a divorce, and litigation over a couple of movie projects—
made him feel like a criminal, so that it was easy for him to

identify with Mac. (And those who have read interviews with him won't have much trouble spotting drug dealing as a metaphor for script doctoring, a lucrative sideline that his associates wanted him to mainline—his rewrites were a convenience for directors and producers. Drug dealing can also serve as a tidy metaphor for the messier matter of drug use, which also makes you feel like a criminal.)

The movie has a lot of talk about friendship, and whether the bond between Mac and Nick, who's the head of the narcotics squad in L.A. County, can withstand the pressure from the Feds to bust Mac, or can withstand Nick's wily maneuvers to extract information about Mac from Jo Ann. But the characters aren't centered enough for their subterfuges to amount to much—they're just vagrant impulses that lead to romantic misunderstandings. Towne's actual legal troubles involved old, close friends, but in the movie he doesn't supply the injuries that have been done to Mac and doesn't pin them on anybody in particular. (Nick hasn't done any real harm to him, and even when they argue their voices have the rhythm of friends arguing.) Yet Mac is melancholy, as if betrayal were in the air he breathed. We do see that he's bled dry by his ex-wife (Ann Magnuson), who's out for everything she can get and won't let him see his son if he doesn't deliver his payments. But his grievances seem cosmic, and he longs for a decent, respectable life. His character is a victim fantasy.

The picture may have a special erotic appeal for women, because Mac is waiting for the true-heart woman, the woman whose love is limitless and unconditional, the woman whose only need is to be a helpmate. That's Jo Ann, a woman who never lies. (She's the opposite of Brigid in *The Maltese Falcon*.) Jo Ann, who, with her brother, operates an elegant Italian restaurant, is soft-spoken and refined—a lady. She has her own code of honor, her own gallantry. At the restaurant, she's a pro: she's thoroughly in command of seeming in command. And the film equates her smoothness with the best of traditional values. She isn't up to anything, so

Mac can put himself in her hands. And she falls in love with him, supposedly, because she believes that he's been more truthful to her than Nick has been. It's a priggish, vacuous ideal-woman role, but Michelle Pfeiffer bursts right through it. She activates Towne's romantic dream of the good, kind woman.

Kurt Russell's worldly jokester Nick—a calculating charmer—gives the plot a little bit of motor, or, at least, an occasional push. And the movie badly needs Russell's brazenness and his slippery grin; it needs his sly, shiny eyes. Nick locates us in a wisecracking movie tradition, especially when he razzes the high-muck-a-muck from the federal Drug Enforcement Agency. (J. T. Walsh makes this clown villain the quintessential flatfoot; it's a classic turn.) But Russell's main function is as a contrast to Mac, who's the male ingénue here. Both Nick and Jo Ann want to protect Mac, because he's a-hurtin'. And because he's a saintly stud.

The movie is a confluence of fantasies, with a crime plot that often seems to be stalled, as if a projector had broken down. A good melodramatic structure should rhyme: we should hold our breath at the pacing as the pieces come together, and maybe smile at how neat the fit is. Here the pieces straggle, and by the end you're probably ignoring the plot points. Raul Julia, who turns up as the Mexican Comandante Escalante, has a big, likable, rumbling presence; his role recalls the Leo Carrillo parts in movies like *The Gay Desperado,* with a new aplomb. And for a few seconds here and there Raul Julia takes over; he's funny, and he detonates. (The character's lack of moral conflicts gives his scenes a giddy high.) Then the film's languor settles in again. An elaborate government sting operation waits while Mac and Escalante play Ping-Pong, and waits again while they sit in a boat and Mac talks drivel about bullfighting. (It's the worst dialogue in the film; for sheer inappropriateness it's matched only by Dave Grusin's aggressive, out-to-slay-you score.)

Most of the dialogue is sprightly—it's easy, everyday talk

that actors can breathe to. But Towne's directing is, surprisingly, better than his construction—maybe because when he plans to direct he leaves things loose. He says, "I make the character fit the actor, I don't try to make the actor fit the character." That sounds as if he's highly variable, a modernist. But he isn't. He likes bits from old movies, such as having the cops who are planning to surprise Mac be so dumb that they leave peanut shells wherever they've been posted. The difference between the way Towne handles the peanut shells and the way a director of the thirties would have (and did) is that he doesn't sock the joke home; he glides over it. He wants the effect, yet he doesn't want to be crude about it, so he half does it. Almost everything in the action scenes of the last three-quarters of an hour is half done. Often he gives you the preparation for action and no follow-through; sometimes the reverse.

Towne's memory is stocked with movie tricks, but what he really treasures is the rhapsodic buzz of those moments when two stars hooked into each other's eyes. That's what saves *Tequila Sunrise.* His obsessions about friendship and betrayal don't mesh with the plot (which is off somewhere floating in cloudland), but his understanding of how movies work for audiences lightens this movie, keeps it happy. It's about a guy who wants to say, "I'm dying from loving you so much," and a girl who knows that in a hot tub he's "like a world champion." Traditionally, these feelings are disguised, or kidded, before they're presented in public. Robert Towne puts them right out on the table. (Both Mac and Nick approach Jo Ann through the pain her beauty causes them. Nick phones and tells her, "I'm going to die if I don't see you.") By rational standards the movie is flimsy and stupid, but by romantic standards it's delectable. The three talented stars are smashing, and the film's paranoid narcissism is dreamy and pretty. Hollywood glamour has a lot to do with a moviegoer's braving out the silliness that's part of it. This is a lusciously silly movie. It has an amorous shine.

Mississippi Burning

The director Alan Parker likes to operate in a wildly melo-dramatic universe of his own creation. In *Mississippi Burning,* which is set during the Freedom Summer of 1964, he treats Southerners the way he treated the Turks ten years ago in *Midnight Express.* And he twists facts here as he did there, with the same apparent objective: to come up with garish forms of violence. We see the white Southerners burning and beating and lynching, but Parker isn't content with that. He wants to give the audience violence it can cheer. A black F.B.I man is introduced so he can threaten to castrate a white man, and the F.B.I strings up a suspected Klansman to scare him into testifying against his buddies. Then, there are the inventions that jack up the plot. A dep-uty sheriff (Brad Dourif) brutally beats his tiny wife (Frances McDormand) while his K.K.K. pals watch to make sure he does a thorough job. She has succumbed to the overtures of an F.B.I. man (Gene Hackman) and told him where the bodies of three missing civil-rights workers were to be found. (Actually, the F.B.I. informant was a man, and he was given a thirty-thousand-dollar reward for his help.) The en-tire movie hinges on the ploy that the F.B.I. couldn't stop the K.K.K. from its terrorism against blacks until it swung over to vigilante tactics. And we're put in the position of applauding the F.B.I.'s dirtiest forms of intimidation. This cheap gimmick undercuts the whole civil-rights subject; it validates the terrorist methods of the Klan.

When black people here are on a march, they look with-drawn, dead-eyed, blank; there's no elation or glory in their progress down the street. The Civil Rights Act had just been passed in the Senate, and during that Freedom Summer, when roughly a thousand students and activists arrived in Mississippi to set up schools and register blacks to vote, blacks themselves were busy in the fight for desegregation; they were holding rallies, staging protests, and forming picket lines. They were training themselves to take verbal and physical abuse without being provoked to violence. In the movie, the blacks are sheeplike and frightened; they seem totally unprepared. The events here took place eight and a half years after Rosa Parks refused to go to the back of the bus, but Alan Parker is essentially putting blacks at the back again. The picture opens with a fictionalized re-creation of the murder of the three civil-rights workers—James Chaney, the local black who was working for CORE, and two young Jewish activists from up North, Andrew Goodman and Michael Schwerner—who were in their station wagon and were stopped by Ku Klux Klansmen and lawmen. Chaney was driving; in the movie, he has been replaced at the wheel by one of the whites. It's a small detail, but the details add up to a civil-rights movie in which blacks don't do much of anything except inspire pity and sympathy in the two F.B.I. men (Hackman and Willem Dafoe) who are the heroes.

Hackman's Anderson and Dafoe's Ward arrive in the small town where the three men were last seen; their mission is to find out what happened to them. Anderson is a burly, big Mississippian who grew up dirt poor and knows that for whites to feel that they're better than blacks may be the only point of pride they've got. He understands, but it disgusts him. He's a complicated, lonely man who no longer feels at home in the South yet isn't at home with Northerners, either. (Actually, Hackman, a Midwesterner, had never been in the Deep South before, but you wouldn't guess it from his performance.) The pale, bespectacled Ward, who is in charge of the investigation, looks small next to Anderson. He's formal, conscientious, and deeply courteous. A Harvard Law School man who was at the Department of Justice before joining the Bureau, he represents the idealism of the Kennedy era—he's brave and dedicated, but rigid.

The man has no common sense. And he inadvertently sets off a brief war between the Bureau and the Klan.

When the local people, black and white alike, won't tell Ward anything, he thinks the answer is to bring in more agents, and after he's got a huge manhunt going and still has no results he brings in Naval Reserves. The K.K.K. fights the invasion by attacking black people and burning their churches. Anderson, who knows how to nose around town and pick up leads, keeps arguing with Ward, showing him that he's making the situation worse. At one point, they face off as if they were going to kill each other, and the movie turns into a bad imitation of a Western. But what's involved in the running battle between the two is the central cheat of the movie. Parker, working from a script by Chris Gerolmo (which he says he rewrote), sets up Dafoe's Ward as a high-principled official with no resourcefulness or flexibility or canniness, and says that he represents the only legal way to tackle the problems. The only alternative, according to Parker, is the illegal, underhanded methods that Anderson insists must be used. And, of course, Anderson—an uncommon common man, whom Hackman plays with humor and buried rage—is the man we identify with. Hackman draws us to him; he's the star here—he's vivid. And he's the spokesman for brutality. There isn't even a whisper of a suggestion that Anderson may get any undue satisfaction from the brutal methods that Ward, recognizing his own defeat, finally allows him to employ. No—they're employed righteously, for Biblical vengeance. (The common man knows what those gents from Harvard Law are too educated to understand.) Parker uses the civil-rights movement to make a wham-bam Charles Bronson movie, and, from his blithe public statements, he seems unaware that this could be thought morally repugnant.

He justifies his small inventions and his big, crude ones in terms of fiscal responsibility to his backers. Presumably, the audience needs a whomp in the gut every two minutes. But if it does, that's because whomping is Parker's basic way of reaching people, and he sets up a pattern. He pounds you, in scenes like the one of the K.K.K., armed with clubs, gathering outside a church in which black people are singing. He won't let go of effects like the lowing of cows in a barn that's been set on fire. (He takes the title very literally; the sets keep going up in flames.) Yet, despite the heaviness of *Mississippi Burning,* it doesn't necessarily stay with you— it's too mechanical, too inexpressive. (There are exceptions: a night shot of the station wagon, with the three young men, coming over a wavy, hilly road, followed by two cars and a truck with no lights; the lovely shades of regret in some of Hackman's scenes with Frances McDormand; the cheeriness of the actress Park Overall's remarks in the town beauty parlor.) Parker is a slicker—a man with talent and technique but without a sustaining sensibility. Each time I heard the pulsating music start working me up for the next bout of violence, I dreaded what was coming. The manipulation got to me, all right, but the only emotion I felt was hatred of the movie.

DECEMBER 26, 1988

THE COMEDY
OF EVIL

Dangerous Liaisons

In the prologue of *Dangerous Liaisons,* the Marquise de
Merteuil (Glenn Close) and the Vicomte de Valmont (John
Malkovich) are in their homes, with fleets of servants preparing them for the start of their daily social engagements.
And as they're massaged and are given their facials and are
made up and dressed and bejewelled it's as if they were
being readied for a play—or a war. It's a wonderfully shrewd
opening. The director, Stephen Frears, and the screenwriter, Christopher Hampton, who reworked his theatrical
version of the Choderlos de Laclos novel *Les Liaisons Dangereuses,* take us right into a world of artifice—the customs
and pleasures of French aristocrats in the late seventeen-
seventies—and keep us so close to these people that we can
examine their lace and their wigs and their skins. The novel,
which was originally published in Paris in 1782, condemned
in court in 1824, publicly burned, and banned for the rest
of the nineteenth century, has a tone and a texture unlike
those of any other novel. Written in the form of highly confidential letters, it is principally about the erotic power

games played by the Marquise and Valmont, who were once lovers but are now allies and co-conspirators. Laclos, an artillery officer who eventually, under Napoleon, rose to be a general, shows these two aristocrats planning sexual conquests with the cunning and deviousness of military masters, and with far more cruelty, since their victims don't know that they have been made pawns in a campaign. The implication is that the depraved pair stand for their class (and for what after 1789 was to be known as the ancien régime). The success of the movie is that in taking you so far into this systematic debauchery it gets you to feel the emotions under the clever, petty calculations. (It's like uncovering the carnal roots of chess.) By the end, the artificiality has dissolved and something forceful and shocking has taken over.

All along, you see the duplicitousness under the Marquise's wholesome, open-faced, pink-and-creamy exterior. That's what gives the material its comic austerity: you see what's under her farm-fresh smile, you know the heart that beats under her charmingly freckled bosom. Lighted by the marvelous cinematographer Philippe Rousselot (*Diva, Hope and Glory*), she looks as "natural" as a Fragonard. But she's playacting when she makes herself the sympathetic confidante of the conventional-minded ladies of her circle; she feels utter contempt for them, and she twists and turns them to her purposes. The storytelling isn't clear enough at the start: it glides over the plan the Marquise outlines to Valmont. A recent lover who has deserted her is going to marry a rich virgin, the fifteen-year-old, convent-trained Cécile (Uma Thurman); to get back at him, the Marquise has hatched the idea that Valmont should seduce the girl. But Valmont isn't stimulated by the suggestion; he thinks the defloration so easy that it's unworthy of his talents. He takes Cécile on, but only as secondary to a more prestigious target he has chosen for himself: a devout young married woman who's a citadel of virtue—Mme. de Tourvel (Michelle Pfeiffer). Somehow, the Marquise's request of Valmont and the matter of their former relationship and current alliance aren't sufficiently weighted, and you're not fully drawn in; for a long time, you watch the movie as if it were a charmingly wicked marionette show. And that's how you watch it even after everything is lucid and you begin to be fascinated. The Marquise has a grandeur in her manipulativeness: she ruthlessly sets about destroying Cécile, whose mother (Swoosie Kurtz) is her close friend. The girl herself adores her; to the Marquise, this is simply an advantage to be used—she'll use anything to get back at the lover who rejected her.

There are times when the Marquise—a happy widow— sounds much like a modern, "liberated" woman. This is basically faithful to Laclos, who reads like a feminist if you don't pick up the nuances. Here is a passage from Letter 152, in which the Marquise reprimands Valmont for his "connubial" manner with her: "Do you know, Vicomte, why I never married again? It was certainly not for lack of advantageous matches: it was solely so that no one should have the right to object to anything I might do. It was not even for fear that I might no longer be able to have my way, for I should always have succeeded in that in the end: but I should have found it irksome if anyone had had so much as a right to complain. In short, I wished to lie only when I wanted to, not when I had to." In both novel and movie, the Marquise is liberated to lie and scheme, and her primary motive is vicious, vengeful jealousy. At the start, she wants to pay back the lover who prefers a virgin; near the end, she wants to destroy Valmont, because he has fallen in love with the pious prude he set out to amuse himself with. When he describes his ecstasy in bed with Mme. de Tourvel, the Marquise recognizes that he's in love, and the color drains from her face; she's a victim of her feelings, like the men and women she despises for their weakness. She's enraged; she feels left out.

The Marquise is actually the opposite of liberated: she is one of the most formidable examples of hell-hath-no-fury-like-a-woman-scorned in all literature. Childless, of course, she's woman the destroyer, and, despite her reserve and her control, and her superficial rationality, she pulls the lowest kind of "feminine" treachery: she cancels the game she has going with Valmont after he has won, and pins the blame on him. She's a power-hungry, castrating female as conceived by an eighteenth-century male writer. She's also a great character, in the way that Richard III is great. She's polished in her savagery, and the straight-backed Glenn Close, looking matriarchal and pure (even her teeth are perfect), gives a smooth performance that is by far her best work onscreen. She may lack the ravaged intensity that Jeanne Moreau brought to the role in the 1959 modern-dress version by Roger Vadim, and she's rather bland (though less so in the second half), but she has terrific bearing, and her arch Marquise, with her immaculate simulation of propriety, provides a balance to Malkovich's outré Valmont.

Malkovich takes a little getting used to, because of his furtive eyes, his pursed lips, his slight speech impediment (is it a lisp?), and his little moues. Though he wears a powdered wig, he's weirdly far from the conventional movie image of a French nobleman of the pre-Revolutionary period. Some reptilian men are very successful sexually, but reptilian and fey make an odd combination. Still, off-putting as the casting of Malkovich is, it works cumulatively—even triumphantly. He brings the movie a clowning wit; this Valmont is a cutup and a boudoir farceur. (He uses a trace of effeminacy as an all-purpose lubricant for a tricky gesture or line reading.) And when his dark hair is long and loose it seems to propel him sexually; it helps you make sense of his conquests. When Gérard Philipe played the role, in the Vadim version, he was near death, and he didn't suggest the energy that Valmont requires, but he still had remnants of angelic good looks, and that helped explain women's attraction to him. (It's generally assumed that angelic-looking men can get away with plenty—that that's how the devil fools us.) With Malkovich in the role, Valmont's warped soul is on the outside. Yet Malkovich gives you the sense that Valmont is a priapic freak, and the movie needs that. The Vicomte is the freak who grows into a romantic. (Once he does, he's no good to the Marquise.) And, maybe because this Valmont's depravity is on the surface, along with his mocking humor, he's likable—he's funny, and his swinishness is fascinating. You can see before the Marquise does that he's in love with the serious-minded bourgeoise. And you can see that he's foolish enough, and vain enough, to try to live up to what the Marquise expects of him, in order to be thought irreproachably heartless. (He has a left-handed sense of honor.)

As Mme. de Tourvel, who clings to her conception of honor, the paradisially beautiful Michelle Pfeiffer is caught in frightened closeups. Stiff in her tight bodice and her crisp bonnets, this modest little wife, generous and philanthropic, seems almost plain. But when passion hits her it overpowers her. Her face is damp; she's sweaty—Valmont has set her on fire. And when he rejects her brutally (he just flat out lets her have it), and she breaks down crying, she's helplessly human, a real person caught in a maze of deception. This is when the movie comes together. Mme. de Tourvel's suffering cuts through the decorative formality; suddenly, the marionettes have blood in their veins. The comedy goes out of the game, and the viewer may feel slightly stunned at the impact the movie begins to have. Mme. de Tourvel's collapse is what all that choice cruelty was pointing toward. The transition is so affecting partly because of the traplike construction of the story and partly because Pfeiffer's performance is very simple—it feels true. She makes it totally convincing that the rake Valmont would experience ecstasy while releasing Mme. de Tourvel from her Puritan timidity, yet would be afraid of being laughed at for loving this woman from a different class—a woman without guile or wit.

From then on, everything that happens—and it happens bam, bam, bam—seems part of an unstoppable chain of events. Frears might almost be letting the story tell itself as he moves right through the Marquise's declaration of war, the casualties that follow, and on to the hooting scene (described in Letter 173). Frears' technique is remarkably unaffected. Using American actors (instead of following the Hollywood tradition of casting British actors as French aristocrats) gives the film a directness, an emotional immediacy. (Mildred Natwick is admirably straightforward as Valmont's aged aunt.) So do the speedy, encircling camera movements, and the ravishing closeups, with every facet of the women's earrings picking up light. This must be one of the least static costume films ever shot. (The play version has eighteen scenes; Hampton says the screenplay has two hundred.) But, then, by the end this doesn't feel like a costume film: though the locations include several châteaus near Paris, and the clothes are magnificent, *Dangerous Liaisons* is brisk and unsentimental. There's a minute of a Gluck opera in the background of two scenes, and when a pause is needed there's a brief, blissful interlude of singers at a musicale, but the movie has the let's-get-on-with-it quality that's Frears' signature.

Possibly there's no way to make a picture this fast (it was shot in ten weeks) and achieve something comparable in greatness to the elegant comedy of evil that Laclos left us. There are dismal clinkers in Hampton's dialogue; he strains to give the Marquise and Valmont witty dialogue to underline their perversity. (He's saying they're too clever by half.) And the scenes between the Marquise and Valmont miss out on sensual excitement: you don't feel an electrical current crackling between them. But the casting is still strong. (It's clear that the Marquise has poisoned her capacity to love, and that she has no means left to express her feelings for Valmont except by destroying him, the woman he cares for, and herself.) This is a first-rate piece of work by a director who's daring and agile. The unfussiness of Frears' approach is tonic. The movie gets at the important things and doesn't linger over them. It's heaven—alive in a way that movies of classics rarely are.

Working Girl

The first ten minutes of Mike Nichols' *Working Girl* is laid in very deftly, preparing us for a bouncy, updated version of the Cinderella comedies that Ginger Rogers made in the thirties between her musicals with Fred Astaire. Tess McGill (Melanie Griffith), a poor but enterprising girl from Staten Island, fights off the sleazoid bosses and struggles to break through the educational-background barriers and climb from Wall Street secretary to executive. But the Cinderella feeling must all still be in Nichols' head; the emotion has been relegated to an idea, and a rather grim idea, at that. We're supposed to be cheered by watching Tess become part of the establishment: she makes it into the world of mergers and acquisitions. Her victory is certified when she's ensconced in a cubicle high up in a skyscraper; on the soundtrack, Carly Simon and a women's choir sing exultantly. No, there's no irony—only fatuity.

Lest we get the wrong idea, the picture makes it clear that the victory is only for a sweet, feminine girl like Tess—not for anybody forceful or butch. The villain is Tess's sneaky, upper-crust boss, played by Sigourney Weaver: she doesn't just try to steal Tess's big, career-making radio-network idea; she's also unwomanly. At first, Weaver is a confident, entertaining cartoon of moneyed egomania; she's a genuinely game actress, eager to be funny. But then the picture demeans her, by making her a ludicrous witch who can't hang on to her guy or her job. (It even demeans her in small, gross ways: when she's in the hospital, doctors try to look under her nightie.) Weaver looks stranded in the last part of the movie. The director seems to have abdicated, and the staging is so broad you can't tell whether satire is intended or just dumb jokes; even with sharp editing, nothing has any edge.

Is this really the work of the Mike Nichols who is said to be a miracle man with actors? Tall, skinny-legged Melanie Griffith is warm and, yes, down to earth and very appealing, and she has funny bits all the way through. She carries what there is of the picture. But her funky (and infinitely preferable) performances in De Palma's *Body Double* and Jonathan Demme's *Something Wild* are the skeletons rattling in this picture's closet. The subtext of *Working Girl* is that Mike Nichols is trying to let a little bit of tackiness into a big-budget movie—a little bit of John Waters and *Something Wild*. It must have been the funky Melanie that this picture with its double-entendre title was meant to be about. But Nichols may be afraid of swinging the door open, and so Melanie Griffith is ostensibly used for "vulnerability." This is the kind of star performance in which the heroine's misty eyes and soft-focus smiles are supposed to turn our brains to jelly. Since Tess keeps beating her head against a wall trying to succeed, it wouldn't be inappropriate for her to look bleary and depressed. But the moviemakers try to conceal Griffith's being out of condition. The camera goes lyrical; it babies her, making her a cuddlebug, and showing us her firm, round haunches while pretending it isn't doing what it's doing. (One of the things it's doing is catching her in black garter belts, push-up bra, and bikini panties; there's even a peeky porno tease when she bustles about cleaning Weaver's house while wearing undies.) As the investment-banker hero, Harrison Ford tries for the casualness of a big-time smoothie, and he has some style, but, whether because of what he's attempting or because of the director's listlessness, the film's pacing slackens just when he appears. Ford does manage to be diverting in moments that have nothing to do with the tinny plot: a scene where Tess has passed out and he makes small talk in her direction, and, later, a scene when he gets a food delivery at the door and goes back to Tess in bed, whistling "If I Only Had a Brain." (He suggests a man who keeps himself amused.)

The picture does better by some of the players in minor roles: Joan Cusack (of the euphoric grin) as Tess's happy, rowdy best friend; Kevin Spacey as a coke-snorting arbitrageur who's an irrepressible lech; and Nora Dunn as the office suckup and priss. But Nichols must have a cummerbund around his head: the directing is constricted—there's no visual inventiveness or spontaneity. And in his hands the script (by Kevin Wade) has no conviction: the lines have a lot of surprise, but the situations (and digressions) are moldy. After Tess gives up her tattooed Staten Island boyfriend (Alec Baldwin), she returns and has more scenes with him—as if the tattoos hadn't already told us everything. When Tess and her investment man get overheated by a deal they've got going, and rush from a business meeting to their big sex scene, the movie pokes only the mildest fun at them. The plot hinges on Tess's making an impression on a fatherly tycoon (Philip Bosco), who materializes out of an earlier era of movies; this dear old geezer sees that justice is meted out to everyone. Yet the way the wedding of the tycoon's daughter is set up suggests that he lives among twerps and has spawned a bumpkin. There's a classic piece of inept plotting: the last-minute introduction of a disk jockey who's the linchpin of the network deal. It's as if somebody ran onto the stage waving a telegram just as the curtain came down on his head.

This Cinderella story seems to have been concocted by people at the top of the skyscraper who have no fellow-feeling for losers. The film makes the point that Tess, like the other working-class secretaries, tries to get attention and does exactly the wrong thing: she puts on so much makeup she looks like a brainless bimbo, and then she wonders why the Ivy League graduates get jobs over her. The secretaries wear their hair scooped up high in front and hanging down around their shoulders, and it's all teased and whipped and snarled. Another director might have shown us how pretty they are in their purple and green and blue eyeshadow and dishevelled Marie-Antoinette hairdos, but Nichols has them looking like procuresses. The discrimination against them should be by the blind Ivy League bosses; here it's by the blind director.

JANUARY 9, 1989

FOGGED IN

The Accidental Tourist

The Accidental Tourist begins with the numb grief of a Baltimore man, Macon Leary (William Hurt), whose twelve-year-old son was randomly killed by a gunman in a Burger Bonanza the year before. A travel writer, Macon turns out guidebooks for American business people who have to go abroad but don't want to feel they've left home. Macon has always been punctilious, a man who likes his comforts; he hasn't been after pleasure—he's been concerned to avoid the pain of disorder or the unknown. Now he's gone past his usual standoffishness: he's become such a depressed loner that his wife (Kathleen Turner) can't bear the way he has split himself off from their loss, and leaves him. Stiffly, timorously, he goes on about his work—an only half-awake man. The movie, which closely follows the 1985 Ann Tyler novel it's based on, is about Macon's coming to life.

This happens through the agency of Edward, his dead son's Welsh corgi, who becomes unpredictable and snappish and, in a fluke accident, causes Macon to break his leg. Unable to care for himself, Macon has the excuse he needs to move into his grandfather's handsome Victorian house, where he grew up, and where his sister, who's in her late thirties, and his two brothers, in their forties, like him, live together playing the card game they devised as children. They're four polite, methodical stick-in-the-muds and one unmanageable dog. It isn't until Edward has become a terror that Macon sends for a dog trainer, Muriel (Geena Davis)— a fiercely eager oddball who lives in a slum neighborhood with her sickly seven-year-old son. Muriel, who has Fu Manchu fingernails and wears plastic jewelry and jungle prints, reaches out to Macon and pulls him into her bed; her scruffiness and the messy confusion of her life turn out to be his salvation. The plot construction is that of a screwball comedy of the thirties: poor working girl has the life force that upper-class prig needs. But everyone here seems catatonic— even Muriel, whose tense talkativeness is as panicked as Macon's recessiveness and silence. Is she meant to be a forward version of Macon's shy family? Or does she seem near-grotesque because we're seeing her from Macon's stuffy, upper-middle-class perspective? I wasn't sure.

Parts of the picture seem to be taking place in a parallel universe, where people talk a formal, affected English that sounds counterfeit. And this cheerless universe (it lacks oxygen) seems to belong to William Hurt. Slowed-down, withdrawn Macon isn't just the central character; he's the only full character. Hurt is made up to look older and very pale; he gives a shrunk-inside-himself performance. He keeps us aware of a droll intelligence under the priggishness and the pain, but it's hidden. Most of the time he does his acting behind his eyes, as if he expected the camera to pick up his brain waves, and now and then it just about does that. The rest of the time, it doesn't, and he pressures you with all that sad-sack passivity. He's too mopish, too flat-voiced dull. (Macon must know that his guidebooks are at some level amusing, that they're self-satires. Hurt could use more resiliency.) It's true that when you're reading the novel everything except Edward's barking and biting does seem to go on behind the characters' eyes. But in the novel you know what's happening back there. Watching the movie is like trying to read a book with the covers closed.

If you're going to write a novel of sensibility on the screen, it had better be your own novel, your own sensibility. It may be a disaster, but the viewer isn't as likely to get the empty feeling of being on the outside staring reverently at not very much. There are, of course, ways for moviemakers to get inside a novel of sensibility—even one that's about loss and inertia—but the voice that attracts the moviemakers is what almost certainly dooms them to failure. They become dubbers. And in the case of Anne Tyler's novels, voice is everything; she has a fluky sort of precision—a fidelity to everyday eccentricity—that makes her writing enjoyable. The discreet, painstaking Lawrence Kasdan, who directed, and wrote the screenplay with Frank Galati, is so conscious of how he could go wrong by obtrusiveness that he hangs back. Temperamentally, he may have a real affinity with Tyler—they both like schematic whimsy. And Macon neatly packing his suitcase is almost uncannily like the dressing of the corpse in Kasdan's *The Big Chill*. But Tyler keeps perking along, while Kasdan is cautious—paralyzed. He doesn't risk dubbing in his own voice (which isn't a strong one anyway). This *Accidental Tourist* has no voice. It's mute.

The minimal fun of *Tourist* has to do with our not having seen people like the Learys on the screen before. And toward the middle of the movie, when we get into the big family house and hear the four anesthetized siblings saying the things they've said a thousand times, Kasdan catches a wry, pixillated family humor. (It's close to Tyler's tone and to her patented compulsive families.) Amy Wright as the hopeful, organized sister and Ed Begley, Jr., and David Ogden Stiers as the glum, serious-faced brothers make Hurt's Macon more believable; they're a fogged-in, reclusive family unit—they hold to their routines, like the travellers who follow Macon's guidebooks. They're all trying to keep senseless killers at bay. And when Macon's publisher (Bill Pullman) meets the sister and joins the unit you can see why the family's genteel lethargy appeals to him: he fits in; he

has his own drollness, and the movie becomes funnier when
he's around. The interactions of the Learys, snug in their
home (it's their shell) and dedicating their hours to trivial
pursuits, clearly touch Kasdan right on his funny bone. And
there's something about this family of overgrown children that may touch all of us who grew up among siblings.
But then Kathleen Turner, as the wife, shows up again, and
there's no telling what she's doing or why Macon was married to her or what sort of life they had together before their
son's death. (Did Macon function at normal speed then?)
Turner is the director's worst miscalculation; the novel offered no guidance, and you can't tell what he's directing her
to show. She might be in a different movie, and you begin
to wish she were.

The viewer's hopes all center on Geena Davis's skinny,
volatile Muriel; in this ponderous, dead-zone atmosphere,
the screwball-comedy structure gives you a rooting interest
in her. She's the moral core of the movie—the person with
inferior social status who recognizes the possibility of Macon's becoming a caring person. And once you've seen Macon show some feeling for what her undersized son goes
through living in the slums among bullies you can't help
wanting him to be a father to the boy, especially since Robert Gorman, as the kid, never gives an inch—he's a tough
little weakling. (He isn't photographed to be a shiny-haired
princeling, like the boy in Paris who reminds Macon of his
lost son—a scene that has an almost homoerotic idealiza-
tion.) Kasdan gets a clear-cut performance from Gorman,
but he seems divided about how he wants Muriel to come
across. A six-foot beauty, Geena Davis is cast against her
looks; no one in the movie seems to notice that she's a full-
lipped goddess. Davis has been given frizzy, lopsided hair,
and has been directed to be twitchy and to talk in ungram-
matical bursts (much like the Muriel in the novel). At the
same time, Kasdan knows that Geena Davis has a lit-up quality, and he uses her to radiate a number of scenes. By the
end, I was grateful that the cinematographer, John Bailey,

made her so vivid, because in this movie once you're away from the comically inexpressive faces in the family house there's nothing to sustain you except looking at Geena Davis. (By then, Edward has gone the way of Hollywood dogs who have outlived their plot function.)

In a movie with such hesitant tempos, and a rippling John Williams score that's like some semi-serious Frenchie on a binge, it's impossible to tell if the desperate Muriel is meant to be spontaneous. But it's clear that she symbolizes change, and so moviegoers can extract something inspiriting from *Tourist* and see it as a lesson movie like *Ordinary People.* That may help to account for some of the good press the picture has been racking up and the long lines at theatres. I found *Tourist* hell to sit through, but it has an audience appeal: it provides a new romantic myth of the eighties—a time of widespread remarriage and hoped-for rebirth. The film's gloominess doesn't keep it from being a crowd pleaser, because it leads to that final moment when Macon makes his choice—his "commitment." In the movie, as in the novel, he abandons his old emotional luggage. Essentially, this is a dating movie, like Claude Lelouch's *A Man and a Woman,* but for darker times, for times of lowered expectations. The audience response indicates that the movie does get at some of the appeal of a novelist who writes of Macon's wife telling him that he and Muriel would be "one of those mismatched couples no one invites to parties," and of Macon's thinking that "he saw now how such couples evolved. They were not, as he'd always supposed, the result of some ludicrous lack of perception, but had come together for reasons that the rest of the world would never guess."

Beaches

Sisters aren't just doing it for themselves—they're also doing it to themselves. *Beaches,* the first film from Bette Midler's All Girl Productions, probably started out trying to be truthful to women's experiences. As a mission, that can really snarl you up. The movie is about the lifelong friendship between two women of contrasting backgrounds—Midler as CC Bloom, the show-biz-crazy Jewish redhead from New York, and Barbara Hershey as Hillary Whitney, the repressed wealthy Wasp from San Francisco. They're eleven years old when they meet on the beach at Atlantic City, in 1957; they write to each other during their girlhood, then share a bohemian apartment on the Lower East Side—yes, they bang on the radiators, and they also fall in love with the same man (John Heard). Over the decades, they're together in times of crisis, such as the birth of Hillary's baby daughter, and finally the movie turns into an all-girl *Love Story,* with CC (now a singing star) staying at Hillary's side as she becomes ghoulishly pale from heart disease and lingeringly expires. Through this (slow, slow) deathwatch, CC learns to transcend her self-involvement; she becomes a better person, and—implicitly—a bigger star. The two friends, I think we're meant to understand, are two halves of an ideal woman. And by the end CC's indomitable spirit is in Hillary's child. (Is this New Age Egyptian—a twist on metempsychosis?)

There's a cadaverous feeling to the movie even before Hillary starts turning up her toes. Midler's CC has the living-every-minute quality that makes Midler such a vibrant presence, but Hershey's face has been wiped clean of experience. Even if you've seen her in *The Stunt Man, The Right Stuff, The Natural, Hannah and Her Sisters, A World Apart,* and other pictures, she's a stranger. Her newly puffed-up lips are only part of the change—her face looks as if it had been carved out of a bar of Ivory soap. And the creepy, behind-the-screen story of a talented woman turning herself into a Barbie doll (and acting like one) runs in your head along with *Beaches*.

The picture is rich in worst moments. Everything to do with CC's work at "a little theatre on the West Side" qualifies. And then there's CC in a musical number from her hit show; the berserk staging is a stunner—I haven't seen anything like this since the "Satan's Alley" number in Stallone's *Staying Alive*. There's Hillary, who has (temporarily) broken away from her background, reciting "Free at last." Her other big scenes are dillies, too. And there's a dinner party, with the two friends and their husbands at Tavern on the Green, where CC is hailed as "the toast of Broadway." Almost any scene qualifies except the scenes with Mayim Bialik as CC at eleven; this scrawny kid, with carrot-red hair and charming protruding teeth, has a show-biz humor that matches up with Midler and parodies her, too.

Midler also parodies herself. She overdoes herself: her bubbly life-lovingness is too professional and assured; her warm inspirational faucet keeps running. She's in good voice, especially in her pop-ballad version of "Under the Boardwalk," but the score is maudlin, like the movie. Midler is showing us her soulfulness the way she did in her bag-lady mime in *Divine Madness*. Her instincts take care of her, and she's never really bad here, but if you ran *The Rose,* the first three-quarters of *Divine Madness,* or *Down and Out in Beverly Hills* and then looked at *Beaches,* I think you'd want to bash your head against the wall.

In one scene, CC is in Hollywood working in the movies; when the director, who's a vicious bum, insults her, she punches him in the face. This reference to the bad experience Midler had on the career-damaging *Jinxed!* might have more impact if by then you weren't thinking back on *Jinxed!* almost fondly. Sometimes the nice-guy directors do the performers in, too. Garry Marshall, who directed this picture, has no feeling for the material—not even false feeling. *Beaches* has no outstanding scenes, no highs; it just slogs along—those worst moments are the film's texture. The script, by Mary Agnes Donoghue, from Iris Rainer Dart's novel, outlines the emotions for you. CC and Hillary tell you things like "We've grown apart." Why are people in the audience weeping and applauding? It's the idea that gets to them, not the quality of the rendering. They've been primed to cry by *Love Story* and ten million hours of TV viewing, and maybe even by the sappy side of the women's movement. They've been primed to respond to singing stars who bare their emotions. Midler's CC is so down to earth it's a great-lady performance.

Dirty Rotten Scoundrels

I should have known better, but I looked forward to *Dirty Rotten Scoundrels*. Michael Caine and Steve Martin as con men on the Côte d'Azur, in a remake of the 1964 *Bedtime Story*—it sounded plausible. And there's nothing the matter with the performances. Caine is the slick Continental who operates very discreetly, very romantically. His confederates drop a few words into the ears of pre-researched middle-aged rich American women; they let it be known that he's a deposed prince, and when the women learn that he is hard-pressed to support the anti-Communist troops who are trying to liberate his country they press greenbacks and jewelry into his reluctant hands—enough lucre to keep him in a great villa high on a cliff overlooking the sea. Martin is a happy-go-lucky American spaz in wrinkled baggy pants; he's an improviser, a vagabond who chases after the most attractive young women he spots, and shamelessly, in a loud, whiny voice, cadges meals and a few bucks off them. He has never set his sights any higher—not until he stumbles into Caine's smooth terrain. Then a light dawns in his face; it visibly flashes on. He blackmails Caine into serving as his mentor, and, in the movie's most artful, most Buster Keaton-like scenes, he stands and walks and lounges in a simulation of Caine's nonchalance. But the picture doesn't seem to have any faith in its own setup. After we watch Martin training to be dapper and imperturbable, we expect to see him screwing up and displaying his new sang-froid just when he shouldn't. Instead, the picture cuts to Caine, as the prince, discouraging one after another of the amorous women who want to take a royal husband home to the Midwest; he displays his brother—Martin as mad Prince Ruprecht, who is locked in the cellar. As Ruprecht, Martin is a simian, bent-over combination of the young Jerry Lewis and William Hickey in *Prizzi's Honor*. This was the funniest part of the 1964 version (with David Niven as the sophisticate and Marlon Brando as the Hapsburg idiot), and, though misplaced, it's funny here, too. What it isn't is fresh or new.

The movie is mildly pleasant; it has amusing moments and a sunny sheen. But it's unexciting—it has no fangs, no bite at all. The original version had two big laughs (the Hapsburg idiot and a shin-whacking scene), and, with all the gloss that's been added, those are still the big laughs. Frank Oz, who directed, and Dale Launer, who reworked the 1964 script, by Stanley Shapiro and Paul Henning, are trying to get the public to buy the same package twice. They retain some of the worst ideas in the original, in a barely altered form. Caine is supposed to observe a code: he fleeces only those who can afford it. And he explains that he's a failed artist who takes care of beautiful things—the villa and the grounds and his wines and his art collection. We're supposed to accept him as a basically honorable fellow who's the custodian of a cultural tradition. (Do the moviemakers even know they're treating us as suckers?)

Oz and Launer had the chance to spark the women's roles,

by giving the gullible do-gooders distinct personalities. The prince takes them to bed, and it might have been jolly to see this man who has such pride in his good taste adapting himself to their various dreams of a sheik. (If they were matches for him, he could have been forced to use his wits.) Couldn't the women at least have been smart and lusty? As marks, they're too easy—you just don't believe it. They're dithering dummies, and Oz directs all this neutrally, blandly, without any comic drama. (If the women didn't blur together, the film's ending would have more point.) Caine and Martin make a bet on which one can fleece a visiting young American "soap queen" (Glenne Headly), and she, too, is sweetly trustful as she listens to the hard-luck stories that gush out of Martin and the advice she gets from Caine. Headly's face is a comic mask, but she has no lines that bring laughs; she suggests a Maggie Smith robbed of her wit. (It isn't until the very end that she gets a chance to show some tartness.)

When the two men first meet, the boastful Martin says that he tells women "what they want to hear." There's a shade of contempt in the remark, but it's presented as simple, self-serving chatter, and the movie doesn't follow through. Here are two swindlers who live off women—who treat women as prey—and the question of how they feel about them never comes up. If Caine felt put upon by the aging women's demands or if he were lubricious and enjoyed the game, or both, the movie might not be so square. It might absorb more of your attention. I've sat through a lot of worse movies, but this one actually seems proud of its mediocrity.

It's disappointing to see Caine and Martin with nothing to do but show off their styles. They preen beautifully. Caine's comedy is in his tiny jaundiced, disdainful reactions to the American's antics: he has it down to a faint glimmer in the eyes, a slight tightening of the mouth, and the radar from his gleaming hair. The less he does, the more of a master actor he appears to be. (But if he carried urbanity any further he'd be dead.) Steve Martin's blank-eyed vulgarian is wonderfully moronic and crude. Martin takes his cue here from Caine and plays low comedy with high-comic finesse. At their best, they're like a vaudeville team zapping each other and doing a soft-shoe. But the script is such a lazy ripoff of the past that there's not much juice in the roles: we seem to be watching the last pressing of the grapes.

JANUARY 23, 1989

STUNT

Rain Man

Rain Man is Dustin Hoffman humping one note on a piano for two hours and eleven minutes. It's his dream role. As the autistic savant Raymond Babbitt, he's impenetrable: he doesn't make eye contact or touch anyone or carry on a conversation; he doesn't care what anybody thinks of him. Autistic means self-involved, and Raymond is withdrawn in his world of obsessive rituals. So Hoffman doesn't have to play off anybody; he gets to act all by himself. He can work on his trudging, mechanical walk and the tilt of his head and the irascible, nagging sameness of his inflections. Autistics aren't known to be jerky like this (they're more likely to move slowly and fluidly), but Hoffman's performance has an intricate consistency. Even his tight voice fits his conception.

In dramatic terms, what distinguishes autism from other behavioral syndromes is that you don't get a direct emotional response from an autistic person. Even after Raymond is kidnapped by his younger brother, the slimeball Charlie (Tom Cruise), who hopes to get hold of some of the three million dollars their father has left in trust for Raymond's care, Raymond shows no awareness of what's happening to him. Yet because of the way the director, Barry Levinson, sets up the situations there's nothing for you to do except watch Hoffman intently, microscopically, searching for clues to Raymond's feelings. And you may begin to think that you're reading him, that Levinson is bootlegging you teeny glimmers. What you definitely get is the zigzags of Raymond's head that suggest panic at the violation of his daily routines. And now and then he lets out a primal bleat or squawk that alerts you to his terror of a new situation.

The heads of autistics seem to be wired in a closed-off way, as if their brains were divided into little boxes—little worlds unto themselves. And this is especially puzzling in the small percentage who, like Raymond, have surreal talents; he's a wizard—a sci-fi computer mutant—at some mathematical-memory functions. Hoffman gets to play it all: a disconnected, pesky child with inexplicable powers. For close to an hour, it's an entertaining comic turn. Intuitively, Hoffman seems to understand that we'd enjoy identifying with Raymond's obstinacy—it's his way to win out over his crummy brother—and when the audience laughs at Raymond the laughs are always friendly. He's accepted as a harmless, endearing alien—E.T. in autistic drag. But then the performance has nowhere to go. It becomes a repetitive, boring feat, though the boringness can be construed as fidelity to the role (and masochists can regard it as great acting). Slightly stupefied as I left the theatre, I wondered for a second or two why the movie people didn't just have an autistic person play the part. (In the seventies, when Robert Wilson staged his *A Letter for Queen Victoria,* he used an actual autistic teen-ager in the show, with babbling, trance-inducing music that seemed to evoke the fixations of an autistic child.) But with an actual autistic there would be no movie: this whole picture is Hoffman's stunt. It's an acting exercise—working out minuscule variations on his one note. It's no more than an exercise, because Hoffman doesn't challenge us: we're given no reason to change our attitude toward Raymond; we have the same view of him from the beginning of the movie to the end.

Hoffman's crabbed intensity worked marvellously when he played the paranoiac paroled robber in *Straight Time,* and it worked as nippy self-satire when he played the perfectionist actor in *Tootsie.* But it doesn't feel right here. This is the fanatic, uncompromising actor in *Tootsie* playing an autistic the way he played a tomato. (In his mind's eye he's always watching the audience watch him.) It's a determinedly external, locked-in performance (and Levinson makes no attempt, like Wilson's, to take us inside the character by Expressionist means). We're on the outside staring at this virtuoso apparatus. Hoffman doesn't allow Raymond a minute of simple relaxed sluggishness; he keeps you conscious of the buzzing of anxiety in Raymond's brain. He keeps his actor's engine chugging and upstages the movie.

The kidnap plot is no more than a barefaced contrivance to get the two brothers on the road together. *Rain Man* has to get outdoors, or it's just a TV sickness-of-the-week movie; it cinematizes a TV theme by moving the brothers from place to place. Their father has left Charlie a 1949 Buick Roadmaster convertible, and they travel in it, with many a stop, from Cincinnati to L.A. In the first days, the materialistic Charlie is tantrummy and almost insanely callous; he shouts crude insults at Raymond. Obviously these scenes are intended to show how self-centered Charlie is, and how far he has to go to become a sensitive, loving person; he's meant to be spiritually autistic. But, oddly, Charlie's jeering at Raymond doesn't cause you pain. Levinson's directing is too flaccid for you to feel the scenes sharply; there's no conviction in them. (This makes the movie easy to swallow, on a TV level.) And Cruise as a slimeball is just a sugarpuss in Italian tailoring. He doesn't even use his body in an expressive way. His performance here consists of not smiling too much—so as not to distract his fans from watching Hoffman. (This could be called "restraint.") Cruise is an actor in the same sense that Robert Taylor was an actor. He's patented: his knowing that a camera is on him produces nothing but fraudulence.

Charlie has felt sorry for himself for years. That's been his justification for his cheap huckstering; he runs a shady business in L.A., selling imported sports cars that don't quite meet American regulations. But during the trip—Charlie's voyage of self-discovery—he has no one to hustle, and (according to plot calculation) is forced back on himself. Levinson lays it out for the audience on a platter: Charlie has the capacity to change. In due course, after he vents his exasperation at Raymond's inflexibility, he begins to understand himself better and he learns to care about Raymond. And when the two brothers touch heads it's clear that the time they've spent together has affected them both. They've regained the bond they had when Charlie was a baby and Raymond sang to him. This heads-together image has its poetry. It also sums up the film's anti-sentimental sentimental bilge.

Rain Man is getting credit for treating autism "authentically," because Raymond isn't cured; in a simple transposition, it's Charlie who's cured. Actually, autism here is a dramatic gimmick that gives an offbeat tone to a conventional buddy movie. (*Rain Man* has parallels to several scenes in *Midnight Run* and *Twins,* but the standard buddy-movie tricks are so subdued that they may squeak by as "life.") The press has been full of accounts of the research into autism done by Hoffman and Levinson and the principal scriptwriter, Ronald Bass, but what's the use of all this research if then they rig the story and throw in a big sequence with Raymond using his whiz-bang memory to make a killing in Las Vegas that takes care of Charlie's money troubles? And what's the point of setting up Raymond's avoidance of being touched if Charlie is going to hold him while showing him how to dance and Charlie's warm-hearted Italian girlfriend (Valeria Golino) is going to teach him how to kiss? (Is that something Raymond is likely to be called on to do?) Everything in this movie is fudged ever so humanistically, in a perfunctory, low-pressure way. And the picture has its effectiveness: people are crying at it. Of course they're crying at it—it's a piece of wet kitsch.

Levinson—it's his temperament—stretches out the scenes until they yawn. You may sit there thinking "And more?" "And again?" and "We've already been here!" This is the kind of moviemaking in which you've been there before you get there.

In the context of a hit like *Rain Man*—it's the top box-office film in the country—it may seem almost naïve to suggest that if Raymond is the central character, and the given of the material is that he can't express his mental state, then it's up to the moviemakers to do it. Movies have often been at their most eloquent when the writers and directors and designers and composers used the possibilities of visual and aural stylization, of imagination and fantasy, to envision how the world might be perceived by disordered psyches. (Examples: just about any film noir you can think of, the 1981 M-G-M musical *Pennies from Heaven, Blue Velvet, Raising Arizona, Dreamchild, The Stepfather*, De Palma's *Carrie*, the BBC miniseries *The Singing Detective*.) If moviemakers don't risk shaking up audiences and making our nerves tingle, they're likely to fall back on hauling an autistic savant to Las Vegas, duding him up, and teaching him to kiss.

FEBRUARY 6, 1989

MARRIAGES

True Believer

A fast, tense thriller like *True Believer* can quicken your senses. It can jazz you up and make you feel a little manic. The director, Joseph Ruben, has great timing, and the story has some elation built right into its structure. It's about a Manhattan lawyer with a rancid practice: he's been defending drug dealers and getting paid in cash. His new associate arrives, fresh from law school, and looks at him with disgust. The lawyer is goaded into taking on a case that's outside his drug specialty, and soon his eyes widen at the possibility—just the bare possibility—that the man he's defending might be innocent. Ruben, who directed the 1984 political-suspense fantasy *Dreamscape* and the 1987 suburban shocker *The Stepfather,* has a deft ironic tone. He knows not to overdo the theme of a disillusioned idealist's rediscovery of his belief in justice. He just lets it seep through the plot.

In the sixties, the lawyer, Eddie Dodd (James Woods), was a hero of the counterculture; he had the reputation of being a fearless champion of civil rights. That's why the just hatched lawyer, Roger Baron (Robert Downey, Jr.), who was top man on the Michigan *Law Review,* wanted to work with him. Rog made the naïve mistake of thinking that Eddie

Dodd was still the white knight he'd idolized; the movie itself is naïve about Eddie's golden age. The script, by Wesley Strick, is sharp and gritty, but it mythologizes its William Kunstler-like figure. Eddie is meant to be a once-authentic hero, the protector of the weak, who has lost his self-respect. As a figure, he comes perilously close to the aging, drunken lawyers of old Hollywood who found their humanity again. (Eddie is a pothead.) But Ruben's moviemaking avoids sogginess: Eddie's tawdry, barbed view of the world whips you along. And, as Woods plays him—angry, insomniac, unclean—Eddie has listening posts on the back of his head. He would hear a whispering mention of his name in Madison Square Garden. Eddie's graying ponytail, fastened with turquoise terry cloth, is the vanity he clings to, the emblem of what he once stood for. It's surprisingly dignified and handsome, like the chignons of the Founding Fathers.

When I tried to tell a friend how sensational James Woods is in *True Believer,* the friend said, "Yeah, but no matter how good he is he knows he's better." I can't disagree, exactly, yet it's the impression he gives of hyperbolic self-regard that makes him seem perfectly cast here (as it did in *Salvador*). Almost anyone else I can think of as Eddie Dodd would be too hammy warm; Woods' flamboyance helps to dry out the role. If Eddie weren't written as a heroic radical—if he were conceived as a more realistic version of the blowhards who exploited the protesters of the sixties—Woods could play him more complexly. That would be a different movie, but this one does at least recognize that Dodd has a blowhard tendency. In one scene he gets heady on the excitement of having a bunch of reporters around him, and he brags about what he's going to prove in court; when he sees Rog listening, he's suddenly shamefaced, like a kid who's been caught out.

The case involves a young Korean immigrant, Kim (Yuji Okumoto), who was convicted of shooting a member of a Chinese gang on the street in Chinatown; Kim has been in

Sing Sing for eight years, and has just killed a convict who attacked him. Kim's mother thinks that Dodd may be able to get him a new trial, because a witness to the original murder claims that the murderer wasn't Oriental. This witness (played winningly by Tom Bower) has been a patient in a mental hospital, and he's very obstreperous about his knowledge that the phone company killed John F. Kennedy. But Dodd manages to use his testimony to wangle a new trial. Then he's stymied when Kim won't tell him anything. Something, though, must be fishy about Kim's conviction, because the district attorney (Kurtwood Smith) offers Dodd a deal: Kim, who faces forty more years in prison, will be out in five if Dodd agrees not to bring the case to trial. Dodd tells Kim about the D.A.'s offer, and Kim turns it down. That's when Dodd becomes passionately dedicated to Kim's defense; he feels that Kim gave up the offer for him—that Kim knew he was itching to fight the authorities. And this case becomes all he cares about. He gets so hyper that he's shouting in people's faces. (One guy, appalled, says, "Jesus, jump back!")

True Believer can be said to be about Dodd's finding his lost ideals, but it's basically about pace and drive. The director doesn't use the movie to congratulate himself on sharing Eddie's ideals; he uses it to make us share the excitement of Eddie's recovering those ideals. The picture is about Eddie Dodd's body chemistry—the energy and charge that go into the investigation of what happened eight years earlier. Eddie doesn't want sleep; he lives off the excitement of having a cause. It's a marriage of purpose and adrenaline. He hurtles from one illicit source of data to the next, and Rog and a private investigator named Kitty (Margaret Colin) hurtle alongside him. The picture keeps your brain active processing the information they turn up, and the hardboiled dialogue is always telling you something twisty and unforeseen. The cinematography, by John W. Lindley (who also did *The Stepfather*), has a tabloid harshness. Flashbacks to the eight-year-old crime, which is seen in bluish-tinted black-

and-white, are ominous, grungy. And the prison killing is staged with breathtaking assurance. This is true teamwork: the movie pulses.

Joseph Ruben (he's still in his thirties) works in popular forms, but there's nothing formulaic about his characters. Part of the stimulus of *True Believer* is the rush that you get from the minor players who keep being brought into the investigation and the trial. Ruben has a marvellous intuitive grasp of just how long we want to look at a self-righteous ex-convict (Miguel Fernandes) who runs a plumbing-supplies factory with ex-con labor, or at an ex-con (John Snyder) who picks a fight with Eddie. This isn't the kind of movie that builds suspense by working up your dread of what's coming next. Ruben and the editor, George Bowers, get at you viscerally without sacrificing the sophisticated stuff that's going on all the time. They do it by the vitality of their craftsmanship. As Rog, Downey is never too much of a baby-faced hayseed; Rog is hip enough to cover up his gaffes. Margaret Colin gives a fillip to her line readings; she makes comedy out of cynicism. And Ruben trusts us enough not to make Kim a soft-eyed sweetie. It's a pick-me-up of a movie. Nothing great, nothing terribly distinctive, but the aliveness of the texture can keep you fascinated. And the case raises an issue that may be new to movies: how legal trade-offs violate the system of justice. This is one thriller where you almost never feel you're ahead of the story.

High Hopes

Mike Leigh's wacked-out comedy-drama *High Hopes* is exuberantly likable without actually being very satisfying. It's a loosely joined series of sketches about class distinctions in Thatcherland, which is populated here by rich twits, pushy yups, and the working poor, who are soulful and full of humor. The representative figures are three couples: a shiny-faced champagne dealer and his cool socialite wife; a boorish, money-making car salesman and his shrieking hysteric of a wife; and a despairing Marxist who scrapes by as a motorcycle messenger and his companion of ten years, who works for the city. Nobody produces anything of value or is creative except waifish Shirley (Ruth Sheen), who lives with the messenger. I hate to say this, but, yes, she likes to grow things. Her job is planting trees, and she keeps a garden in a corner of the roof of her apartment building. And she longs to have a child. Put this way, the movie sounds like a liberal-left horror, but almost all the lachrymose social consciousness is side by side with loony, knockabout satire. This is one English tradition that—we can be thankful—has not died even among the serious left: delight in extreme, preposterous silliness. The characters keep turning into absurdist cartoons.

"Devised and directed by Mike Leigh" is the customary credit for Leigh's work in the theatre, television, and films. His method is to set up "a structural surrounding" and then ask his actors to "find their characters." He explains, "Characters develop, then relationships, and these I monitor and follow and push toward a dramatic conclusion of some kind, so that you get a microcosm of society through improvisation." This doesn't explain how he gets so much rambunctious comedy out of the actors, but it does help to explain why *High Hopes* limps along: it isn't really conceived as a narrative film. It's conceived as a group of skits that the director will extend and fuse. Yet the best things the actors do—such as the twits' pixieish sex play—often resist Leigh's fusing; they're funny out there on their own.

As the twitty nymph Laetitia, Lesley Manville (she was the young wife in *High Season*) is a cutup, like Andrea Martin or Catherine O'Hara, with a little of Mary Beth Hurt's pertness. She has the manner of a colonial master in the section where the messenger's forgetful old mum (Edna Doré), a "council tenant" who lives next door to Laetitia's gentrified abode, has mislaid her key and asks for help. This passage combines cabaret humor (the unfeeling Laetitia) with kitchen-sink realism (the tired, confused mum), and even though the disparity between the two modes is funny I kept waiting for the modes to come together—for the old woman with her wandering mind to score off smug young Laetitia. A skit like this might be liberated if it were in a revue. The way Leigh uses it, it has a significance that curdles it. Almost everything in the movie that's jokey and distorted and grotesque plays off the "reality" of the failing old woman's misery.

The film's virulent contempt for Martin (Philip Jackson), the newly rich car salesman, goes way beyond his slobby insensitivity and horniness and Toryism. It probably goes back to the bohemian left's traditional snobbish hatred of the prospering middle class (and people who move to the suburbs). The left can be really good haters, aristocrats of hatred. But Martin's scenes don't do anything except indict him. On the other hand, the pretentiousness of his social-climber wife, Valerie (Heather Tobias), is so hog-wild that it has a shrill, comic-strip kick to it. She's a laughing case of nerves.

As if to confound the viewer, scenes that our instincts tell us shouldn't work—the ones, for example, that show the sound, loving relationship between Cyril, the messenger, and his dark-eyed, dark-haired Shirley—are the bedrock of the movie. Ruth Sheen's Shirley is long-legged and has protruding upper teeth that give her a little-kid grin, and Philip Davis's Cyril is stocky, with scroungy blond hair and beard, and specs and buckteeth. Sheen once played Olive Oyl on the stage, and Shirley towers over her man in that gauche, lanky way; she's both plain and beautiful, a Madonna who has been deprived of a babe. Everything that Shirley does is expressive, and clearly Cyril appreciates her. They're believable mates, even though the irony that the only true marriage is that of the unmarried pair can stick in your craw, along with their spontaneity, their unforced smiles, their open eyes turned to the future, and the pot smoking that marks them as good people.

Mike Leigh is an original; he doesn't just bring out characters—he brings out eccentric personalities. And his work with the cinematographer Roger Pratt is simple yet visionary. The film is never drab, never ordinary. Leigh is a real filmmaker, and his political vision gives his work substance and conviction. But he's shaping sentimental screwball microcosms. If an artist can be said to be corrupting absurdism, that's what he's doing. He uses absurdism to modernize realism, to syncopate it. It still drags its feet.

Three Fugitives

The Touchstone/Disney executives must make a coach's speech to cheer on their writers and directors: "Your movie will succeed only if it's the dumbest movie of the decade." Francis Veber, who wrote and directed *Three Fugitives,* went at the task strenuously, and, having already made the French film this one is based on, he had a jump start. Veber offers a lout's value system and queasy pedophiliac overtones. Big, gruff Nick Nolte plays a veteran armed robber, just released from prison, who goes to a bank to open a small account and is taken hostage by slight Martin Short, a terrified twerp of an amateur holdup man. Short's motive isn't meant as a joke: he needs money, to keep his six-year-old daughter (Sarah Rowland Doroff) in a special school—she has been mute since her mother died, two years earlier. That's the setup: the three are variously chased, and chase each other. During all this, Nolte keeps whamming Short on the head, using him as a punching bag, and the child—she's a poker-faced miniature Isabelle Adjani—ignores her devoted father. He's too small for her. She's smitten by big, blond, blue-eyed Nolte. One night, when he collapses, she cuddles against him; she speaks when she's in danger of losing him, and in a near-obscene moment she looks into his eyes adoringly, touching her face to a pale-blue stuffed animal he had given her, rubbing against it teasingly, seductively. There's a lewd sneakiness about this crumbum farce. Everything in it seems designed to humiliate the father, and you can't tell what's going on when Short—ostensibly for purposes of disguise—is dressed as a woman and the three form a nuclear family.

Veber made his reputation by adapting Jean Poiret's play *La Cage aux Folles* to the screen: the movie made fun of macho pretensions. *Three Fugitives* is a salute to macho. (The head of Disney is a big guy.) My guess is that Veber desperately threw in his repertory of tricks, and that, working in this country, he didn't have the instinctive understanding to blend the different elements. (Maybe nobody could have blended them; certainly nobody should have.) Even Haskell Wexler's wonderfully realistic cinematography doesn't fit the movie: it doesn't go with the stylized people-getting-banged-in-the-face material and the oozing pathos. He lighted something that shouldn't have seen the light of day.

FEBRUARY 20, 1989

KILLERS AND COUSINS

Out Cold

Out Cold is trim and smart—a handsome, dispassionate murder comedy that's kept in equilibrium from beginning to end. The picture has what Dashiell Hammett's Casper Gutman might have called "a nice malice." It's an American movie, set mostly in and around San Pedro, California, but the calm with which the young English director, Malcolm Mowbray (who made the 1984 *A Private Function,* with Maggie Smith and Michael Palin), keeps everything in check doesn't seem American, exactly. Mowbray's deliberateness has a lunar dimension. Laughs gurgle out of you unexpectedly. I think this has something to do with the fact that Mowbray lays things out for us privately. The film's black jokes don't explode; they don't go public. The film is so evenly paced it's almost secretive.

Sunny (Teri Garr) can't think of anything except the money that her vain, beefy husband, Ernie (Bruce McGill), is spending on other women. She hires a private detective (Randy Quaid)—a supreme jerk—to get the goods on him, so she can clean him out in a divorce action. But she's too restless to give the detective even a few days. She grabs a chance to kill Ernie and make his business partner, Dave (John Lithgow), think he did it. Ernie and Dave worked as butchers in the Army, and when they got out they ran a butcher shop together. Big, shy Dave, a bachelor and a slave to the business, has always been in love with Sunny; convinced that he killed Ernie by accidentally locking him in the freezer, he prostrates himself before her, and the movie is under way.

Lithgow's Dave suggests the mousy young Alec Guinness in the body of a giant. Dave has a big mug but small, babyish features. He's a trusting person with a slow-motion brain: he's just what Sunny needs. There's cleanup work to be done. Ernie is upright in the freezer, with the chocolate-covered ice-cream bar he was eating frozen to his forehead, and the lunkhead detective, who thinks he's got pictures of Ernie's paramour visiting him at the shop, has actually photographed Sunny on the night she stiffed him. As Sunny, Teri Garr is slim and fast. She moves like a darting goldfish. And she's like a psychic in reverse: we can read the workings of her mind. We follow her slapdash, opportunistic scheming as clearly as if her thoughts were comic-strip captions. But neither Dave nor Lester Atlas, the detective—each of them a hulking six feet four—can read the writing. Quaid's Atlas, who's sly but doltish, gets everything wrong. And he's seedy to the core: his professional pride in his work is expressed in a lecherous smirk. Atlas's emotional needs are just about satisfied by photographing husbands with their pants down.

Teri Garr plays her role with a savage, twinkling joy. Why doesn't her skill get more recognition? I think it's partly because she holds nothing back, and emotions so shallow yet so fully communicated belong to caricature, to sketches. She seems two-dimensional, crisp, weightless. That's why she's perfect for this movie. A few glints of Sunny's eyes and a slight nibble of her lip and it's clear just what she's up to. (When she wants something, she sends out rays.)

Sunny doesn't feel an instant's remorse for killing Ernie; she's getting her own back. She doesn't feel any pity for dumb Dave. (Neither do we.) And clumsy, oafish Lester Atlas is just an inconvenience to be got rid of—albeit a big inconvenience. (His tenacity provides a motor for the plot.)

These monsters are all acted so impeccably that there's nothing crude about the movie. The repeated shots of hamburger coming out of the grinder are like macabre mood music. And the clear, clean morning light and the Edward Hopper streets and storefronts create a world where the script, by Leonard Glasser and George Malko, plays itself out in all its linear precision. This small, disingenuous comedy has been buffed to shine like a jewel; the smoothness of it keeps you giggling.

Parents

In *Parents,* Randy Quaid is terrifyingly outsize. As Nick, who works as a defoliation expert at Toxico, a chemical plant, in 1958, he's swollen with well-being; when he puffs out his cheeks, he recalls Zero Mostel in *Rhinoceros.* Nick has everything he wants: an adoring, obedient wife, Lily (Mary Beth Hurt), who spends her days working cheerfully in the kitchen of their split-level home. Situated in suburban Indiana, that house is like a shrine to conformist America of the fifties. Nick and Lily are both in tip-top shape; they're a lovey-dovey pair of married sweethearts, like the couples in *Life.* And Nick has his golf and his wine cellar (robust red wine only). All's right with the world—a man's world—except for that miserable, finicky little kid Michael (Bryan Madorsky), Nick and Lily's ten-year-old son, who won't eat his meat to grow up as big and strong as Daddy.

Parents—in which we're always looking up at Nick through the eyes of scrawny, scared Michael—starts as a satiric comedy set in the polite repressiveness of the Eisenhower period. Michael intuitively knows that more than this clean, upbeat, all-American stuff is going on in his home, but he doesn't know what. He wrestles with nightmarish visions in which sex and eating meat are all one smeary chaos. He has no one to turn to until his school psychologist (Sandy Dennis) calls him in. She wants to know why, when the children in his class were asked to draw pictures of their families, he smudged his all over with red crayon.

The first feature directed by the actor Bob Balaban, *Parents* is a stunning début, even though the story finally lapses into gory banality. The script, by Christopher Hawthorne, is quite good until then. But Hawthorne seems to have got into a metaphorical plot he couldn't work out: confused little Michael is a budding version of the hippies of the sixties who thought that their keeping-up-with-the-Joneses middle-class parents incarnated man-eating capitalist imperialism. The script carries this counterculture fantasy into horror-movie effects, leaving the satire undeveloped, and doing away with the ingenuity we've been enjoying. Balaban has the help of some witty people, such as the art director, Andris Hausmanis, who's given Nick and Lily a dawning-of-the-space-age open-plan house that's an Expressionist jamboree. And the costume designer, Arthur Rowsell, has put Mary Beth Hurt into a series of full-skirted, pinch-waisted outfits that lampoon the ideal housewife of the era. The house itself makes low, organic sounds, like a dragon in a dream; here and elsewhere, Balaban and his team have learned from David Lynch.

Balaban doesn't need to bow to anyone in his handling of the actors; his work with the young performers, especially, is wizardly. One look at Michael and we know that everything about him is a disappointment to his father, and that Michael knows it. The boy's scenes with Juno Mills-Cockell, who plays his new school friend, Sheila, are inexplicably flaky. And his scenes with Sandy Dennis (who, the man next to me said, suggested "Shelley Winters crossed with Jeanne Moreau") go into comedy heaven. This blowsy psychologist is aware that she gives the impression of being askew, but she's just naturally uncoördinated—she can't get herself together. Michael trusts her instinctively just because she's not together, like his parents. Or, as he puts it to her, "you're not a real grownup."

Michael's mother is definitely a grownup. He can't get past her vacuous, picture-perfect role-playing, though he knows that she loves him. Mary Beth Hurt's Lily is trying so hard to be a flawless wife that it's like a daily performance. In her spearhead bra and flouncy skirts and spikes, she's armored for peppiness; her teeth flash in her pointed mouth—she's *on*. Hurt turns herself into a corky cartoon, using every chance she gets to modulate it with hints of desperation. Lily's brittle dinky curls could almost be squeezing her head; she's insanely chipper—she's pitifully sweet.

Balaban seems to have the knack of encouraging performers to bring out new sides. Quaid shows a spooky wit in the scenes where Nick reassures Michael about his fear of the dark: the father's face is impassive, faintly smiling, sinister. And Nick carves meat with an enthusiasm that is unlike any expression I've seen on Quaid's face before; he has a new red-bloodedness in this role. (The worst thing Nick can say to his wife is "Your son, the vegetarian.") Few screen actors have shown the range that Quaid has in recent years: his L.B.J. on television was a phenomenal piece of work, and he carries it with him—the partly buried joke is that as Nick he foreshadows the President as defoliator. In *Parents*—the right title, yet a hopelessly prosaic one, and a clue to the unresolved emotions that bring the picture down—Quaid is Father the Provider as a helpless, neurotic boy sees him: as devil, as archenemy. He's the father who threatens to give up on his kid. Quaid has a major comic presence here; his grin is pure audacity.

Cousins

Isabella Rossellini and Ted Danson are at the still center of *Cousins,* smiling serenely while the others in the cast busily bang away at their joie de vivre. The pair's quiet normality gives moviegoers a peaceful sensation: you're not being asked to identify with the dingalings and obsessives and high-energy sexpots who surround them—you can simply rest your eyes on Rossellini. She doesn't have the animation or the temperament of a trained actress, but this lack of technique seems to work for her; her unforced expressiveness has a grace—it's as if she were too friendly and sensible to go in for the usual affectations. In some ways, the less she does, the better: we're not distracted from gaping at her eerie pearliness. And since the story gives her an infantile, skirt-chasing husband (William Petersen), who doesn't see in her what we do, we feel superior to him—even sorry for him, when we're not exasperated by him. He's wearing himself down, cluttering his days by sneaking out for quickies, like the one he has with Danson's frantic, obnoxious wife (Sean Young). They're rabbits: they meet at a family wedding and hop off together.

That's the day Rossellini and Danson become cousins: her widowed mother (Norma Aleandro) marries his uncle (George Coe). It's a union of Italian and Polish families, in the Pacific Northwest. When the new cousins are left behind, they speak to each other; they're too tactful to mention it, but they know they have something in common—they're the injured parties. It turns out that neither has a happy marriage, and in the weeks that follow they're attracted to each other. But they don't become lovers—partly because of self-consciousness about their cheating spouses, and partly because their relatives are so sure they're having a hot furtive affair. The scenes that show the friendship that develops between them are easygoing and likable, but the plot rigging sticks out: they're not like their spouses—they're made of finer stuff. (Rossellini, with her childlike gaze, damn near makes you believe it.) They take pristine, romantic walks in the country. And when their ardor can't be contained and they do go to bed together they don't hide their adultery—they're not hypocrites, they're open and honest. You can't be much more decent and heroic than they are. Extramarital sex has never been made more innocently pretty. They've been good for too long. So they kick up their heels: their tryst in a lakeside cabin is blissfully madcap.

Cousins is a canny Americanization of the celebrated French makeout movie *Cousin, Cousine* (1975), which was so life-affirming it treated the open-hearted lovers' adultery as frolicsome, free-spirited nonconformity. There was no dark, turbid side to this sex comedy—nothing concealed or scary in the characters. That's what gave the French film its giddy appeal, and Joel Schumacher, who directed the American version, and Stephen Metcalfe, who wrote the adaptation, have kept it that way. In this romantic fantasyland, the Petersen and Sean Young characters, who are aggressively anxious about money and getting ahead, are treated satirically; the free spirits, Rossellini and Danson, who are indifferent to worldly success, don't lack anything. Life is a party, and everybody lives well. I found this American version (it was shot in British Columbia) somewhat easier to take than the French one—less pleased with itself, less arch about the characters' cuddly eccentricities. But the lyrical prosperity, the dewy, grassy vistas—it's all so thin. And as the picture goes on and on, and you get its box-office formula—sex without messiness, family without oppressive closeness—you may begin to feel as if you were in a carefree pink padded cell.

Bland, dreamy effervescence is what's being sold. The only break in the whimsical tone comes in the episode of the videotape that's made by Danson's adolescent son (Keith

Coogan). The boy has shot the initial family wedding, catching as much of the happy, drunken misbehavior as he could,
and when he displays his video at the next big family gathering the relatives are upset to see that he has turned it into
a heavy-handed social-protest art work by crosscutting the
footage with scenes of starvation and calamity. Though this
sequence is lifted from an infinitely funnier sequence in the
film of Mordecai Richler's *The Apprenticeship of Duddy
Kravitz,* it still has a satirical kick. But Schumacher knows
that his job here is to smoothen any rough edges and keep
the movie restful; he goes right back to staging more wed-
dings, a jolly funeral, and so on. This is the kind of movie
in which the hero blows blues on the trumpet, and his uncle
says of him that he's "a failure in everything except life."
The movie conditions the audience, so that it actually laughs
appreciatively when Danson's father (Lloyd Bridges) tells
him to follow his heart: "You've only got one life to live.
You can make it chickenshit or chicken salad."

People used to respond to the Doris Day sex comedies,
too, and that's what *Cousins* (with its postponed sex) resembles—except that it isn't so insistently bright, and it's more
woodlandsy, more radiant and idyllic. There are no villains:
the spouses to be cast off are just screwed-up sillies. Petersen's frizzy-haired Don Juan is so anxious that he looks as if
he might scratch himself bald. He chimes with the Sean
Young character. Overdressed and curled and frazzled, she's
a gorgeous wreck. She's also generally lively. But she's subdued compared with Lloyd Bridges, who comes on in roar-
ing good form. (Yes, he overdoes the lusty heartiness, but
the picture can use the shot of energy he brings it.)

Danson's Frankenstein-monster overhanging forehead
saves him from being just a vapidly handsome horn-blower,
and he's quite proficient. He hovers near Rossellini, an affable escort; the script gives him a little flipness—it helps.
And Rossellini, limply "natural" and madonna-like, in simple, loose clothes, a minimum of makeup, and her own hair
(she isn't coiffed up to the sky), brings some kind of reality

to this pink tosh. Toward the end, when, for a time, her character is depressed and her eyes show that she has been crying, a pall is cast over the movie; everything is flabby while we wait for the restoration of the character's happiness. The only suspense the movie has is: How soon will she light up again? Rossellini's artlessness holds everything together. Soft as she is, she's got a collarbone like Garbo's.

MARCH 6, 1989

TWO-BASE HIT

New York Stories

As an artist in Martin Scorsese's *Life Lessons,* the first part of the anthology film *New York Stories,* Nick Nolte is more bricklayer than aesthete, and that's what's great about him. After the artist's girl tells him she's leaving him, he gets into a rhythm as he spreads bright colors on a huge horizontal canvas, and you can see that he has the energy to breathe life into it. This isn't a matter of physical size; it's his conviction, his sureness. Scorsese is a skinny little guy, but he's got this energy, too. And he uses Nolte's Lionel Dobie for good-humored self-satire. Still, Nolte's towering stockiness does help: he's a wonderful sculptural object—a loping, gray-bearded beast spattered with paint. He pads up and down in front of the canvas moving his brushstrokes to rock and roll, played loud enough to drown out distractions. Dobie works fast. Smiling, he's dancing with his brushes, painting to the music. Scorsese knows that painting to rock is a cliché, but he also knows that it's a good way for an Action painter to work. The music turned up high like that unifies Dobie's impulses. His sensuality is all working together, exciting him, keeping him going.

That sensuality is also the story's comic spirit; Scorsese is laughing at Dobie while identifying with him. That's what makes the little, forty-five-minute film so intensely enjoyable. Even Dobie's possessive love for Paulette (Rosanna Arquette), his assistant, who lives and works in an enclosure in the loft, is comic. She's just a slip of a girl. Roughly fifty, he's almost two and a half times her age; he's at least twice her size. And, though her eyes still shine when she watches him paint, she's fed up with him—with his slack belly, his slyness, his genius. She's ready to move on. (It's too bad that her work doesn't suggest his influence; if she painted wan imitation Dobies, her plight would have a bit more pungency.) Dobie is lucky: he's drawn to girls he can impress—he's drawn to groupies. And he's famous enough to attract an endless supply of them. But he can't let go. He's so sneakily determined to hang on to Paulette that, like Dostoyevski, whose life is the source of the screenplay that Scorsese sketched for the writer, Richard Price, Dobie solemnly pledges that if his protégée will go on living with him he won't touch her.

Dobie torments himself; he torments her. To some extent, he knows what he's doing: he needs to keep his turbulence up. He fetishizes every part of her, and especially her leg, with its fine gold-chain anklet, indolently extended on her bed. It's a perfect piece of erotic calendar art; he yearns to kiss that foot. He thinks that it's all he can think about; we laugh at his roiling frustration, because he somehow pours it into his work. He's a laboratory: he manufactures the tumult he needs for his painting. Appraising a possible replacement for Paulette, he tries to gauge whether he can fetishize this girl, too. She doesn't matter to him any more than Paulette does. We enjoy watching this ego furnace of his. (Staring at Paulette's foot, he remarks, "Nothing personal.") The girls aren't hurt by his manipulations: they're getting what they want—they're getting entrée into the big-time art world. And we enjoy the rich downtown impasto: the not-surprised-by-anything dealer (suave and grouchy Patrick O'Neal, with his parched voice), the performance artist (Steve Buscemi), the young painter (Jesse Borrego), the cops, the celebrities, the celebrity hounds. It isn't just Dobie's colors that are squeezed out straight from the tube (they land on his matted hair, his glasses, his Cartier watch, his belly); Nestor Almendros lights the crowds and parties so they have this same thick brilliance. No doubt Scorsese feels an affinity with the Abstract Expressionist idea that the canvas should be exciting all over; there's a visual buzz going on throughout the movie. This is the SoHo carnival as Scorsese sees it, zeroing in on objects the way the painter does. He keeps it all swarming to the (often parodying) music.

I was caught up in the passionate thrashing around that Scorsese did in *The Last Temptation of Christ*. His ambivalences and confusions became visible; they were right there on the screen. And he seemed to have gone straight through to the sources of his love of moviemaking. He told stories about a man (he looked like a Flemish Christ) who was perhaps a bit of a fool, and maybe a charlatan, and yet performed miracles, and such is the nature of movie-watching that (even if you're not a Christian) you wanted more and more miracles. You wanted him to show those doubters. Now it's as if Scorsese, having put his fanatic adolescent perplexities on the screen, had cleared his head. Maybe his films will no longer have to swing between passivity and violence.

Life Lessons is his most genial work: if jealousy and rejection fuel Dobie's art, happiness fuels it, too. Everything that keeps him jumping goes into it. The fun of the movie is in its not taking Dobie or his art too seriously. He's not a man of much depth, but the picture doesn't wring its hands about that. Scorsese has lightened up, and in a satisfying way. He's developed a sense of horseplay. We don't feel he's scoring off Dobie, because he's scoring off himself. He sees the comedy of his own compulsiveness in love and art, and he's able to sustain this vision.

Price's script is rather broad, but, given a halfway-good role, Nolte takes it all the way. He's a master of the inchoate, the deeply mixed up. He's like the man with a hoe: you can read his muscles. And he gives this little picture scale and heft. Dobie, preparing for a new show, stays up all night painting, aware that Paulette is entertaining a young lover in her partitioned mini-loft inside the huge loft. He lets up on the blaring rock and listens to Mario Del Monaco singing "Nessun dorma," from Puccini's *Turandot.* For a minute, his energy flags, and he sits bare-chested, spent—trying to come to terms with both his fatigue and the pulsating sensations that drive him on. The tenor lifts up his voice in the sweet anguish of "Nessun dorma"—no sleep, no sleep until he has possessed the woman who eludes him. And, with Nolte sitting there listening, you don't have to know what the words mean to roar with laughter.

The middle story, the thirty-four-minute *Life Without Zoe,* directed by Francis Coppola, from a script he wrote with his seventeen-year-old daughter, Sofia, attempts to use New York as a city out of the Arabian Nights. The conceit never takes hold; Vittorio Storaro's fabled golden light comes across as an aberration; Coppola's head doesn't seem to be in his moviemaking. Let's not linger over it—just note that Don Novello brings a little snap to the role of Hector (the butler who tends to the twelve-year-old heroine, in her apartment at the Sherry Netherland), and that Carmine Coppola plays a street musician (a flutist) with a tawdry vigor that actually says something about the city. What about the plot? Well, it's like those long, boring anecdotes that used to end with "Isn't it amazing what the mind of man can conceive!"

There are some genuine laughs in Woody Allen's thirty-nine-minute *Oedipus Wrecks.* He stars in it as Sheldon Mills, a quiet, dignified lawyer, who, distraught, says to his analyst, "I'm fifty years old . . . and I still haven't resolved my relationship with my mother." When his mother, Mrs. Millstein (Mae Questel), appears, it's clear that nobody could resolve a relationship with this demon. A tiny woman, she seems harmless until you hear her voice: it drills into your skull and sucks out your brains. There is no answer to anything she says. Poor Sheldon, who has tried to escape the hideously familiar sound by de-Jewishing his name and becoming engaged to a Gentile (Mia Farrow), doesn't stand a chance.

His deepest wish is fulfilled: his mother disappears—but only to return in punishing nightmare form, discussing his engagement with crowds of people. Clearly, she understands—as we do—that he'd be afraid of dating a Jewish woman, afraid that she'd turn into his mother. He feels that if he marries his shiksa he'll escape his mother; he'll grow up—he'll gain his dignity.

This is Woody Allen's kind of comedy—the situation harks back to his earlier, funnier films, and the audience is grateful. But what was once peppy and slobby-spirited has become almost oppressively schematic. This film (with cinematography by Sven Nykvist) is too cleanly made for what it's about. It just doesn't have the organic untidiness that was part of Woody Allen's humor. Even his jokes are clean now, and his malice has been airbrushed out. He can't really revive the kind of comedy he used to do. For one thing, when a man in his thirties is befuddled it can be charming—you figure he'll work it out. But when he's in his fifties even his befuddlement has a weight. The little film itself is too deliberate. It has been a while since Allen directed out-and-out comedy, and here and there his timing is off. (When the magician is onstage putting swords through the Great Chinese Box that Mother is in, the scene is flabby right up until the cut to Sheldon, in the audience, smiling.) If Allen's pacing were speedier and more casual and erratic, maybe we wouldn't get the occasional feeling that we're watching waxworks—that he has already done too much of this. (We especially don't need his sortie into the Chaplinesque; he reaches for high emotion with something so derivative it cancels itself out.)

But even with the wax, the fumbles, and the absence of

the kind of moviemaking excitement that Scorsese charges us up with, this short-story comedy is very appealing. (It might be more appealing, and it would definitely be messier, if the mother wasn't simply a demon—if maybe she was a likable force of nature, with wit and gusto, but still made Sheldon feel ashamed of being her son.) The movie does take a surprisingly amiable—if somewhat ambiguous—turn. From what we see, Sheldon's relationship with his fiancée is polite and bland; it has no color or warmth—it has no silliness. And he gives no sign that he knows he's missing out on anything. But when, at his therapist's suggestion, he consults a clairvoyant, Treva (Julie Kavner), he finds himself responding to qualities that mark her as the opposite of his fiancée. Treva is like a high priestess of slobbiness. Devoted, caring, anxious, solicitous—and, above all, weepy—she's everything he has been fighting off.

Woody Allen has written the role that Julie Kavner deserves: she's the cartoon Jewish woman redeemed, and she plays it superbly—she's a Yiddishe Olive Oyl, a hopeless involuntary comic. And, even in the guise of Sheldon the lawyer in tweeds, Woody Allen recognizes her as his soul mate. The movie is a Freudian vaudeville, worked out with details such as Sheldon's loose, improved sex life during the period of his mother's disappearance. It's just after he acknowledges to his analyst that he's happy without her that everything clamps down on him. Freud was a Jewish comic, too (and his jokes also went on too long).

MARCH 20, 1989

TOO HIP BY HALF

The Adventures of Baron Munchausen

If Terry Gilliam's special-effects extravaganza, *The Adventures of Baron Munchausen,* puts you in a querulous, punitive frame of mind (What did he think he was doing? Couldn't he at least have drawn us into the movie at the start?), you may be able to restore your spirits by thinking about the backers' fury. These financiers from several countries must want to kill this guy who spent, it's estimated, fifty million dollars. And, in a way, that has to be what he wants them to feel.

Baron Munchausen, who lived from 1720 to 1797, was a German cavalry officer who in his later days sat around telling whoppers about his exploits; he was a fibber of genius—a fabulist. When books about him began to come out, starting in the early seventeen-eighties, he became a prototype of the fabricator; the movies about him include UFA's lavish color epic, in 1943, and the Czech animator Karel Zeman's version, in 1962. After you see the new film, you can reconstruct what Gilliam had in mind: he identifies with Munchausen, and he sees his theme as the liar as artist. His

Munchausen (John Neville) is a poet, a lover, a man of imagination. Gilliam pits him against the practical men who believe in facts and compromise and conformity; their leader is the chief official, Jackson (Jonathan Pryce), the man of reason. It doesn't take much intuition to recognize that Jackson, who orders the execution of a military hero (Sting) for his valor in saving lives—for being outstanding, for accomplishing too much—represents the movie moguls who have tried to trim and shape Gilliam's work. Specifically, Jackson could be standing in for the head of Universal, whom Gilliam addressed in a full-page ad in *Variety* late in 1985: "Dear Sid Sheinberg—When are you going to release my film, *Brazil?*—Terry Gilliam."

While you're watching *Munchausen,* the theme of the liar as artist doesn't emerge. You're not sure what the picture is about. Somehow, Gilliam is too distracted to indicate who the Baron is and what his legend is. For a few seconds here and there, you feel you're in a Piranesi dream world, or you're frolicking with ancient gods, but the entrancement never lasts long. You keep being jerked back to a nameless walled city under siege by the Turks in the late eighteenth century.

The images are packed, but what's going on in them isn't directly involving—it's at a remove. For long stretches, just about every shot is a special effect, and the scenes have the deadness of special effects without a clear narrative. A huge production was built on a script, by Charles McKeown and Gilliam, that seems perfunctory—an assortment of bits. This is a movie about a storyteller's tales made by a director who shows no feeling for the magical pleasure an audience experiences at a comedy when the timing is a jamboree, the episodes have a dramatic shape, and everything dovetails in a perfect surprise. The elements are here for a fantasy on the order of *The Wizard of Oz* and *Pinocchio* and the 1940 *Thief of Bagdad,* but the conflict—the definition—is missing. So is the innocence. In some area of themselves, Disney and those who made the other children's classics (and Spielberg, who made *E.T.*) never grew up. Gilliam, whose style is bad-boy antic and frenzied, may not have grown up, either (he puts sappy, unfunny wigs on people), but he seems to deny himself a child's sense of wonder. This movie isn't for kids.

It should be, though. The Baron, who assesses the threat of the Turks by riding a cannonball over the battlefield, tells the besieged townspeople that he can save the city if only he can locate his four "extraordinary servants," who were dispersed after the film's first adventure, in the Turkish sultan's palace. The mighty four are the world's fastest runner (Eric Idle), the world's strongest man (Winston Dennis), the man who can see the farthest (McKeown), and the man who can blow hurricane winds (Jack Purvis). Searching for the four, the Baron travels in a balloon made of women's silk knickers; he is accompanied by a stowaway, the ten-year-old Sally (Sarah Polley), who's part of a troupe of actors. The Baron and Sally voyage to a city on the moon; they fall into the fire god Vulcan's foundry inside the belching Mt. Etna; they're swallowed by a sea dragon. And they find the four—now aged—prodigies, who have all lost their powers. But Gilliam didn't bother to give these prodigies individual introductions when we first met them, and we hardly seem meant to care that they are reunited with the Baron and then regain their gifts. We aren't asked to be sad for them or happy for them, either. The story is almost devoid of emotional shading.

Except for Eric Idle, who wears shackles and weights to keep himself on the ground when he isn't whizzing by in a Road Runner routine, the four are almost faceless. Though the idea of their looking old in defeat and young in victory has juicy possibilities, it doesn't come to much. That's the case with John Neville's perpetually rejuvenated Baron, too. The movie wants us to see his renewed youth as his reward for believing in fantasy, but there's no magic in his cycles of shrivelling and freshening. Neville's courtly performance seems just what was wanted of him, and yet there's nothing elating in it, no zest. The conception verges on shaggy-dog preciousness.

This movie is short on characterization and personality. Whenever a high-energy performer, such as Robin Williams, as the King of the Moon, or Oliver Reed, as the rampaging Vulcan, has a chance to dominate the screen, it's like a reprieve. When Vulcan sees the Baron flirting with his wife, Venus (Uma Thurman), the steam that comes out of his ears has a burlesque-show kick to it. It hits the spot. That can't be said of anything that's done by the horses, the elephants, the thousands of soldiers, or the ladies of the sultan's harem. At a press conference that Terry Gilliam gave when *Brazil* was finally released here, he said, "I like working within limitations on the budget of a film, so that I can't have everything I want. Say, if we were making *Holy Grail* again, and we had all the money we wanted, we would have had real horses, we wouldn't have had coconuts. I think, given enough money and time, I could be really mediocre." No coconuts here.

What saves *Munchausen* from mediocrity is that you sense that Gilliam is brainstorming. He goes hippety-hoppety all over the place. The picture is too dry and too busy to be considered merely mediocre. And he has his gifts. He retains an edge of Monty Python's cranky, warped slapstick, and he has a painter's eye (so does Michael Cimino). There are fleeting camera moves with real surprise in them, like one toward the end when the camera pulls back from the site of a scheduled beheading and rushes through the crowd. In the red-tinted volcano scenes, Vulcan and his giants (who— in a neat quirky touch—turn out to be shorter than the Baron) are marvellously hairy and bestial. There are also scenes that are near-inspired, like the sight of the Baron and Venus dancing in the air high above cascading waterfalls in an immense, deep-in-the-earth ballroom; but a bit of conviction—of ardor and awe—is missing. Gilliam isn't a poet. We perceive the romantic idea; we don't really feel it. And when the Baron is in the belly of the sea monster, with ships of many nations marooned there, and the sailors are passing their time playing cards, Gilliam leaves out the hypnotic, surreal element that would make the vision indelible.

Maybe the reason we don't feel that the Baron is a rhapsodist, an artistic figure, or that the ending represents the triumph of the poetic imagination, is that Gilliam isn't a lyrical director. It's not just that he's disjointed and weak as a storyteller, and that he has a defective sense of rhythm. It's that his gifts—his gagster's prankishness and his sense of beauty—don't harmonize. At least, they don't here. It's as if he rejected the effort needed to make a sequence flow. He throws things together, trashing his own inspirations. The city on the moon that Dante Ferretti has designed and the big, airy, creamy scenes that Giuseppe Rotunno has lighted don't stay in the memory; they're static and then they're gone. Gilliam uses banal symphonic music over the battle scenes to give them the illusion of movement. And the climax of the film—in which the Baron demonstrates that you merely have to believe in imagination to make the Turkish siege disappear—is an inept cheat, lacking even the logic of a dream.

It's my impression that Gilliam was temperamentally more in tune with the retro-futurist nightmare of *Brazil* and its chaotic pop version of Kafka and Orwell. What's called for here is comic romanticism; that's what the sets are designed for—they're like architectural drawings made in a dream. And the quixotic Baron, a ladies' man, hands red roses to each new woman he meets and is in love with them all. He's in love with exploring; he's fighting off death because there's more he wants to see. Gilliam limits him by trying to pin him down as the opponent of the "man of reason"— a term that has no contemporary point. (We don't really believe in the man of reason in that sense anymore.) What Gilliam seems to have in mind is the businessman who looks at the figures Gilliam is piling up, and pulls the rug out from under him—the materialist who, in Gilliam's view, doesn't have the imagination to believe in his vision and support it all the way. He's made a fifty-million-dollar movie about why he can't get along with the men who back movies. (It's because he makes fifty-million-dollar movies about why he can't get along with the men who back movies.) Clearly, he feels thwarted and trapped: the film features a blind executioner and is full of cages and other images of imprisonment, such as the monster's belly and the walled city itself.

The closest Gilliam comes to coconuts here is in the rolling, manually operated ocean waves and the other curvy, ruffled stage effects of Sally's theatre company, before the play that's being performed (a play about Munchausen) opens out to show the gigantic scale that movies make possible. This opening out has dazzling potentialities, because instead of giving us "nature" he gives us tricky false perspectives and enormous painted sets. There's something of Méliès in this scenic approach, and something of Fritz Lang, too. And Gilliam displays each new set proudly, with a flourish. But it's not enough to have great design and effects—you must know what to do with them. (Those who say that the fifty million is all on the screen are giving the director a dubious compliment.) In *Brazil* Gilliam attacked reality; he does it again here. But at some point reality bites you on the nose.

APRIL 3, 1989

LIKE MAD

The Dream Team

Speed freaks will sometimes respond to what you're about to say; they'll answer a question before it's out of your mouth, and keep on riffing a few jumps ahead of you. The air seems electrified by some brilliant form of madness. In *The Dream Team,* Michael Keaton's Billy is intuitive in that wired, double-quick way, and without stimulants. His perceptivity is on overdrive. The mercurial Billy, formerly a writer, is a wisecracking violent lunatic. Tossing out zingers because he can't keep them in, he does a running satirical commentary on what's going on in the New Jersey mental hospital he's in, and on what's in the minds of the three other psychotics in his group. He's bored with them; their phobias and compulsions are old jokes to him. But he's touchy. If one of them says something he resents, he explodes and smashes things; kicking is his specialty.

Michael Keaton takes his role—the hero of a screw-loose farce—and makes it funnier than the director, Howard Zieff, and the writers, Jon Connolly and David Loucka, are likely to have envisioned, by making it totally plausible. In picture after picture (*Night Shift, Touch and Go, Beetlejuice, Clean and Sober*), Keaton's acting feels uncensored—freehand. Wearing jeans, a T-shirt, and Nikes, Billy is ready for anything; he bursts into a room like a storm. His velocity is part of his problem.

The Dream Team has a pip of a comic idea (it's indebted to an incident in *One Flew Over the Cuckoo's Nest*). Dr. Weitzman (Dennis Boutsikaris), the therapist for the group, decides that the men could benefit from a break in their routine, and arranges to take them, by van, to a game in Yankee Stadium. At a pit stop, he witnesses a murder, is knocked unconscious by the killers, and is hauled away in an ambulance. The four, stranded in New York City, draw on their reserves of sanity (and their weird recesses of dementia) to save the Doctor from the killers and take care of each other. The flaw in the idea is that the quadruple therapeutic story line, which is almost surreally upbeat, makes the picture seem less quirky than it is.

In the New York streets, the four stay close to the van, and if they leave they return to it—it's their connection to the hospital, where they felt safe. Hyperactive Billy becomes the organizer, the whip. He's a fantasist, and his grip on reality loosens now and then, but he's got a sense of responsibility. Man Mountain Peter Boyle is also in the group. He's Jack, a onetime topflight advertising man who went berserk and has become an exhibitionist with religious delusions. (He thinks he's Jesus.) Boyle has some of his best moments onscreen since he was the hulking monster singing "Puttin' on the Ritz" in *Young Frankenstein*. On the way to the city, Dr. Weitzman turns on the car radio and Jack suddenly breaks free of his mania and bounces to the rhythms of "Hit the Road, Jack." The scene is too short, but it's a tribute to the restorative powers of shared enjoyment. Billy can't believe the change in the others: for a few seconds, the usual bickering of the group stops. Jack has a terrific moment at the opposite extreme (i.e., pure lunacy) when he joins in the clapping to gospel music at a black people's storefront church: the maniac feels vindicated—he thinks that he's the source of their joy. Through much of the picture, Jack keeps flipping from sane to crazy, and when he visits his swank agency and renews his old antagonisms, sane and crazy merge.

Zieff's directing is less ingenious with Christopher Lloyd as another member of the group—Henry, a former postal employee, who truckles to authority figures. Maybe the role is just too close to other parts Lloyd has played; maybe the finicky Henry is simply too miserably unhinged to be entertaining. (He's pesky rather than funny.) And the fourth—fat, infantile Albert (Stephen Furst)—isn't up to the film's level of invention; he belongs to the world of sitcom. He transcends it in at least one scene, though: when he's arrested, he blushes with pride that the police are taking his picture.

Zieff has a knack for mellow slapstick (as he shows in a hospital-corridor scene where big Jack plays Jesus the healer), and although he often falls into standard cornball staging, he'll come up with surprising changes in tone, like the scene in an Army-Navy store where the aging shopkeeper (Jack Duffy), a veteran of the urban madhouse, calmly adjusts to the men's insanity. Zieff has a relaxed touch with the blithe, bearded Dr. Weitzman, and he gives Lorraine Bracco, as Billy's onetime girlfriend, a chance to build a character who might love Billy for his manic fantasy life. And when Zieff falters, there's Keaton demonstrating what a star can do for a picture. In a restaurant scene, he's like James Cagney—doing something bad while his face tells us how thoroughly he's enjoying it. The film isn't the knockout it might have been if it had a few big wild routines. And, yes, it's sentimental. But the sentimentality isn't overplayed, and Keaton's fast rap cauterizes much of it. He's a cross between a mouth and a moonbeam.

Crusoe

Caleb Deschanel's Fridayless *Crusoe* is a variation on the famous story. This version centers on Aidan Quinn as a Tidewater Virginia slave trader whose eagerness for profits leads him, in 1808, to charter a ship in the dangerous autumn months. On board, Crusoe boots the ship's dog, Scamp—a scrawny, predominantly Airedale mutt—off his bunk. But when a storm casts the ship against dark rock formations off an island and only Crusoe and Scamp are swept onshore alive, the dog becomes his companion. Having Scamp nearby helps him stay rational and hopeful as he salvages provisions and tools from the wrecked ship, and this new, tender relationship with Scamp is the prototype of what happens to the slaver when he encounters natives.

He discovers that cannibals use his island for burial rites and human sacrifices, and, horrified at witnessing a murder ritual, he fires a shot, which enables the next scheduled victim to escape and take refuge with him. Crusoe is a little batty with joy at having this fellow for a servant, a pet, and a companion for a few hours, and is shattered at losing him. When Crusoe is caught in a trap and again when he's sinking in a bog, a native warrior (Adé Sapara) frees him; they become friends as equals—until the warrior is caught by white men and dragged on board their ship. It's up to Crusoe to save his black friend from slavery.

This is a movie about how an immature, unfeeling money-grubber discovers reverence for life. In terms of its ideas, it's a late-sixties fable made in the late eighties. The narrative is genuinely childish, in a hippie way. It's laid out in a series of short scenes (marked by blackouts or simple cuts) that show the changes in Crusoe and the passage of time. Time passes plainly, artlessly. Deschanel, who was the cinematographer for Carroll Ballard's 1979 *The Black Stallion* (as well as for *The Right Stuff* and other pictures), has directed only once before—*The Escape Artist,* in 1982. He has an instinct for image magic, but he doesn't know how to make narrative magic happen, and he doesn't want to know. His lack of skill is frank and deliberate—he's like somebody with a vocabulary of two hundred simple words. Yet his emotionality and his feeling for atmosphere can carry a viewer along. He has a style; it comes out of the meekness in the way he works.

Maybe the film's ambience is affecting partly because Aidan Quinn's Crusoe is a hippie Christ figure—a young man finding the way to be gentle. Quinn is an intense, romantic actor, with a touch of the amnesiac about him—especially in his choked, slurry voice. We're used to hearing stage-English diction in movies that are set in the nineteenth century, and he sounds like a careless and apathetic modern actor. It takes a while to adapt to the idea that a man who's essentially talking to himself might not clip his words, and might sound as if he were sleepwalking. That dazed voice can get to you; it has an eerie way of suggesting a lost child. Quinn makes it work in roles as different as the hate-filled psycho in *Stakeout,* the AIDS victim in the TV film *An Early Frost,* and the accuser Chris in the American Playhouse *All My Sons.* Slim and curly-topped, with fixated blue eyes, he isn't hardened; he's a boyish presence on the screen—open, receptive, a New Age Montgomery Clift. He's the right actor for Deschanel's conception.

Deschanel isn't concerned about Quinn's talking like a modern man, because he doesn't really expect you to believe in the period. He's hoping you'll take the movie as a child's illustrated book, and accept the period as a convention for the fable. His style—it's like finger painting—represents a revulsion against professionalism. He's like Werner Herzog, but without metaphysics. And without metaphysics hippie craftsmanship is a lot more palatable.

The Robinson Crusoe story has been reimagined so that it's not a wilderness test of survival—it's a stripped-down search for values, an enforced spiritual retreat. Based on a script by Walon Green, this *Crusoe* is spare and evocative; it tends toward wordlessness and suggests a haiku movie. Essentially, it's all images of entrapment and freedom—it's about Crusoe's learning to be a free man. We see the black warrior's beautifully rounded muscles and powerful frame; we perceive his physical superiority to Crusoe, who's skin and bones. Crusoe perceives it, too. And as they work together to build a little sailboat for the warrior it's clear that Crusoe admires the warrior's intelligence and resourcefulness. Each of them sings a song from his past life, and then, in perhaps the film's most idealized moment, they swap songs. If you were in a cynical frame of mind, you might proclaim this the Brotherhood moment—and, of course, it is. (The movie is a revised *Tempest,* in which Prospero and Caliban find out they're brothers.) But Deschanel is so sweetly softheaded—so uncorrupted—that even this scene isn't inflated.

I love Luis Buñuel's 1952 *The Adventures of Robinson Crusoe,* with the rich-voiced Dan O'Herlihy calling out his loneliness. Deschanel's *Crusoe* doesn't have the poetry of that film, or the delirium and passionate sexual longing. But its innocence is likable. The images recall Ballard's *The Black Stallion,* with a more matter-of-fact sense of wonder. During the storm at sea, there are cuts to the frightened geese and goats who are penned up below deck. After the shipwreck, when Crusoe first opens his eyes onshore a crab walks by his face and we see it as he does—huge. He looks at anything that moves autonomously: a snail, a chameleon, a centipede. He tries to eat them but gives up on the centipede and tosses it to Scamp. Ballard's scenes complete an action and achieve a fullness, an exaltation; Deschanel cuts away without anything much happening, yet each homely detail has a trace of awe. *Crusoe* is a movie made by a child— or, at least, a child at core. I can't say that it's great, but it's touching. I kept watching with pleasure.

Heathers

The satirical black comedy *Heathers* is set in Westerburg High in Sherwood, Ohio. I assume that's for Sherwood Anderson, whose "Winesburg, Ohio" stories the movie evokes. It evokes a bunch of movies, too: *Lord Love a Duck, Carrie, Massacre at Central High, River's Edge,* the John Hughes pictures, and maybe the W. C. Fields *Million Dollar Legs,* where all the girls were named Angela. Here Westerburg High's three rich beauties—the élite group who do their damnedest to make life hell for those less gilded—are all named Heather. Their reluctant associate in bitchery, Veronica (Winona Ryder), confides to her diary that she dreams of "a world without Heather." And a psychotically fearless juvenile delinquent, J.D. (Christian Slater), shows up at the school and does a Jack Nicholson-devil impression. This cocksure demon may have materialized out of what Veronica has written: he goads her to become his accomplice in making her dream come true.

Heathers arrived with a very smart promotion, rave reviews, and the widespread suggestion that it would be a rallying cry for youth but was so diabolically audacious it would antagonize adults. It doesn't live up to the advance word. Yes, it's a collection of barbs and sick jokes, but it's not fun, and it lacks a punch line. The script, by the first-time screenwriter Daniel Waters, has a lot of prankish, spiky dialogue and some ingenious slapstick situations; despite some harshly obscene (invented) Valley Girl slang, it suggests that the picture will lift off into the junior division of Blue Velvetland. But layers of didacticism weigh it down, and the young, inexperienced director, Michael Lehmann, doesn't find the right moods for the gags. Lehmann uses hyper-bright colors for a facetious artificial effect; he's razzing the material, hoping for irony.

The premise of the movie is that Westerburg High (which stands in for all our high schools) is run by the Heathers because they're the most popular girls in the school: the other girls want to be them, and the boys want to be the jocks who get to date them. And so the Heathers' cruel snobbery is seen as proof of the worm in the American apple: cliques and castes undermine democratic values. The movie is about how terrible this rule by social popularity is and how it makes the other students perceive themselves as miserable failures. But, from what we see, the Heathers aren't popular—they're just rich bitches. And, from what we know, high school has many different groups—no one clique runs the whole shebang.

The script has its wacko inspirations: Veronica and J.D. disguise the murders they commit as suicides, and the media, the teachers, the parents, and the students deliver plasticized sentiments about "the tragedy of teen-age suicide." And the middle of the movie—a slapstick sequence in which two football heroes are killed and their deaths are arranged to suggest that they were lovers in a suicide pact—has a good rowdy nastiness. One boy's father assumes the guilt for not having understood his son's tendencies; the writer has a malicious talent for pinning down psychological cant. But the movie doesn't stay a black comedy.

In her heart Veronica doesn't believe the killings are justified. She's in on them, yet she isn't quite in on them. The picture doesn't know how to end, so she has to save the school. This turnaround finishes off the satirical possibilities. By then, you may miss the tall, blond Heather Chandler (Kim Walker), who pelted her victims with vicious one-liners. (Walker has a glittering teen-age bravado, especially when she drinks her death potion.) Winona Ryder is lovely-looking, but her role is too wobbly and "real" for the mock outrages that surround it. The pieces of the picture don't fit together. The writer and the director pull back from their sadistic gaudiness (which might be more entertaining if it didn't seem self-congratulatory). Veronica represents their we-don't-really-mean-it side—we don't want to hurt anybody's feelings. Where's the sting?

APRIL 17, 1989

FASCINATION

Let's Get Lost

Since the beginning of movies, what has made a screen performer a star has usually been that he or she functioned as a dream love object for multitudes of people. There are other kinds of stars, of course, but the glamorous figures have been the lifeblood of the movies. (And possibly American films have been popular around the world because the figures we fetishized travelled so well: they fit right into the amorous longings of many other cultures.)

As a young man, in the nineteen-fifties, the cool jazz trumpeter and singer Chet Baker had the casual deviltry and the "Blame It on My Youth" handsomeness to become a screen idol. He looked like James Dean, with deep-set eyes and a Steve Canyon jaw, and he was slated to appear opposite Natalie Wood in an M-G-M movie based on his own rise to stardom in the West Coast jazz scene. But Baker, who was taking drugs at the age of twenty-four—he later acknowledged that his favorite high was speedballs of heroin and cocaine—was in so much trouble with the police by then that he skipped out to Europe. (Robert Wagner played the jazz-trumpeter role written for Baker; the movie, *All the Fine Young Cannibals,* came out in 1960.)

Baker was busted over and over; he served time in Italy,

in the United States, and in Britain, and he managed to get himself deported from several countries. He also got beaten up, and on one momentous occasion, in San Francisco in 1968, his teeth were knocked out; it was three years (most of it "on public assistance") before he learned to blow his horn wearing dentures. But with his face caved in he still had his musicianship and his romantic glamour, though in the seventies and eighties it was the glamour of a ravaged dreamboat. In May, 1988, just a few months before *Let's Get Lost*, the documentary about him that Bruce Weber was preparing, was first shown, at a European film festival, he died, at age fifty-eight, after a fall from a second-floor window in an Amsterdam hotel near the drug dealers' section of town. His road manager said, "It was a hot night. He was probably just sitting on the windowsill and nodded out. One time too many."

Let's Get Lost isn't primarily about Chet Baker the jazz musician; it's about Chet Baker the love object, the fetish. Weber, the photographer who does the advertising spreads for Calvin Klein featuring well-muscled male torsos, has a definite "type." His earlier, 1987 documentary, *Broken Noses*, centers on the theme of macho as it's exemplified by a lightweight boxer, Andy Minsker, who coached a club of kids ranging in age from ten to sixteen. But Minsker comes across as a lightweight in too many ways. Whatever Weber was trying to indicate about macho was elusive, and the footage becomes somewhat discomforting when the camera lingers on the little boys' beautiful scrawny chests. Near the start of the film, Minsker is said to look like a young Chet Baker, and he does—he's got the jawline and the build. But he doesn't have Baker's theatrical aura. And when Baker's languorous music—cool but with a pop sweetness—is heard on the track while Minsker and his brother roughhouse, you may feel that Weber is trying to eroticize footage that doesn't really have much kick. My guess is that by the time Weber finished *Broken Noses*, and dedicated it to Baker, he'd realized that it was a warmup, and that his real subject was the young trumpeter who had fascinated him since he was sixteen and bought his first Chet Baker record.

Weber proceeded to collect still photographs and film clips from Baker's early days in L.A. with Charlie Parker (in 1952), Gerry Mulligan (1952–53), and others; from TV appearances in the fifties and sixties; and from quickie movies that Baker acted in in Italy and Hollywood. These finds are intermingled with footage of Weber (off camera) hanging out with the older, ruined Baker and interviewing his friends and associates, his mother, his wives and children and lovers. (Sometimes Minsker turns up alongside Baker.) Behind it all is a soundtrack made up of Baker recordings that span more than three decades—the idealized essence of the man. And maybe because Weber, despite his lifelong fixation on this charmer, knew him only as a battered, treacherous wreck, in the two years before his death, *Let's Get Lost* is one of the most suggestive (and unresolved) films ever made. It's about love, but love with few illusions.

Self-destructive beauties like Chet Baker are attractive to us in ways we can't quite pin down. When we see him as he was in the early fifties, on the West Coast, he evokes terms like "Beat," "cool," "dangerous"—all of them tinged with doomy romanticism. And the Santa Monica palm trees, tall against dark skies, are a magical evocation of that smoky era. Weber's visual intuitions are as lyrical and right as Baker's melodic instincts. (I dug through my dusty pile of 45s and found ten Baker records; he doesn't sing on any of them, but you could almost swear you heard the words coming out of his horn.)

You see Chet Baker as a kid who was out for adolescent pleasures: convertibles, pretty girls, booze, drugs. He didn't have to goad himself to master the horn; it came easy to him—he was a natural. He was out for adolescent pleasures all his life. And you see how blank his beauty is and how corrupt he becomes. Weber documents his own obsession with a beauty who had turned into a sunken-eyed death's-head long before he met him. (The film recalls the scene in

Ugetsu when the artist finds that his dream Lady is an evil wraith.)

The early photographs of the smooth-chested Baker holding his trumpet aren't by Weber, but they have something of the animal magnetism of the expressionless, athletic models in Weber's fashion layouts. Baker's soft voice can be heard on "Imagination [Is Funny]," and he sings in a glossy pastoral scene from an Italian movie, posed among youthful picnickers. In his later years, Baker was given to beating up on women (and he is said to have ratted on his friends to save himself from arrest). All this time, he was singing romantic songs.

Toward the end, there was an unmistakable whiff of Skid Row con artistry about him, even though he made two hundred thousand dollars his last year. We get to see what drew audiences. He went to the Cannes Film Festival in 1987, when *Broken Noses* was screened there, and his performance at Cannes, singing Elvis Costello's "Almost Blue," is part of *Let's Get Lost*. Wrapped in his romantic myth, he was always a jazz crooner—his voice was always small. Now it's a breathy murmur, yet his stoned, introverted tonelessness is oddly sensuous. He sings very slowly, and the effect is dreamy—the impeccable phrasing sounds like something remembered from the deep past (though the song is new). He does what he's been doing for more than thirty-five years, and the crowd is hushed. He's singing a torch song after the flame is gone; he's selling the romance of burnout. (It's a new kind of Dionysian image—not of frenzy but of oblivion.)

Weber included some rather undistinguished color sequences in *Broken Noses;* this time, working again with the cinematographer Jeff Preiss, in 16 mm., he sticks to black-and-white, and it's reticent yet expressive, impassioned. The film has its lapses, though. At one point, we hear Baker singing on the track while we see him, haggard and sinister (like a Jack Palance villain), in the Santa Monica sunshine bumping carnival cars. The scene is reminiscent of student films, and it sticks out, because Baker isn't being fetishized here—just pointlessly photographed. Toward the end, Weber throws in a collage of celebrities at Cannes (past and present) which doesn't belong here. It's padding, and it wrecks the organization of the last half hour. (At two hours, the film is slightly long.)

There are also lapses in moral judgment: badgering the women being interviewed, and setting them against each other. When the singer Ruth Young, who's from a show-biz family, is questioned about her relationship with Baker, she's delighted to perform for the camera, and she's lively, witty, and tough. (When she sings, it's clear that she modelled her style on Baker's.) But Carol, the Englishwoman who's the mother of three of his children, isn't part of show biz, and she feels awkward when she's asked similar questions. She doesn't want to bitch about her children's father, and she doesn't want to offend Baker's mother. (So she blames Ruth for everything that's gone wrong.) When Carol and also Baker's mother make it clear that they don't want to talk about certain matters, Weber keeps the camera on them while they plead for privacy. Is there perhaps an element of hostility in the way he presses the women? It's obvious that Baker has been hell on those close to him—why pry and compound their pain? Weber is an artist when he directs so that the imagery appears to be one with Baker's music. When he becomes more aggressive (and more petty), as he does with the women, the sequences are just skillful boorish cinéma vérité.

Weber spent his own money on *Let's Get Lost* (over a million dollars), and, of all movies made for obsessive reasons, this is one of the most naked. It's naked even in the way that this man in thrall to his "type" shows no bond of sympathy with the women who are similarly in thrall. Maybe it took a photographer-director to aestheticize his fetish to such a degree that it's impossible here to separate Chet Baker the scrupulously observed subject from Chet Baker the erotic dream. *Let's Get Lost* is shamelessly true to the (per-haps universal) experience of infatuation.

Field of Dreams

Field of Dreams is a crock—a kinder, gentler crock. If the Reagan era was Eisenhower II, this picture could be con-strued as the opening salute of the Bush era: Eisenhower III. (Baby boomers talk counterculture and vote conservative.) As a rebellious teen-ager of the sixties, the hero, Ray (Kevin Costner), rejected his father's outlook and the absorption in baseball they had shared. (His father was a minor-league player.) Now Ray is a New Age farmer in Iowa, with a hip, loving wife (Amy Madigan), whom he met at Berkeley, and a bright little daughter (Gaby Hoffman). But he can't get over the way he treated his father, who's dead. Walking among the cornstalks, Ray hears the whispered command to build a baseball field. When he does it, mowing down the corn and sinking the last of the family's money into lights for night games, the spirits of Shoeless Joe Jackson (Ray Liotta) and the other White Sox who were barred from baseball for life after the 1919 World Series scandal arrive and play on the field. Eventually, Ray and his father get their second chance, too, but not until after he has a mystical encounter with James Earl Jones as a reclusive writer who's sacred to the sixties generation (in the 1982 book *Shoeless Joe,* by W. P. Kinsella, the writer is J. D. Salinger), and also a mystical encounter with Burt Lancaster as Doc Graham, who played one inning for the New York Giants.

At some level, the writer-director, Phil Alden Robinson, must have really believed in this material and felt he had to make the movie. He may be treating people as if their brains were mush, but he'd just about have to be sincere to work so methodically, putting each new miracle in its narrative slot. It's not difficult to imagine moviemakers setting out cynically to make *It's a Wonderful Life* on the baseball field, but the result wouldn't be likely to have this (perfectly appropriate) stiff, pictorial cinematography or this just-one-miracle-after-another feeling. And it probably wouldn't have this doggerel emotion, these corn-fed epiphanies.

All the clumsy elements go together, and they give the movie a kind of authenticity that puts a strain on a viewer; you may feel like a pariah if you're not moved. After all, Ray's Berkeley-trained wife gets to make a riled-up speech against book burning, and Ray gets to bring his father back and make him happy—gets to make peace with himself. (And you can hear the sobs of people in the audience who haven't been so lucky. Or are these just the usual weepers?) That the film is sincere doesn't mean it's not manipulative; it so desperately wants to be liked that it's manipulative with a clear conscience.

Ray runs around the country (and into the past) carrying out the orders of the Great Whisperer in the sky. He doesn't give any thought to the farm, though it's about to be lost and he and his family ruined. Brainless Ray doesn't have to do much of anything except smile at Shoeless Joe and crinkle his shiny eyes. He's like a flower child who thinks that if you remain a child you'll wind up as William Blake. And that's the point of view of the picture.

The wonderfully hard-edged, bittersweet Amy Madigan does quick, amused line readings, and in the early scenes she and Costner spark each other. He's a first-rate romantic actor, and though for the rest of the movie he's playing an earnest, visionary boob, he does it with conviction. He's James Stewart (who is seen in *Harvey* on the farmhouse TV) and Gary Cooper in their Frank Capra roles; this is the kind of American-hero acting in which only good thoughts enter the hero's mind and moonlight bounces off his teeth. The other stars lend the film their personalities, but are misused.

James Earl Jones is made such a hearty great writer that his every moment seems fraudulent. And Lancaster is given fourth-rate lines and presented as a noble old man. With that tender, gravelly voice of his, which echoes through our moviegoing lives, and his cloudy eyes, he doesn't need to have the audience's responses programmed.

This whimsical fantasy isn't just removed from all reality; it's removed from its own subject matter. The great baseball players from the past are simply out there in the mowed-down cornfield doing something or other; there's no competitive excitement in it, and no rhythmic beauty. Are Robinson and his producers so afraid of the supposed box-office curse on baseball movies that they don't want to risk bringing baseball into the foreground? We never get to feel for ourselves what it was that made Shoeless Joe and the others love the game so much they had to come back from the grave to play it. We never get to feel what Ray's father could express while tossing a baseball to his son that he couldn't express any other way. The kick of the game is missing.

Maybe that's because baseball here is a metaphor for the "old" American values—conformist values. Asked if there is a Heaven, the spirit of Ray's father replies, "It's the place dreams come true." Ray looks at the farmhouse and his wife and child, and says, "Maybe this is Heaven." And the music soars as Ray and his father play catch—the communion Ray had refused as a teen-ager. Is the movie saying no more than that if you challenge your parents' values you may regret it later? Not exactly, because the religioso context gives Ray's spiritual distress a cautionary impact. The movie is pretty close to saying: Don't challenge your parents' values, because if you do you'll be sorry. It's saying: Play ball.

MAY 1, 1989

YOUNG STUFF

Scandal

Scandal, Oscar Wilde said, is "gossip made tedious by morality," and that's a pretty fair description of *Scandal,* the new English film about the Profumo affair. It's understandable that the (first-time) director, Michael Caton-Jones, and the writer, Michael Thomas, try to avoid the spirit of tabloid sensationalism. It was the tabloids that, in 1963, exploited a sexual indiscretion: During July and August of 1961, John Profumo, the Secretary of State for War in Macmillan's Tory Government, visited the teen-age showgirl Christine Keeler at the West End flat of an obliging osteopath, Stephen Ward. Since Christine also dallied with a Russian who was the assistant naval attaché of the Soviet Embassy, the papers took up the cry of the danger to national security. Profumo, who at first, in an address to the House of Commons, denied any impropriety, had to confess his lie, and he resigned from his Cabinet post. But the hullabaloo about ruling-class depravity would not die, and eventually the government fell. By then, Ward, who had been thrown to the mob—tried on trumped-up charges of living off the earnings of prostitutes—had killed himself. But *Scandal,* in keeping a tasteful distance from the prurient tabloids, has replaced spicy dirt with an oversympathetic tone and the easy irony that the generous-hearted Ward (who ran with the upper class but wasn't born to it) had been made the scapegoat. Ward the victim, played by John Hurt, is the hero of the picture.

Hurt is an absolute master of pathos, and at first the shadings in his manner are unexpected, but the moviemakers' soft interpretation of Ward turns *Scandal* into just one more English film about the cruelty of the class system. As Hurt plays him, Ward has a dreamy, awed look in his eyes when he's girl-watching on the street; he seems to regard life as infinitely benign. And he has a carefree, giddy vacancy when he's among lords and ladies. He's highly regarded as an osteopath (Ward massaged and manipulated a number of royal backs, and many celebrated ones: Averell Harriman's, Winston Churchill's, Elizabeth Taylor's), but he's not very strongly driven, in physical terms. He seems almost neuter (like the film itself), and a voyeur rather than an active participant. Where I think the movie goes off is in presenting Ward as the noble underdog. Even though he wasn't the paid pimp that the court accused him of being, he pandered to the sexual appetites of the aristocrats. He picked up hedonistic young working-class girls and trained them to tempt and tease the upper class; the girls he supplied to the wealthy and powerful were his ticket into society. (His weekend cottage at Cliveden, Lord Astor's estate, was rented to him for one pound a year.)

And Ward's voyeurism had a side that the movie doesn't show: his sitting room was equipped with a two-way mirror, so that he and his guests could observe the action in the bedroom. He may not have slept with his houseguests, such as the seventeen-year-old Christine Keeler (Joanne Whalley-Kilmer) and her sixteen-year-old showgirl pal Mandy Rice-Davies (Bridget Fonda), but he probably got what he wanted out of them. Ward the social-climbing panderer couldn't handle success: when he became part of the circle he'd aspired to, he got so carried away that he began to fancy himself a diplomat and a James Bond. *Scandal* sacrifices the rich comic possibilities in the sort of self-loathing man who's sexually turned on by being in close proximity to wealth and power. Instead, it makes Ward a warmly tolerant fellow who just wants to be liked, and tries to turn the material into a love story between him and Keeler. That leaves us puzzled; there's something missing. It's the blundering side of this ultra-nice peeper, Stephen Ward. Without it, what might be a satirical slice of history is a sentimental docudrama.

Visually, the movie is fairly supple and efficient, but it's intellectually mediocre. There must be a better angle on the Profumo affair than humanizing Stephen Ward. *Scandal* shows (and tells) us the obvious, and posts little flags at the sites of groundwork for future plot developments. Stephen recollects his schoolboy experience of being flogged for a petty offense that the schoolmasters knew he didn't commit—a scapegoat even then, always the outsider. Some of this is based on factual material, but it's presented in an exhausted dramatic format. We observe this kind and loving man who sorrows for the confused Keeler (after she has done him in by chattering to the press—for money), and we observe that yes, Stephen's idle-rich friends desert him when he's in trouble.

What sustains a viewer is the narrative, with its evocative details—how Keeler, bored with the middle-aged dignitaries that Ward introduced her to, took on a West Indian lover and then another West Indian, and how, as a result of a violent quarrel between the two, a newspaperman got on her trail. (She then offered up the story of her earlier gentleman callers, Profumo and the Russian.) There are also details of the public indignation over the decadence of the "Establishment"—over sadomasochism and spies and naked bathing in Lord Astor's pool. The movie skims the years from 1959 to 1963, and there's Ward introducing Christine to hash and her becoming spacey, and the music changing, and the kinky Victorian repressiveness giving way to London's Swinging Sixties.

Ian McKellen's Profumo, with two bald streaks running

up his skull, may be reminiscent of Martyn Green as the Lord High Executioner, but he has a wry dignity. No doubt Profumo's lines had to be written with care that he would have no grounds for a lawsuit; McKellen doesn't say much—he communicates the character's thoughts by teeny flickers of expression. He's rather marvellous at suggesting Profumo's awareness of the risks he's taking when he whips around town in his Rolls with his ladylike trollop. And the Dutch actor Jeroen Krabbé, who plays the Russian attaché, has a great camera face and physique. (He can bring a theatricality—a whiff of danger—to a scene.)

But, finally, the movie comes down to the girl: How is she? And the answer is: Not quite right. Joanne Whalley-Kilmer is a skilled actress, and she was doe-eyed perfection as the nurse in *The Singing Detective,* but she seems too polished, too refined here—a little wan. She's incredibly pretty, the way Olivia de Havilland was when she played in *The Adventures of Robin Hood*; you look at her as Christine Keeler and never quite "get" her. You don't get a fix on why she obliges older men whom she isn't attracted to, and you don't believe the film's explanation that she does it for love of Ward. By the end, we seem meant to find Christine tragic, but most of us will probably just think her vaguely unhappy. Deep down, under her genteel exterior, the Christine Keeler of the movie has to be a harlot, and the only time I felt that Whalley-Kilmer got close to that was in her first scene, when Christine is doing her act, among the nightclub showgirls, and eying the customers. She has a tarty coquettishness; you can believe that she's a kid playing at harlotry—trying it on—and this game plan gives her a cheap, raw-edged gorgeousness, but she loses it almost at once. The later Christine is appealing but elusive, unreadable; maybe that's what the moviemakers wanted, but it doesn't seem enough.

Bridget Fonda's impudent platinum-blond Mandy—a teenage "kept woman" with the hawk eyes of an old madam—is the movie's only wild card. Fonda shows some of the comic flair that her aunt Jane showed in movies such as *The Chapman Report;* her dryness has a provocative, taunting assertiveness. She's gauchely young and tall, and when she's flouncing around the night-club dressing room in her spangled scanties she's like an adolescent drag queen. Fonda is onscreen just briefly, but her gamine crispness makes you aware of how sickly-holy the film's point of view is.

Say Anything

As the nineteen-year-old jock Lloyd Dobler in the high-school romance *Say Anything,* John Cusack goes around Seattle with a hipster's deadpan and question marks in his eyes. He has a crush on the class valedictorian, Diane Court (Ione Skye), who is a dedicated student and has never socialized with her classmates; she's Lloyd's ideal, and he's determined to ask her to go to the graduation party with him. His friends advise him that she's out of his reach; they're sure she'll turn him down, and under his mask of confidence (which fools nobody) he's terrified of rejection. When he gets Diane on the phone, he can't keep up a sequential conversation; he babbles, and talks in spurts—he riffs. He's irresistible; she says yes. When he's out with her, his heart is in his mouth, but he knows to talk when he's nervous, and he makes Diane feel protected and happier than she has ever been. As for Lloyd, he's found bliss. He wants to hang on to her—for life.

Say Anything is unabashedly romantic about Lloyd Dobler's capacity to make a commitment. It's a slight movie, but that's not a put-down. Its slightness has to do with the writer-director Cameron Crowe's specialty: he's wired into teen-age flakes and the sloppy, exuberant confusion of high-school dating. Crowe is great here on oddity and fringe moments; the comedy helps to dry out the romanticism—to give it lightness and a trace of enchantment. And John Cusack's performance is distinctive enough for you to think you might remember the name Lloyd Dobler—that he stands for something, like Jacques Tati's Mr. Hulot. There's a sequence with its own pop magic: when Lloyd feels he's lost Diane he tries to puzzle out what happened—he talks into a tape recorder, going over the events of their time together, as he drives through all the places they went to. And I've never seen anything like the image of the forlorn Lloyd serenading Diane with a boom box: he stands in the secluded area outside her house holding the box over his head, with Peter Gabriel's "In Your Eyes" resonating among the trees.

Some of the film's best characters and scenes could be mistaken for throwaways. There's the girl (Lili Taylor) who comes to the graduation party with her guitar, prepared to sing sixty-five songs she has written about the perfidiousness of the ex-boyfriend who drove her to attempt suicide. Crowe lets the scene run long enough for us to see the self-dramatizing elation that's crowding out her self-pity—she's burstingly angry that she was cheated on, and she wants the world to know that she's alive now and making music. Crowe—he wrote *Fast Times at Ridgemont High*—keeps faith with teen-agers; he doesn't generalize about them (or about the older generation, either).

A couple of astonishingly fluid scenes between Cusack and his real-life sister Joan suggest the love and the tensions between Lloyd and his older, divorced sister, whom he lives with—the two of them are Army brats. She crabs at him for a second when he does a comedy routine with her small son, and he reminds her that she used to be "warped and twisted and hilarious." You feel the sourness of her divorce and her single-parent situation; everything clues you in to why Lloyd wants stability and why he's determined that his love for Diane last forever. But none of this is overdone. John Cusack underplays Lloyd's decency and strength— takes them for granted. And Crowe and his editor, Richard Marks, know when to nip a scene off; the movie has abrupt, eccentric rhythms. You don't feel like a ninny for watching a high-school movie.

This first picture that Crowe has directed is a lovely piece of work—despite a dumb idea at its center. When Lloyd is asked what his goal is, he says, "To be with Diane." He doesn't know what he wants to do yet; that makes sense. But there's too much emphasis on Diane's braininess—her genius. It's as if she were going to be his higher calling, as in a magnificent-obsession novel. And all the solicitude about Diane's future as a member of some cosmic think tank is puzzling, because as Crowe has written her, and as Ione Skye plays her, she's just a nice, intelligent, industrious girl— a model grind. The talk of her brilliance seems like some kind of mistake; there isn't a lick of flash or fun in the character. Mostly, she just smiles big.

Diane's father (John Mahoney) has been pushing her to ever higher academic achievement all her life; they have had a mutually adoring relationship. Her shift from being close to Daddy to being close to Lloyd is almost a parody of the lives of properly raised girls who went directly from their fathers' houses to their husbands' houses. (In giving Diane a new protector, the movie seems to be using the excuse of her high intelligence to treat her as a frail creature.) The story turns into a battle of wills between Lloyd and the father. John Cusack and Mahoney have to carry the unconvincing melodramatic portion of the plot, but they carry it stunningly. Mahoney never tries to turn his character into a lovable fellow; there's a mean, self-serving streak in his Mr. Court that's almost dazzling. And Cusack is a wonder: Lloyd's (nearly) blank look tells you that a lot of things are going on inside him—he has a buzz in his blank face. Cusack is a joyous performer, and at the party he's joined by the radiant, blond Kim Walker; Loren Dean, as the face that launched sixty-five songs; Jason Gould, as an amiable drunk; Eric Stoltz; Amy Brooks; and Chynna Phillips, among many others. Every one of them makes you smile. There's no special moviemaking excitement in *Say Anything,* but Cameron Crowe is a real director—he loves actors.

MAY 15, 1989

TRAMPLED

The Rainbow

Describing the landscape where the heroine, Ursula Brangwen, walks toward the woods in *The Rainbow,* D. H. Lawrence wrote, "It was very splendid, free and chaotic." That's true of *The Rainbow* itself. It doesn't have the dramatic clarity (or the greatness) of its successor, *Women in Love,* but it's a passionately heated landmark novel about marriage. This chronicle of three generations of a farming family is an attempt to show how marriage worked in the Victorian and Edwardian periods and why it became subject to new strains in the industrial age. Ursula, who experiences those strains— and is aware of them—flails at everything around her. While still in her teens, she's in conflict between her drives and the repressive claims of conventional marriage. It isn't just sex she wants; she yearns for sexual and spiritual union. The novel, which was completed and published in 1915, was prosecuted for obscenity and ordered destroyed. It's not hard to understand why. The writing is intensely sensual and often ecstatic; it's potent—Lawrence makes you feel that the whole world is panting in rhythm with his language. And Ursula, trying to break free, challenges Christianity and colonialism, and questions the other ideas that her fiancé, Anton—an attractive man with a fine, slender body who's

137

in the Royal Engineers—casually accepts. When she expresses her feelings, he hates her. Finally, he wants to marry her, he wants to kill her. The new movie version, by Ken Russell (who filmed *Women in Love* in 1969), doesn't impose an artificial pattern or plot on the material, but it isn't splendid. Amorphous and unsatisfying would be more accurate.

The pastoral locations are grassy vistas that seem to melt before your eyes. The Midlands look the way a reader wants them to look, and the images suggest that the material is being approached with humility and seriousness. This isn't one of Russell's lurid, campy pictures. But his underlying attitudes haven't really changed; the campiness is simply more restrained. The adaptation, which he did with his wife, Vivian, is a slapdash job—speeches are borrowed from one set of characters for another, and incidents are thrown in. So the themes don't cohere. It isn't clear what the story is about, besides the one theme that the "modern" woman's desire for independence leads to turmoil, and that there's hope in this turmoil. (If Ursula married the officer, who has no deep connections with her, she'd shrivel.) The movie's most powerful section is the treatment of Ursula's first job— when, at seventeen, she takes a teaching post at a school where the children of the poor are beaten into whining submission. Russell seems relieved to get away from the difficult, blind anger that's woven into the sexual experiences of Ursula (Sammi Davis) and Anton (Paul McGann). He plunges into the Dickensian miseries of the school, where the contending forces are clearer.

The ads for *The Rainbow* feature a banner line from the review in the *Times*: "Ken Russell is the purest interpreter D. H. Lawrence could have hoped for." In his worst nightmares. Russell's fidelity (to roughly the second half of the novel, the part that moves from the previous generations of the Brangwen family to concentrate on Ursula) is staggeringly superficial. The fault isn't just in the script; it's in how he has directed Sammi Davis, and how she plays the role.

She made a smart, sunny impression in relatively small, teen-ager parts in *Mona Lisa, Hope and Glory, A Prayer for the Dying* (less sunny), and other movies; and, as the cunning little schemer—a starring role—in the BBC's Thomas Hardy adaptation, *The Day After the Fair,* she had an authentic horror. (But she didn't have to represent the consciousness of the Hardy material.) As Ursula, she has a scrappiness that works well in the school-teaching scenes, but in the rest of the movie nothing she says seems to have any substance: her rude, angry lines just pop into her mouth right out of the script. This Ursula is blank-faced and lightweight. It makes sense that she should seem surly and withdrawn to her family and the other characters, but she can't be merely that to us, or who's going to give us what is the glory of the novel—Lawrence's intuitive exploration of her feelings and her imagination? That's what's missing. One of the pioneer-ing feminist heroines—a woman who represents an advance on previous generations, a woman on a quest—has been turned into a snippy, closed-off brat.

As if to make up for the passion that's omitted, Russell adds an episode in which Ursula (when she's still a school-girl) poses nude for a dirty-old-man painter (Dudley Sutton), who becomes furious when she won't let him beat her. And Russell adds such details as the headmaster maneuvering the young teacher Ursula into displaying her bottom for him. But Lawrence's material isn't about scruffy lechery; it's about sexuality and spirit. Russell's additions detract from the poetic intensity of what Lawrence was up to, and muddy the conflicts. Since it's Winifred, the teacher that the school-girl Ursula has a crush on, who dares Ursula to go to the painter's studio, without warning her about his kinks, Win-ifred seems callous and sadistic. The scenes involving Win-ifred (Amanda Donohoe) are fairly weird anyway, since Donohoe, who was the serpentlike fanged vampire in Rus-sell's 1988 *The Lair of the White Worm,* retains some of her viperishness here. She's a leering mannish lesbian, who se-duces Ursula with soft caresses and anti-male talk, and then turns about and marries Ursula's plump and prosperous mine-owner uncle, played with smiling finesse by David Hemmings. (You couldn't guess from the movie that in the novel Ursula is the matchmaker.)

Glenda Jackson and Christopher Gable are surprisingly relaxed as Ursula's parents, and (in small details) they show us how different their sexual life is from hers. The mother keeps having babies; the father is proud of being able to support his family, and finds his other joys at the church organ and in wood carving. The parents' lives are eventful yet peaceful in ways that Ursula will never know. But will anybody who hasn't read the novel be able to understand Ursula the dreamer? Or will they just think she's an impossibly petulant twerp?

Funny thing about this movie: Russell, notorious for overheating most of his pictures, has left the heat out of this one. He seems to be trying to serve the novel without recognizing what a blazing vision it is, how it stirs a reader. And he seems to have run out of bravura. (The climactic scene, in which Ursula is in danger of being trampled by horses—and perhaps by a marriage based merely on sexual attraction—is emotionally inert.) The most sensuous moment is very brief. Just after Ursula and Anton meet—when she isn't quite sixteen—they go into a church that's being restored. They're secluded there; he opens several of the miniature buttons on one of the gloves she's wearing, exposing a small bit of flesh, and kisses it. That's at least the beginning of something.

Miss Firecracker

The playwright Beth Henley is a fey, witty observer, with a knack for impish parody. But her themes are sometimes poetic—she wants us to feel exalted—and she's not a poet. She doesn't transform her material; the transformation process goes no further than turning everything into slightly fermented local color. Set in Yazoo City, Mississippi, *Miss Firecracker*—she adapted it from her 1984 play, *The Miss Firecracker Contest*—is a farce about Southern eccentrics that's at the same time (and here's the death knell) a loving tribute to the indomitability of screwed-up, lonely dreamers.

Holly Hunter is the waif Carnelle, who was orphaned at eight and raised with her classier cousins Elain (Mary Steenburgen) and Delmount (Tim Robbins). After tall, willowy Elain married a wealthy Atlanta businessman and Delmount went away, Carnelle stayed on alone in the big, decaying family mansion. Yazoo City isn't rich in opportunities for Carnelle; she works the gutsucker machine on the assembly line of a catfish-packing plant. She has just one rhapsodic memory: it's of the time, back in 1972, when she watched the triumphal big parade featuring her idol Elain, who had won the Fourth of July beauty pageant—the Miss Firecracker Contest. Carnelle isn't considered much to look at, and her effort to gain acceptance by hopping into bed with local boys has already got her the title Miss Hot Tamale, but she thinks that if she can just win this year's contest (it's the last year she'll be eligible) she'll be respected, and she'll be able to leave town "in a blaze of glory." The movie is about what Carnelle goes through for the chance of winning (and, yes, how she discovers true values).

The contest is a rambunctious "This Is Your Life" freak show. The patrician Elain returns home; she's been asked

to deliver the keynote speech. Delmount, a dilettantish aspiring poet-philosopher, has just been released from the asy-
lum that Elain had him committed to; he comes back to try
to sell the tumbledown house. And he is soon charmed by
Popeye (Alfre Woodard), the black seamstress who's working on the shiny outfit for Carnelle to wear in the talent
competition. (To the tune of "The Star-Spangled Banner,"
Carnelle marches, tap-dances, does cartwheels, and twirls a
red-white-and-blue wooden rifle—all pretty much simultaneously.)

Thomas Schlamme, directing his first feature, has tried for
vividness, and it should be acknowledged that the movie is
never plain boring. But its comic pathos and Southern-gothic
cuteness can grate on you. Almost everything to do with
Carnelle's dream is like some quaint form of torture—it's as
if somebody behind you were whacking you on the head
and saying "Isn't this priceless?" in one ear and "Doesn't
this girl have gumption!" in the other. Henley over-
individualizes the characters; you get the feeling that a whole
summertime seminar of creative-writing students has gone
to work on each one of them, punching them up. Then
Schlamme directs the actors to brighten them up even more.
Holly Hunter initiated the role of Carnelle on the stage, and
she gives it a determinedly virtuosic stage performance; she
cries and smiles almost as much as Luise Rainer did, and
Rainer wasn't feisty. Schlamme compounds this folly with
closeups of Hunter acting full tilt. Probably from the best of
motives—admiration of Hunter's talent—he force-feeds us
Carnelle's desperation, her courage, and her heartbreaking
pint-size gallantry. So it's just about impossible to laugh at
her.

But even if he didn't—even if he brought the emotions
down a few shades—the material still might not work, because there is something off in Henley's technique. In some
aberrant way (which can work on the stage), her writing is
all exposition; everything is told to us, and it all feels like
anecdotes that are already set from previous tellings—that

are finished. Henley is too meticulous a student of playwriting: she positions all the skeletons in the funky closets and prepares us for each thing that happens—Carnelle and Elain enter amid a flutter of briefing papers.

Mary Steenburgen, with her calm, deliberate way of talking, isn't bad. At first, she seems to be overdoing Elain's flower-of-Southern-womanhood diction and her self-adoring meanness, but then, as the picture goes on, Elain's twanging pseudo graciousness becomes more effective. You listen to the elegant trickiness of the line readings; since Elain the coquette is a false identity that was confirmed when she won the Miss Firecracker contest, Steenburgen is probably justified in keeping us aware of the gears grinding. (But Elain could have been made funnier; we don't need to see that the actress ''understands'' the character.) Some of the other performers provide texture in the background: Ann Wedgeworth and Trey Wilson as the contest officials who sing during the swimsuit competition; Angela Turner as the blond contestant who delivers the Scarlett O'Hara ''As God is my witness!'' monologue.

But the only element that really makes the movie worth seeing is Tim Robbins' droll, courtly Delmount. When I first saw Robbins in a starring role, he was playing the prim civil-rights worker in *Five Corners,* he was good, all right, but I thought it was a case of sensational casting—I didn't see how he could play anything else. I assumed that the stiffness and the idealist's bulging, bumpy forehead and the squinched-up pug face were the only way he could look. Then, as the flirty, baby-faced rookie pitcher in *Bull Durham,* he showed that he could use his six-foot-four frame for slapstick. And as the ''video visionary'' in (the generally negligible) *Tapeheads* he had an agreeable loose humor. (When he and John Cusack danced together on a roof, the scene recalled the relaxed teamwork of the Laurel and Hardy dances.) But Robbins' Delmount suggests that he could be a major actor.

He has the gift of looking just right for each of his roles, and he has a puckish commanding presence here (though Delmount can't command, because he's a creature of impulses: he never thinks anything out). The role is a baroque contraption, and that's what Henley is good at; she has a wonderfully silly talent—Delmount even suffers from gothic nightmares. Robbins gives the movie some richness; he gives it scenes that flow, that spill over. He uses his full height here, and his sweaty hair, curling from the humidity, provides him with an aureole. Delmount, the misfit prince with a dinky ponytail, has Southern grace and formality along with a wild, infantile sense of fun. When he's quarrelling with his sister Elain—and especially when they swing into a ballroom dance—they have a tingling love-hate intimacy, something voluptuous that they take for granted. As Elain, Steenburgen plays off Robbins with a cool, lofty satisfaction; they're marvellous together. Delmount is completely different in his lovestruck scenes with Alfre Woodard's Popeye: grinning and boyish, he's her heartthrob. The two of them are so nuttily harmonious they're like Shakespearean clown-lovers, or Papageno and Papagena—they're spellbound. I wouldn't have guessed that Woodard (who has played so many put-upon, suffering women) had this kind of lightness in her. The role is a caricature, but so, of course, are most of the other roles (underneath their awful rounding). What makes Woodard's Popeye stand out is that, with a black actress playing the part (it was written in the play as white), Popeye becomes a black caricature. There's naughtiness in the performance: Woodard's rapt gaze evokes memories of Butterfly McQueen at her dizziest.

Tim Robbins brings some comic poetry into the movie. When Delmount is bawling himself out for his own pretentiousness, or watching the pageant and sucking on a little pipe, he makes you feel that behind his sneaky, demon eyes he's thinking thoughts no character in a movie has ever thought before. And he's stimulated by them.

MAY 29, 1989

HICCUP

Indiana Jones and the Last Crusade

A friend of mine who's in his early fifties and is eminent in his field says that when he grows up he wants to be Sean Connery. He doesn't mean the smooth operator James Bond; he means the bluff, bare-domed Connery of *The Man Who Would Be King* and *The Untouchables* and now *Indiana Jones and the Last Crusade.* Connery's physical presence is assured, contained, insolent; that's what makes this burry Scotsman a masculine ideal. In *The Last Crusade,* Connery, in a droopy mustache and a trim grayish-white beard, is Indiana Jones' scholar father, a medievalist who's too engrossed in his studies to pay much attention to his daredevil son's archeological adventures. Tweedy and distracted, in the manner of a Victorian pedant, he's the only surprising note in *The Last Crusade.*

"I look for humor in whatever I'm doing," Connery has said, and he finds it here in his byplay with the man he calls Junior. Harrison Ford is a master of double takes, and Connery keeps occasioning them. He rags the two-fisted Indy as if he were still a kid, and uses paternal authority to outrank him—even to the point of slapping him in the face for using "Jesus Christ" as a swear word. Professor Henry Jones, Sr., is the only man alive who isn't in awe of Indiana Jones.

Each of the two stars carries associations from his past roles; their scenes together are so charged with personality that the atmosphere of parody is almost flirtatious. Connery isn't a subtle actor, but as a presence he has phenomenal subtlety. And he can be silly: He can introduce little-boy mischief, and his masculinity is never in doubt. Amusing himself, he gooses this entire movie along. Ford is a little dull until he has Connery to play off. Then they nudge each other skillfully, and the director, Steven Spielberg, knows just when to cut to the father's sheepish stare, the son's wolfy grin.

The Connery-Ford clowning distracts us from the doldrums of punches and chases and plot explication. The movie isn't bad; most of it is enjoyable. But it's familiar and repetitive—it's a rehash. It makes you recall the old-Hollywood wisdom: If they liked it once, they'll love it twice. The action simply doesn't have the exhilarating, leaping precision that Spielberg gave us in the past (before he became apologetic about it). Great Spielberg action is so brilliant it spooks you; it makes you want to cheer—you leave the theatre laughing at your own excitement. Here Indy punches out so many people that you weary of the amplified sound of fist against flesh. (*Indiana Jones* is this summer's *Roger Rabbit,* but this time there's no distinction between live action and animation.) You watch chases by speedboat and motorbike, tank and airplane and dirigible (it's 1938), but you don't feel kinetically caught up in them. Vehicles keep exploding in flames—who cares?

Right at the beginning, in Monument Valley in 1912, when Indy as a Boy Scout (played by River Phoenix) rescues the jewelled "Cross of Coronado" from archeological looters and, escaping from them, hops onto a circus train, falls into a vat of snakes, grabs a whip from the lion's cage, and is cut on the chin, we laugh in hip recognition that we're seeing how the adult Indy acquired his phobia, his weapon, and his scar, even though there's no real wit in it. And we never get a clear idea of why the head looter resembles the adult Indy, or why Indy adopts the outward tokens of this looter—the brown fedora, the leather jacket. We see the looter give Indy a bit of approval (something he never gets from his father). Is that meant to be enough cause for Indy to turn the looter into some sort of good-bad-guy ideal and to reject his father's soft-tweed-hat tyranny? Spielberg doesn't seem to want the scenes to snap into clarity; he may think this fuzziness is artistic ambiguity. Even a complicated big scene of Indy and a blond art historian (Alison Doody) trapped in a Venetian catacomb that's full of rats isn't shaped satisfyingly. Most of the staging is shabby, routine. (A church stained-glass window that figures in the plot is so glaringly inauthentic you half expect the fakery to be the point.)

A few images make an impact: Indiana's horse is magnificent in motion, his eyes rolling, his mane flying; the vertical compositions that show the ancient city of Petra, which was carved into the rock mountains of Jordan, leave you wanting to see more. I like the device of Indy's father and friends looking down a cliff to what they think is Indy's grave while he has climbed up and is behind them, trying to see what they're looking at. It's a good gag—I've always liked it. And there are funny, wiggy bits, such as Alison Doody's last scene, when, after being misdirected almost consistently, she goes out in glory, with glittering eyes and a lewd smile. But the only real spin is in Connery and Ford's slapstick.

Their teamwork can't save the movie from the tone deafness that has been afflicting Spielberg's work ever since he became a consciously inspirational director, as in his dreadful whimsy about rejuvenation in *Twilight Zone—The Movie,* and as in *The Color Purple* and *Empire of the Sun.* (Offering mystical guidance seems to be his conception of a step toward becoming mature and responsible.) This third film of the Indiana Jones trilogy is virtually a reprise of the first one (*Raiders of the Lost Ark*). Spielberg and his asso-

ciate George Lucas, the producer, appear to be retreating to
the pulpy sincerity of *Raiders* as a way of dodging the rocks
thrown at the second film (*Indiana Jones and the Temple
of Doom*) for being "horrific." They've taken the *Raiders*
mixture of cliff-hanger and anti-Nazi thriller and religious
spectacle even further. Now the Nazis are after the Holy
Grail—the cup that Jesus drank from at the Last Supper,
which was used to catch the blood that spilled from the
spear wound in His side. In the film's theology (which is
murky at best), the Grail heals mortal injuries and confers
eternal life on anyone who drinks from it. (This is a rejuvenation whimsy, too.) And the script by Jeffrey Boam,
based on a story devised by Lucas and Menno Meyjes, shows
us that Indy and his father, in their search for the Grail, find
each other. Their search is also a search for the divine in all
of us, and John Williams' grandiose score tips us when the
searchers are getting hot.

For a while in the twenties and thirties, art was talked
about as a substitute for religion; now B movies are a substitute for religion. (The pulp adventure is the Grail. Con-
necting with your dad is the Grail.) And Spielberg hokes up
his B movie by using the Connery-Ford teamwork for
"heart." (He's trying to put back the heart he literally took
out in *Temple of Doom*.)

Spielberg wants us to feel the two men's yearning for the
father-son relationship they've never had. And to bring them
together he invokes pop Christian symbolism without any
apparent awareness that this may be offensive to those of
other faiths or of no faith—probably to some Christians,
too. Isn't it offensive to him? During a miracle scene, when
Denholm Elliott (as the museum curator who is Indy's superior) crosses himself, it's like a hiccup of old M-G-M.

The Last Crusade is jarring every time it impinges on religious mythology or historical events—as in a scene of a
Nazi rally, with a huge bonfire of books. Spielberg wants to
show his reverence for books, but the slick staging may
make you think that his entire knowledge of history and

culture is filtered through movies. (A man who loved books wouldn't be likely to have approved this follow-the-dots script.) And when he mixes Saturday-afternoon-serial death-defying stunts with "real" feelings that we associate with his own life (such as his pain at having been separated from his father), the movie feels awkward. It's a joke to us that Indy can never please his father, because we see Indy's wild-ass fearlessness. (In a carefree moment, he shoots three men with one bullet.) Indy isn't just relentlessly victimized by one physical attack after another; the verbal abuse he receives from his father—the fiercely robust Connery—adds a second dimension. It's almost as if Indy were being attacked *personally*—there's a giddiness to it. His being treated as a butterfingered kid is better, more original, than the serious archetypal-Oedipal theme the movie is attempting.

Spielberg seems willing to throw anything into the stew (there's even a man who's more than seven hundred years old), but the joyous sureness is missing. He must have begun to distrust his instincts—to think he was doing the wrong thing. Directors who made big commercial hits used to feel guiltless, but Spielberg is too anxious, too well intentioned; he thinks it isn't enough to give the audience pleasure. Trying to give it what he feels he owes it (wisdom), he softens and sentimentalizes the action. And, of course, he's being congratulated for his new, grownup approach: members of the press are responding to the jump from the goofball connotations of *Temple of Doom* to the important sound of *Last Crusade*. This mediocre movie seems destined to be a tidal wave of a hit. Spielberg, who was perhaps the greatest of all pure, escapist movie directors, is being acclaimed for turning into a spiritual simp.

Vampire's Kiss

Usually, when an actor plays a freak you can still spot the feet-on-the-ground professional. Nicolas Cage doesn't give you that rootedness. He's up there in the air, and when you watch him in *Raising Arizona* or *Moonstruck* it's a little dizzying—you're not quite sure you understand what's going on. It could be that this kid—he's only twenty-four—is an actor before he's a human being. That would explain his having had two front teeth knocked out for his role as the mutilated Vietnam vet in *Birdy;* it would explain his eating a plump, wriggling cockroach in his new film *Vampire's Kiss.* These things may not seem very different from Robert De Niro's going from a hundred and forty-five pounds to two hundred and fifteen pounds to play the older Jake La Motta, and De Niro could also be said to be an actor before he's a human being, but they go in different directions. De Niro swells and thickens and sinks down; he walks heavy— he's formidable. Cage strips himself, he takes flight, he wings it. I don't mean to suggest that he's the actor De Niro is— only that, in his own daring, light-headed way, he's a prodigy. He does some of the way-out stuff that you love actors in silent movies for doing, and he makes it work with sound.

In *Vampire's Kiss,* he's the whole show. As Peter Loew, a New York literary agent, he's a fop, a pin-striped sheik with moussed light-brown hair and a pouty, snobbish stare. He talks in a poseur's high-flown accent; it's bizarre and yet right for the character. Locked into all that affectation, Loew has no way to make connections with anyone.

He's all raw, shattered nerves, He takes out his irascibility and his uppity sense of power on his scared, foreign-born secretary (Maria Conchita Alonso), the only person who has a sense of how weird he is; nobody believes her—people tell her all bosses are mean and crazy. But this one is really mean and crazy. His voice gets very high when he's bawling her out; he doesn't feel any need to hide his hysteria from her—he lets himself work up a rage. When he talks to his therapist (Elizabeth Ashley), she isn't alert to how quickly he's coming unstuck.

Loew is so impressionable he has begun to believe that Rachel (Jennifer Beals), a chic seductress he has met, is a vampire who feeds on him. He's sure that he himself is turning into a sunlight-fearing bloodsucker, and he doesn't understand why he hasn't grown fangs. He goes to a novelty store, buys a cheap plastic set, and begins to wear them. And his hair becomes lank, his body is crouched over; he comes to resemble the emaciated, miserly-looking vampire of Murnau's 1922 *Nosferatu,* which he watches on television. He gets that rodent, phantom look.

The title *Vampire's Kiss* may lead you to expect an erotic comedy, and when you first hear Loew's swanked-up Ed Grimley diction you may wait for it to swing into a Transylvanian lisp, but, despite the Manhattan milieu, this is somewhere between a horror picture and a black comedy. It may be the first vampire movie in which the modern office building replaces the castle as the site of torture and degradation. The picture was written by Joseph Minion, who wrote Scorsese's *After Hours,* and this script, too, suggests the avant-garde shorts of the twenties about a young man trapped in a nightmare. Once again, the women (and Loew picks up some dazzling beauties, among them Kasi Lemmons as Jackie) are essentially figures in his fantasy world, rather than characters. The young British director Robert Bierman, who also did the creepy, terrifying HBO film *Apology,* works well with the performers, and an eerie score, by Colin Towns, and the cinematography, by Stefan Czapsky, help to suggest a madman's city. Yet, the picture seems to crumble. That may be because the writer and the director don't distinguish Loew's fantasies from his actual life. Rachel is wonderfully accessorized, with dangling earrings that pick up the highlights on her fangs, but we need to get some tipoff to the difference between the fanged Rachel and the real one, and to what makes her different from the other women he meets. Why does he feel she's drinking his blood? The Hemdale people, who backed the film, made cuts—especially in Loew's sessions with his therapist—and, from reports of people who saw the director's version, key material was removed.

Whether the flaws are the fault of the moviemakers or the money men—and I've never known the editing by money men to improve a picture—we miss seeing how and why the lonely phoney gives in to his delusions. But with Cage in the role we certainly see the delusions at work. This daring kid starts over the top and just keeps going. He's airily amazing. At Loew's maddest, Cage's head is held back on his neckless body and his eyes bulge out like loose marbles. And this apparition is somehow a plausible part of the singles nightlife and the Manhattan street world.

There's a little caustic humor in the fact that Cage doesn't give Loew a single likable quality. When Loew meets Jackie at a bar and condescendingly asks what she does, she says she's a director of personnel. Asked what he does, he replies, "Literature." You look at that spoiled face and you never have to think, "Oh, the poor bastard." I liked the scene in which his lovemaking with Jackie is interrupted by an enormous bat (it looks as big as an owl) that flies into his apartment. He says "Shoo!" to it helplessly, and as Jackie goes out the door she laughs and mimics his "Shoo!" Later, when he's telling his therapist about the incident, he says that he was fighting off the bat and he had this new feeling; he was aroused by the bat. The possibility of its arousing him is less amusing than his saying he fought it off. That's how a wimpy male talks after he goes "Shoo!"

JUNE 12, 1989

STONEWORK

Dead Poets Society

In *Dead Poets Society,* Robin Williams plays John Keating, an eager, dedicated teacher with a gift for liberating his students. Crushed, frightened prep-school boys flower in Keating's class. He talks to them about the passions expressed in poetry, and they become emboldened. The creative impulses they'd kept hidden—or didn't know they had—are released.

Robin Williams' performance is more graceful than anything he's done before. He's more restrained, yet he's brisk, enlivening, a perky, wiry fellow. In class, when Keating gives his attention to a boy who's distressed, you feel that he intuitively enters into the boy's fears. He's totally, concentratedly there (though the camera is too much there), and with his encouragement the shy boy makes up a poem line by line, while standing in class. (In that moment, the young actor shows us the passion that Keating has been talking about—the passion that transcends the conventional.) And even when Keating can't help the boys he listens to them with all his being; he hears them, and he speaks to them directly. He respects them far more than he does the other teachers, whom he treats equably, with a few dry words. Keating's generosity is reserved for the students.

An iconoclastic teacher can be off-putting to some of his charges because he's sure and high-flown and flaky (compared with polite, basically bored teachers). The teacher who stands out is usually a talker, and that can worry students who are anxious about exams and want to know what they're going to be graded on. But Keating isn't that kind of overpowering teacher; he's not like the characters John Houseman played in *Paper Chase* and Maggie Smith played in *The Prime of Miss Jean Brodie*—he doesn't have his students in thrall to him. The scriptwriter, Tom Schulman, has written a character whose center is his rapport with the boys. Keating is simply a former Welton Academy honors student who has just returned from teaching in London, and Williams carries out this conception. Keating is supremely tactful; he has no assertiveness—he tries to help the kids develop on their own—and in emergencies he advises caution.

Williams stays in character, but he understands that a teacher who wakes kids up is likely to be a standup performer, maybe even a comic, and certainly quick on his feet. Williams reads his lines stunningly (he's playing a bright man), and when he mimics various actors reciting Shakespeare there's no undue clowning in it; he's a gifted teacher demonstrating his skills. That's what he's doing when he hops around the classroom and makes the kids laugh. I saw the movie right after reading the just-published *Mudrick Transcribed* (College of Creative Studies, University of California, Santa Barbara, California 93106; $20), a collection of talks on literature by the late Marvin Mudrick, recorded by his students. I can't imagine a better book on how an inspired teacher's mind works; Mudrick's easy rhythms make you aware of how he arrives at the humor that shoots up, geyser after geyser. You know at once why his students would be swept along by his words—he's thinking on his feet, getting high on his thoughts. And that's what Robin Williams shows Keating doing: Williams' performing rhythms reveal the free workings of Keating's mind. If only

Dead Poets Society got into the subject of what Keating gives to teaching and what it gives back to him!

But the movie shifts from one genre to another: the dedicated teacher gives way to the sensitive, misunderstood kid—in this case, Neil Perry (Robert Sean Leonard), an all-A student who wants to be an actor. The link is that the boy, soaring on the confidence he experiences in Keating's class, lacks the shrewdness and courage to deal with his rigid, uncomprehending father (Kurtwood Smith). The shift in genres sidelines the one performer who sparks the viewer's imagination and substitutes a familiar figure: the usual romantic victim to identify with. Many older moviegoers had parents who objected to their artistic inclinations, and for young audiences this may still be an ongoing misery. If you want to be a musician or a dancer or poet or painter and your parents don't think you're being practical, this movie, though it's set in 1959, can feel like your life story. And it can have you sobbing in regret, self-pity, nostalgia.

The title refers to a secret club that Keating founded when he was a student at the school and which is now revived by seven of his boys. On the surface, the club's nighttime gatherings could not be more innocent: the boys recite poetry, tell ghost stories, socialize. But in a deeper sense these clandestine meetings (at a rough cave in the woods) are an act of defiance; this is something the boys have organized for themselves—it isn't controlled by the school. And so, when the boys' new independence leads to a crisis, they're up against the slimy, cunning headmaster (Norman Lloyd) and the parents who have placed them in this exclusive, traditional, disciplinarian setting, and who believe what the headmaster tells them. (The way the movie is shaped, there isn't a perceptive parent in the bunch.)

Everything in the movie has been carefully thought out. The heavy stonework of Welton's twenties-Gothic buildings contrasts with the primitive natural wildness of the cave. The crew of Waspy boys have varied psychological profiles. The doomed Neil Perry is a natural leader. The financially privileged but emotionally deprived Todd Anderson (Ethan Hawke) is afraid to speak in class until Keating soothes his fears. Knox Overstreet (Josh Charles) is comically love-struck. Charlie Dalton (Gale Hansen) has a streak of wild dar-ing—in his best moment he mocks the school's pomposity, saying he had a telephone call from God—but he goes off half-cocked. And so on; it takes a while to sort them out. The young actors are presentable—even admirable—but they're all so camera-angled and director-controlled that they don't have a zit they can call their own.

There are lovely pauses and beautiful transitional shots; the unhurried storytelling is polished. Peter Weir is still in his mid-forties and the editing is swift, yet this is conserva-tive craftsmanship. He works the way some of the major Hollywood directors (William Wyler, George Stevens, John Ford) did as they got middle-aged. The picture draws out the obvious and turns itself into a classic.

It's too lulling to watch a movie in which everything is overprepared. I wanted to claw and scratch at the succes-sion of autumnal images, followed by wintry beauty. Every textured detail falls into place: the mist in the woods outside the mythic cave; the glowing skies; Keating taking his boys outside the classroom; the headmaster's foxy-eyed unctu-ousness; his brute attempt to break the spirit of a boy he paddles. Even Neil Perry's killing himself has no messy, be-wildering motives—you see exactly what drives him to it, just as you see that he's the product of a domineering, guilt-pushing father and a hysterical, helpless mother, whom he resembles. His high cheekbones intensify the poignancy of his death; he's meant to haunt you. Yet the young actor can't make the suicide credible: we don't feel that the boy is holding anything back, we don't feel any buried anger. He's transparent.

When the audience applauded at the end, I was reminded of the audience reaction twenty-odd years ago to *A Man for All Seasons*—a picture with a comparable tasteful romanti-cism. Most recent American movies, in their crudeness, have escaped this kind of middlebrow highmindedness. *Dead Poets Society* is anomalous—a prestige picture. It's on the side of youth, rebellion, poetry, passion. And, like Weir's *Gallipoli,* it has a gold ribbon attached to it. But the film's perception of reality is the black and white of pulp fiction (without the visceral excitement). The picture doesn't rise to the level of tragedy, because it's unwilling to give us an antagonist who isn't hopelessly rigid. (Neil Perry gets all A's, so his father can't even have a rational objection to his extracurricular activities.) There's no other side to anything in this movie—Weir, it appears, is more interested in the elegiac than in the dramatic. And the enthusiasts in the audience seem to be left applauding themselves for being sad, for being uplifted.

JUNE 26, 1989

THE CITY GONE PSYCHO

Batman

In *Batman,* the movement of the camera gives us the sensation of swerving (by radar) through the sinister nighttime canyons of Gotham City. We move swiftly among the forbidding, thickly clustered skyscrapers and dart around the girders and pillars of their cavelike underpinnings. This is the brutal city where crime festers—a city of alleys, not avenues. In one of these alleys, Bruce Wayne as a child watched, helpless, as his parents were mugged and senselessly shot down. Now a grown man and fabulously wealthy, Bruce (Michael Keaton) patrols the city from the rooftops. He has developed his physical strength to the utmost, and, disguised in body armor, a cowl, and a wide-winged cape, and with the aid of a high-tech arsenal, he scales buildings and swoops down on thugs and mobsters—Batman.

There's a primitive visual fascination in the idea of a princeling obsessed with vengeance who turns himself into a creature of the night, and the director, Tim Burton, has given the movie a look, a tone, an eerie intensity. Burton, who's thirty, has a macabre sensibility, with a cheerfulness that's infectious; his three films (*Pee-wee's Big Adventure* and *Beetlejuice* are the other two) get you laughing at your own fear of death.

Seen straight on, the armored Batman is as stiff and strong-jawed as a Wagnerian hero. His cowl-mask has straight-up sides that end in erect ears; he gives the impression of standing at attention all the time. (He's on guard duty.) But something else is going on, too. The eye slits reveal only the lower part of his eyes—you perceive strange, hooded flickers of anger. When Batman is in motion, what you see can recall the movies, such as *The Mark of Zorro* and the 1930 mystery comedy *The Bat Whispers,* that the eighteen-year-old cartoonist Bob Kane had in mind when he concocted the comic-book hero, in 1939. Though the Tim Burton film is based on Kane's characters, it gets some of its funky, nihilistic charge from more recent "graphic novels" about Batman, like Frank Miller's 1986 *The Dark Knight Returns* and Alan Moore's 1988 *The Killing Joke.* This powerfully glamorous new *Batman*, with sets angled and lighted like film noir, goes beyond pulp; it gallops into the cocky unknown.

In the movie's absurdist vision, Batman's antagonist is the sniggering mobster Jack Napier (Jack Nicholson), who turns into the leering madman the Joker. Clearly, Batman and the Joker are intended to represent good and evil counterparts, or, at least, twin freaks, locked together in combat; it was Jack Napier who made an orphan of Bruce Wayne, and it was Batman who dropped Jack into the vat of toxic chemicals that disfigured him. That's the basic plan. But last year's writers' strike started just as the movie was set to go into production, and the promising script, by Sam Hamm (it reads beautifully), never got its final shaping; the touching up that Warren Skaaren (and uncredited others) gave it didn't develop the characters or provide the turning points that were needed. With the young hipster Keaton and the aging hipster Nicholson cast opposite each other, we expect an unholy taunting camaraderie—or certainly some recognition on Batman's part that he and the Joker have a similarity. And we do get a tease now and then: when the two meet, their actions have the formality of Kabuki theatre. But the underwritten movie slides right over the central conflict: good and evil hardly know each other.

At times, it's as if pages of the script had drifted away. The mob kingpin (Jack Palance, in a hearty, ripe performance) is toppled by Jack Napier, who moves to take control of the city, but we're not tipped to what new corruption he has in mind. We wait for the moment when the photojournalist Vicki Vale (Kim Basinger), who's in love with Bruce Wayne and is drawn to Batman, will learn they're the same person. She's just about to when the scene (it's in her apartment) is interrupted by the Joker, who barges in with his henchmen—we expect him to carry her away. The revelation of Batman's identity is suspended (we never get to see it), and the Joker trots off without his prize. After this double non-whammy, a little air seems to leak out of the movie. And it's full of these missed moments; the director just lets them go. Vicki and Bruce, dining together, are seated at opposite ends of an immense banquet table in a baronial hall in Wayne Manor; two thousand years of show business have prepared us for a zinging payoff—we feel almost deprived when we don't get it. Yet these underplayed scenes have a pleasing suggestiveness. The dinner scene, for example, shows us that Bruce is flexible, despite his attraction to armor. (He collects it.) And Vicki quickly realizes that the Bruce Wayne–Batman identity is less important than the question Is he married only to his Batman compulsion or is he willing to share his life with her?

The movie has a dynamics of feeling; it has its own ache. Michael Keaton's poor-little-rich-boy hero is slightly dissociated, somewhat depressed, a fellow who can take his dream vehicle, the Batmobile, for granted. How do you play a guy who likes to go around in a bat costume? Keaton has thought out this fellow's hesitations, his peculiarity, his quietness. In some situations, the unarmed Bruce is once again a passive, helpless kid. (In a triste scene at night, he hangs by his ankles on gym equipment, rocking softly—trying to lull himself to sleep.) Keaton's Bruce-Batman is really the only human being in the movie; he gives it gravity and emotional coloring. This is a man whose mission has taken over his life. The plangent symphonic score, by Danny Elfman, might be the musical form of his thoughts; it's wonderfully morose superhero music.

When Nicholson's Joker appears for the first time, the movie lights up like a pinball machine: the devil has arrived. (Nicholson is playing the role Keaton played in *Beetlejuice.*) The Joker is marvellously dandified—a fashion plate. The great bohemian chapeaus and the playing-card zoot suits, in purple, green, orange, and aqua, that Bob Ringwood has designed for him have a harlequin chic. They're very like the outfits the illustrator Brian Boland gave the character in *The Killing Joke,* and Nicholson struts in them like a homicidal minstrel, dancing to hurdy-gurdy songs by Prince—the Joker's theme music. But the grin carved into the Joker's face doesn't have the horror of the one on Conrad Veidt's face in the 1927 *The Man Who Laughs* (where Bob Kane acknowledges he took it from). Veidt played a man who never forgot his mutilation. Nicholson's Jack Napier is too garish to suffer from having been turned into a clown; the mutilation doesn't cripple him, it fulfills him. And so his wanting to get back at Batman is just crazy spite.

This may work for the kids in the audience, and the Joker's face stirs up a child's confused fear of—and delight in—clowns. (They're like kids made hideous and laughed at.) But possibly the Joker's comic-book dazzle diminishes the film's streak of morbid grandeur—the streak that links this *Batman* to the reverbs that *The Phantom of the Opera* and *The Hunchback of Notre Dame* set off in us. When the adversaries have their final, moonlight encounter, among the gargoyles on the bell tower of Gotham's crumbling, abandoned cathedral, they could be like the Phantom of the Opera split in two, but there's pain in Keaton, there's no pain in Nicholson. The Joker may look a little like Olivier as the John Osborne vaudevillian, but he isn't human: he's all entertainer, a glinting-eyed cartoon—he's still springing gags after he's dead. This interpretation is too mechanical to be fully satisfying. And is Nicholson entertainer enough? He doesn't show the physical elegance and inventiveness we may hope for.

The master flake Tim Burton understands what there is about Batman that captures the moviegoer's imagination. The picture doesn't give us any help on the question of why Bruce Wayne, in creating an alternate identity, picked a pointy-eared, satanic-looking varmint. (Was it simply to gain a sense of menace and to intimidate his prey?) But Burton uses the fluttering Batman enigmatically, playfully. He provides potent, elusive images that draw us in (and our minds do the rest). There may be no more romantic flight of imagination in modern movies than the drive that Vicki and Batman take, by Batmobile, rocketing through a magical forest. Yet though we're watching a gothic variation of the lonely-superhero theme, we're never allowed to forget our hero's human limitations. He's a touchingly comic fellow. When he's all dressed up in his bat drag, he still thinks it necessary to identify himself by saying, in a confidential tone, "I'm Batman."

The movie's darkness is essential to its hold on us. The whole conception of Batman and Gotham City is a night-time vision—a childlike fantasy of the big city that the muggers took over. The caped crusader who can find his way around in the miasmal dark is the only one who can root out the hoods. The good boy Batman has his shiny-toy weapons (the spiked gauntlets, the utility belt equipped with projectile launcher, even the magnificent Batwing fighter plane), but he's alone. The bad boys travel in packs: the Joker and his troupe of sociopaths break into the Flugelheim Museum, merrily slashing and defiling the paintings—the Joker sees himself as an artist of destruction.

Batman and the Joker are fighting for the soul of the city

that spawned them. We see what shape things are in right from the opening scenes. Gotham City, with its jumble of buildings shooting miles and miles up into the dirty skies, is the product of uncontrolled greed. Without sunshine or greenery, the buildings look like derelicts. This is New York City deliberately taken just one step beyond the present; it's the city as you imagine it when you're really down on it. It's Manhattan gone psycho. But even when you're down on it you can get into your punk fantasies about how swollen it is, how blighted and yet horribly alive.

The designer, Anton Furst, seems to have got into that kind of jangled delight, putting together domes and spires, elongated tenements, a drab city hall with statues bowed down in despair, and streets and factories with the coal-mine glow of the castles and battlements in *Chimes at Midnight*. Gotham City has something of the sculptural fascination of the retro-future cities in *Blade Runner* and *Brazil*—it's like Fritz Lang's *Metropolis* corroded and cankered. If H. G. Wells' Time Machine took you there, you'd want to escape back to the present. Still, you revel in this scary Fascistic playground: the camera crawls voluptuously over the concrete and the sewers, and the city excites you— it has belly-laugh wit.

When Gotham City celebrates its two-hundredth birthday, the big parade balloons are filled with poison gas—an inspiration of the Joker's. (He rides on a float, jiggling to the music; his painted red grin has wing tips.) Paranoia and comic-book cheesiness don't defeat Tim Burton; he feels the kick in them—he likes their style. The cinematographer, Roger Pratt, brings theatrical artifice to just about every shot—a high gorgeousness, with purples and blacks that are like our dream of a terrific rock concert. The movie even has giant spotlights (and the Batsignal from the original comic books). This spectacle about an avenging angel trying to protect a city that's already an apocalyptic mess is an American variant of *Wings of Desire*. It has a poetic quality, but it moves pop fast. The masked man in the swirling,

windblown cape has become the hero of a comic opera
that's mean and anarchic and blissful. It has so many unpredictable spins that what's missing doesn't seem to matter
much. The images sing.

Ghostbusters II

Ghostbusters II has a nice, lazy, unforced rhythm. I found
it much more enjoyable than the first *Ghostbusters*—the actors seem more convivial and the special effects less la-
bored. (Actually, the effects are so frowzy you can just about
ignore them.) It's a big comedy, but it's light on its feet, and
the throwaway jokes are weightless—they *ping!* and dis-
solve in the air. You can't remember what you're laughing
at, but you feel great.

The comic premise is that the collective angry energy of
Manhattanites is feeding an underground river of boiling
slime, which is rising; our bad vibes are literally destroying
the city. The Ghostbusters were hounded out of business
five years ago (the city sued them for the mess they made
when they rescued it from poltergeists). They come back
together to drive out a new crop of demons and turn New
Yorkers' attitudes around, so the goo will subside.

Luckily, the director, Ivan Reitman, doesn't need to build
scenes here. The script, by Harold Ramis and Dan Aykroyd,
is a floating crap game, like the scripts for the Hope and
Crosby *Road* pictures. Assorted comedians simply come in
and out of the scenes dropping one-liners. The chief drop-
per, Bill Murray, can perform casual miracles with a simple
joke. He actually gets by in scenes where he just plays with
an eight-month-old baby boy. Murray has changed psycho-
logically since the first *Ghostbusters*: he isn't playing the

grungy, derisive outsider anymore—he's mellowed. Yet he's just as funny. In this movie, he's obviously nuts about the heroine (Sigourney Weaver) and nuts about the kid. But he isn't sentimental. I can't think of any other comedian who has brought off this kind of transition—who has turned into a friendly, responsible guy while retaining access to the sources of his comedy. Murray's humor is still different from anybody else's. (Even when he does a Groucho routine, posing alluringly on a bed, the come-on is his own.)

In the scene where Murray is the cynical, know-it-all host of a cable-TV talk show called "World of the Psychic," and in the courtroom scene, featuring Rick Moranis as the Ghostbusters' attorney, the movie is like a perfectly achieved edition of "Saturday Night Live." Ramis (in a pompadour that makes him look like photographs of George S. Kaufman) has sly, succulent bits as an egotistic sadist; Moranis and Annie Potts make a lovely nerdy team of madly infatuated nearsighted lovers; and Cheech Marin, in a couple of cut-in reaction shots, is a winner each time. Ernie Hudson, who has an agreeable (not particularly comic) presence, gets a big laugh when a ghost train runs right through him and he looks "spooked." Probably the gag is meant to parody old racist set-ups, but you can't be sure, and it may leave you uneasy. Apart from that, the movie, even at its sloppiest (there are a lot of starts that don't go anywhere), produces nothing but the good vibes its heroes are dedicated to.

The goo—it's pink—has an unfathomable connection with an evil seventeenth-century Moldavian whose portrait dominates the room where Weaver restores paintings, under the love-hungry supervision of a geeky bureaucrat named Janosz Poha, played by Peter MacNicol. Poha's Carpathian Upper West Side diction has to navigate through his toothy smile; it's a precarious journey, and the pure silliness of it—all the childish playacting it recalls—can make you surprisingly happy.

JULY 10, 1989

A WOUNDED
APPARITION

Casualties of War

Some movies—*Grand Illusion* and *Shoeshine* come to mind, and the two *Godfathers* and *The Chant of Jimmie Blacksmith* and *The Night of the Shooting Stars*—can affect us in more direct, emotional ways than simple entertainment movies. They have more imagination, more poetry, more intensity than the usual fare; they have large themes, and a vision. They can leave us feeling simultaneously elated and wiped out. Overwhelmed, we may experience a helpless anger if we hear people mock them or poke holes in them in order to dismiss them. The new *Casualties of War* has this kind of purity. If you meet people who are bored by movies you love such as *The Earrings of Madame De . . .* or *The Unbearable Lightness of Being,* chances are you can brush it off and think it's their loss. But this new film is the kind that makes you feel protective. When you leave the theatre, you'll probably find that you're not ready to talk about it. You may also find it hard to talk lightly about anything.

Casualties of War is based on a Vietnam incident of 1966

that was reported in *The New Yorker* by the late Daniel Lang, in the issue of October 18, 1969. (The article was reprinted as a book.) Lang gave a calm, emotionally devastating account of a squad of five American soldiers who were sent on a five-day reconnaissance mission; they kidnapped a Vietnamese village girl, raped her, and then covered up their crime by killing her. The account dealt with the kind of gangbang rape that the Vietnam War had in common with virtually all wars, except that the rapists here, unable in general to distinguish Vietcong sympathizers from other Vietnamese, didn't care that the girl wasn't Vietcong. This indifference to whether a candidate for rape is friend or foe may not really be that much of an exception; it may be frequent in wartime. What's unusual here may simply be that a witness forced the case into the open and it resulted in four court-martial convictions.

A number of movie people hoped to make a film of the Lang article, and, though it was commercially risky, Warners bought the rights and announced that Jack Clayton would make the picture—an arrangement that fell apart. Plans involving John Schlesinger and other directors also collapsed, but the article may have been the (unofficial) taking-off point for one film that did get made: Elia Kazan's low-budget, 16-mm. *The Visitors,* of 1972, which Kazan himself financed. He used a prosecution for rape and murder as background material to explain why a couple of ex-servicemen released from Leavenworth on a technicality were out to get the former buddy who had testified against them. Eventually, in 1987, after Brian De Palma had a success with *The Untouchables,* he was able to persuade Paramount to pick up the rights to the Lang story, which he'd had in the back of his mind since 1969. A script was commissioned from the playwright David Rabe, the quondam Catholic and Vietnam vet who had written *Streamers* and other plays about the war (and had wanted to work on this material for some years), but, when De Palma was all set to film it in Thailand, Paramount pulled out. The picture finally got under way at Columbia—the first picture to be approved by the company's new president, Dawn Steel. Whatever else she does, she should be honored for that decision, because twenty years later this is still risky material.

Lang's factual narrative is based on conversations with Eriksson, the witness who testified against the other men, and on the court-martial records. (The names were changed to protect everyone's privacy.) Rabe's script follows it closely, except that Rabe dramatizes the story by creating several incidents to explain what led to the rape and what followed.

When Eriksson (Michael J. Fox), who has just arrived in Vietnam, is out in a jungle skirmish at night, a mortar explosion shifts the earth under him; he drops down, caught, his feet dangling in an enemy tunnel. De Palma photographs the scene as if it were an ant farm—he shows us aboveground and underground in the same shot. Eriksson yells for help, and in the instant that a Vietcong, who has been crawling toward the dangling legs, slashes at them with his knife, Sergeant Meserve (Sean Penn) pulls Eriksson out. A minute later, Meserve saves him again from that Vietcong, who has come out of the hole to get him.

In the morning, the soldiers enter a peaceful-looking village; they stand near the mud-and-bamboo huts and see a stream and bridges and, a little way in the distance, paddy fields where women and elderly men are working, under the shadow of harsh, steep mountains. The tiered compositions are pale, like Chinese ink paintings. Throughout the movie, everything that's beyond the understanding of the Americans seems to be visualized in layered images; this subtle landscape reaching to Heaven is the site of the random violence that leads to the rape.

Smiling and eager, Eriksson walks behind two water buffalo, helping an ancient farmer with his plowing. Brownie (Erik King), a large-spirited, joshing black soldier, who is Meserve's pal—they're both due to go home in less than a month—cautions Eriksson about his exposed position on

the field and walks him back to where the Sarge is taking
time out, with the other men. They're all relaxed in a clear-
ing near this friendly village, but we become ominously
aware that the villagers in the paddies are evaporating.
Brownie is standing with an arm around Meserve when the
pastoral scene is ruptured: bullets tear into Brownie from a
V.C. across the stream. An instant later, a guerrilla who's
dressed as a farmer runs toward the group and flings a grenade at them. Meserve spots him and warns Eriksson, who
turns and fires his grenade launcher; by luck, he explodes
the V.C.'s grenade. Then the screen is divided by a couple
of split-focus effects: in one, Eriksson, in closeup, rejoices
at his freak shot and is so excited that he lets the grenade-
thrower slip away; in another, Eriksson is staring the wrong
way while behind him a couple of women open a tunnel
for a V.C., who disappears into it. Meanwhile, Meserve fires
his M-16 rifle, and then, his face showing his agony, he uses
his hand like a poultice on Brownie's wound. A soldier ra-
dios for medical help, and Meserve, never letting go of his
friend, keeps reassuring him until he's loaded on a chopper.

In these early scenes, Meserve is skillful and resourceful.
He's only twenty years old, and as Sean Penn plays him he
has the reckless bravery of youth. He's genuinely heroic.
But Brownie dies (as Meserve knew he would), and back at
the base camp the men, who have readied themselves for a
visit to a brothel, are stopped and told that the village ad-
joining the base has been declared off limits. It's too much
for Meserve, who has been put in charge of the five-day
mission to check out a mountain area for signs of Vietcong
activity, and later that night he finishes briefing his men by
telling them to be ready to leave an hour early, so they can
detour to a village to "requisition" a girl. Eriksson half thinks
the Sarge is kidding. It takes a while for him (and for us) to
understand that Meserve is not the man he was; only a day
has passed since his friend was killed, but he has become
bitter and vindictive—a conscious trickster and sinner.

Has something in Meserve snapped? Paul Fussell writes in his new book *Wartime* that in the Second World War the American military "learned that men will inevitably go mad in battle and that no appeal to patriotism, manliness, or loyalty to the group will ultimately matter." So "in later wars things were arranged differently," he explains. "In Vietnam, it was understood that a man fulfilled his combat obligation and purchased his reprieve if he served a fixed term, 365 days, and not days in combat either but days in the theatre of war. The infantry was now treated somewhat like the Air Corps in the Second War: performance of a stated number of missions guaranteed escape." Meserve, who has led dozens of combat patrols, has reached his limit with only a few weeks to go; he turns into an outlaw with a smooth justification for anything. (The kidnapping is a matter of cool planning: the girl can be explained as a "V.C. whore" taken for interrogation.) When Meserve's five-man patrol, having set out before dawn, arrives at the village he selected in advance, he and Corporal Clark (Don Harvey) peer into one hut after another, shining a flashlight on the sleeping women until they find one to their taste—Oanh (Thuy Thu Le), a girl of eighteen or twenty.

The terrified girl clings to her family. Clark carries her out, and her mother and sister come rushing after him, pleading in words that are just jabber to the soldiers, who want to get moving before it's light. They've taken only a few steps when the mother desperately hands them the girl's scarf. It's a pitiful, ambiguous gesture. She seems to want Oanh to have the comfort of this scarf—perhaps it's new, perhaps it's the only token of love the mother can offer her daughter. Eriksson says "Oh Jesus God" when he sees the men's actions, even before the mother holds out the scarf. Then he mutters helplessly, "I'm sorry." He's sick with grief, and we in the audience may experience a surge of horror; we know we're watching something irrevocable. Clark, a crude, tall kid who suggests a young Lee Marvin, is irritated by the girl's crying and whimpering, and he stuffs the scarf into her mouth, to gag her.

The men climb high above the valleys and set up a temporary command post in an abandoned hut in the mountains; it's here that the sobbing, sniffling girl is brutalized. (Thereafter, she's referred to as "the whore" or "the bitch.") Eriksson refuses his turn to rape her, but he can't keep the others from tying her up, beating her, and violating her. He himself is assaulted when he tries to stop them from killing her. Eriksson is brave, but he's also inexperienced and unsure of himself. In the few minutes in which he's alone with the girl and could help her escape, he delays because he's afraid of being charged as a deserter. The opportunity passes, and we can see the misery in his eyes. Meserve sees it, too—sees that Eriksson finds him disgusting, indecent. And he begins to play up to Eriksson's view of him: he deliberately turns himself into a jeering, macho clown, taunting Eriksson, questioning his masculinity, threatening him. Meserve starts to act out his madness; that's the rationale for Penn's theatrical, heated-up performance. He brings off the early, quiet scenes, too. When Meserve shaves after learning of Brownie's death, we see that the hopefulness has drained out of him. Suddenly he's older; the radiance is gone. Soon he's all calculation. Although he was coarse before, it was good-humored coarseness; now there's cynical, low cunning in it. Fox, in contrast, uses a minimum of showmanship. He gives such an interior performance that it may be undervalued. To play a young American in Vietnam who's instinctively thoughtful and idealistic—who's uncorrupted—is excruciatingly difficult, yet Fox never lets the character come across as a prig. The two men act in totally different styles, and the styles match up.

And, whatever the soldiers say or do, there's the spectre of the dazed, battered girl ranting in an accusatory singsong. The movie is haunted by Oanh long before she's dead. The rapists think they've killed her, but she rises; in our minds, she rises again and again. On the basis of the actual soldiers' descriptions of the girl's refusal to accept death, Daniel Lang called her "a wounded apparition," and De Palma and his cinematographer, Stephen H. Burum, give us images that live up to those words—perhaps even go beyond them. Trying to escape along a railway trestle high up against the wall of a canyon, Oanh might be a Kabuki ghost. She goes past suffering into the realm of myth, which in this movie has its own music—a recurring melody played on the panflute.

That lonely music keeps reminding us of the despoiled girl, of the incomprehensible language, the tunnels, the hidden meanings, the sorrow. Eriksson can't forgive himself for his failure to save Oanh. The picture shows us how daringly far he would have had to go to prevent what happened; he would have had to be lucky as well as brave. This is basically the theme that De Palma worked with in his finest movie up until now, the political fantasy *Blow Out,* in which the protagonist, played by John Travolta, also failed to save a young woman's life. We in the audience are put in the man's position: we're made to feel the awfulness of being ineffectual. This lifelike defeat is central to the movie. (One hot day on my first trip to New York City, I walked past a group of men on a tenement stoop. One of them, in a sweaty sleeveless T-shirt, stood shouting at a screaming, weeping little boy perhaps eighteen months old. The man must have caught a glimpse of my stricken face, because he called out, "You don't like it, lady? Then how do you like this?" And he picked up a bottle of pink soda pop from the sidewalk and poured it on the baby's head. Wailing sounds, much louder than before, followed me down the street.)

Eriksson feels he must at least reveal what happened to Oanh and where her body lies. He's a dogged innocent trying to find out what to do; he goes to the higher-ups in the Army and gets a load of doubletalk and some straight talk, too. The gist of it is that in normal (i.e., peacetime) circumstances Meserve would not have buckled like this, and they want Eriksson to keep quiet about it. But he can't deal with their reasoning; he has to stick with the rules he grew up with. He moves through one layer of realization to the next; there's always another, hidden level. The longer Eriksson is in Vietnam, the more the ground opens up beneath him. He can't even go to the latrine without seeing below the floor slats a grenade that Clark has just put there, to kill him.

De Palma has mapped out every shot, yet the picture is alive and mysterious. When Meserve rapes Oanh, the horizon seems to twist into a crooked position; everything is bent away from us. Afterward, he goes outside in the rain and confronts Eriksson, who's standing guard. Meserve's relationship to the universe has changed; the images of nature have a different texture, and when he lifts his face to the sky you may think he's swapped souls with a werewolf. Eriksson is numb and demoralized, and the rain courses down his cheeks in slow motion. De Palma has such seductive, virtuosic control of film craft that he can express convulsions in the unconscious.

In the first use of the split-focus effect, Eriksson was so happy about having hit the grenade that he lost track of the enemy. In a later use of the split effect, Eriksson tries to save Oanh from execution by creating a gigantic diversion: he shoots his gun and draws enemy fire. What he doesn't know is that Clark, who is behind him, is stabbing her. He didn't know what was going on behind him after he was rescued from the tunnel, either. This is Vietnam, where you get fooled. It's also De Palmaland. There are more dimensions than you can keep track of, as the ant-farm shot tells you. And the protagonist who maps things out to protect the girl from other men (as Travolta did) will always be surprised. The theme has such personal meaning for the director that his technique—his own mapping out of the scenes—is itself a dramatization of the theme. His art is in controlling everything, but he still can't account for everything. He plans everything and discovers something more.

De Palma keeps you aware of the whole movie as a com-

position. Like Godard, he bounces you in and out of the
assumptions about movies that you have brought with you
to the theatre. He stretches time and distance, using tech-
niques that he developed in horror-fantasy and suspense
pictures, but without the pop overtones. He shifts from realism to hallucinatory Expressionism. When the wounded
Brownie is flown out by helicopter, the movement of the
yellow-green river running beneath him suggests being so
close up against a painting that it's pure pigment. When Eriksson is flown out, it's at an angle you've never seen before:
he looks up at the rotor blades as they darken the sky. These
helicopters are on drugs.

Great movies are rarely perfect movies. David Rabe wrestles with the ugly side of male bonding; he's on to American
men's bluster and showoff, and his scenes certainly have
drive. But his dialogue is sometimes explicit in the grungy-
poetic mode of "important" American theatre. The actual
Eriksson was in fact (as he is in the movie) married and a
Lutheran. He was also, as Daniel Lang reported, articulate.
This is Eriksson talking to Lang:

> We all figured we might be dead in the next minute, so
> what difference did it make what we did? But the longer I
> was over there, the more I became convinced that it was the
> other way around that counted—that *because* we might not
> be around much longer, we had to take extra care how we
> behaved.

Rabe uses these remarks but places them maladroitly (as a
response to something that has just happened), and he makes
them sound like the stumbling thoughts of a folksy, sublit-
erate fellow reaching for truth:

> I mean, just because each one of us might at any second
> be blown away, everybody's actin' like we can do anything,
> man, and it don't matter what we do—but I'm thinkin' maybe

it's the other way around, maybe the main thing is just the opposite. Because we might be dead in the next split second, maybe we gotta be extra careful what we do—because maybe it matters more—Jesus, maybe it matters more than we even know.

This passage is the heaviest hammering in the movie (and the poorest piece of staging), but it's also a clear indication of Rabe's method. De Palma works directly on our emotions. Rabe's dialogue sometimes sounds like the work of a professional anti-war dramatist trying to make us think. Still, there's none of the ego satisfaction of moral indignation that is put into most Vietnam films and what De Palma does with the camera is so powerful that the few times you wince at the dialogue are almost breathers.

This movie about war and rape—De Palma's nineteenth film—is the culmination of his best work. In essence, it's feminist. I think that in his earlier movies De Palma was always involved in examining (and sometimes satirizing) victimization, but he was often accused of being a victimizer. Some moviegoers (women, especially) were offended by his thrillers; they thought there was something reprehensibly sadistic in his cleverness. He *was* clever. When people talk about their sex fantasies, their descriptions almost always sound like movies, and De Palma headed right for that linkage: he teased the audience about how susceptible it was to romantic manipulation. *Carrie* and *Dressed to Kill* are like lulling erotic reveries that keep getting broken into by scary jokes. He let you know that he was jerking you around and that it was for your amused, childish delight, but a lot of highly vocal people expressed shock. This time, De Palma touches on raw places in people's reactions to his earlier movies; he gets at the reality that may have made some moviegoers too fearful to enjoy themselves. He goes to the heart of sexual victimization, and he does it with a new authority. The way he makes movies now, it's as if he were saying, "What is getting older if it isn't learning more ways that you're vulnerable?"

Cruelty is not taken lightly in this movie. In the audience, we feel alone with the sounds that come out of Oanh's throat; we're alone with the sight of the blood clotting her nose. The director has isolated us from all distractions. There are no plot subterfuges; war is the only metaphor. The soldiers hate Vietnam and the Vietnamese for their frustrations, their grievances, their fear, and they take their revenge on the girl. When Brownie is shot, Eriksson, like Meserve and the others, feels that they've come to fight for the defense of the villagers who knew about the hidden guerrillas and could have warned them. They feel betrayed. Could the villagers have warned them without being killed themselves? It's doubtful, but the soldiers are sure of it, and for most of them that's justification enough for what they do to Oanh. The movie doesn't give us the aftermath: Oanh's mother searched for her and got South Vietnamese troops to help in the search; the mother was then taken away by the Vietcong, accused of having led the troops to a V.C. munitions cache. De Palma simply concentrates on what happened and why.

Meserve and Clark and one of the other men feel like conquerors when they take Oanh with them. They act out their own war fantasy; they feel it's a soldier's right to seize women for his pleasure. Comradeship is about the only spiritual value these jungle fighters still recognize; they're fighting for each other, and they feel that a gangbang relieves their tensions and brings them closer together. When Clark slings Oanh over his shoulder and carries her out of her family's hut, he's the hero of his own comic strip. These men don't suffer from guilt—not in the way that Eriksson suffers for the few minutes of indecisiveness in which he might have saved Oanh's life. He's turned from a cheerful, forthright kid into a desolate loner.

At the end, the swelling sound of musical absolution seems

to be saying that Eriksson must put his experiences in Vietnam behind him—that he has to accept that he did all he could, and go on without always blaming himself. De Palma may underestimate the passion of his images: we don't believe that Eriksson can put Oanh's death into any kind of sane perspective, because we've just felt the sting of what he lived through. He may tell himself that he did all he could, but he feels he should have been able to protect her. The doubt is there in his eyes. (I hear that baby's cries after almost fifty years.) What makes the movie so eerily affecting? Possibly it's Oanh's last moments of life—the needle-sharp presentation of her frailty and strength, and how they intertwine. When she falls to her death, the image is other-worldly, lacerating. It's the supreme violation.

AUGUST 21, 1989

SATYR

My Left Foot

In the middle of *My Left Foot,* the movie about the Dubliner
Christy Brown, a victim of cerebral palsy who became a
painter and a writer, Christy (Daniel Day-Lewis) is in a restaurant, at a dinner party celebrating the opening of an exhibition of the pictures he painted by holding a brush
between his toes. For some time, he has been misinterpret-
ing the friendly manner of the woman doctor who has been
training him, and who arranged the show, and now, high
on booze and success, he erupts. "I love you, Eileen," he
says, and then, sharing his happiness with the others at the
table, "I love you all." Eileen, not comprehending that his
love for her is passionate and sexual, takes the occasion to
announce that she's going to marry the gallery owner in six
months. In his staccato, distorted speech, Christy spits out
"Con-grat-u-la-tions" so that the syllables sound like slaps,
and then he lashes her with "I'm glad you taught me to
speak so I could say that, Eileen." The restaurant is suddenly quiet: everyone is watching his torment as he beats
his head on the table and yanks the tablecloth off with his
teeth.

It's all very fast, and it may be the most emotionally
wrenching scene I've ever experienced at the movies. The

greatness of Day-Lewis's performance is that he pulls you inside Christy Brown's frustration and rage (and his bottomless thirst). There's nothing soft or maudlin about this movie's view of Christy. Right from the first shot, it's clear that the Irish playwright-director Jim Sheridan, who wrote the superb screenplay, with another Irish playwright, Shane Connaughton, knows what he's doing. Christy's left foot is starting a record on his turntable; there's a scratchy stop, and the foot starts it up again—Mozart's *Così Fan Tutte.* A few toes wriggle to the music, and then in a sudden cut the bearded head of the man that the musical toes belong to jerks into the frame, and we see the tight pursed mouth, the tense face, and the twisted-upward, lolling head with slitted eyes peering down. He's anguished and locked in yet excitingly insolent. Day-Lewis seizes the viewer; he takes possession of you. His interpretation recalls Olivier's crookbacked, long-nosed Richard III; Day-Lewis's Christy Brown has the sexual seductiveness that was so startling in the Olivier Richard.

The defiance in Christy's glance carries over when the film flashes back from the acclaimed young author and artist in 1959 to the birth, in 1932, of the crippled, twitching child—the tenth of twenty-two children born to the Browns—who is thought to be a vegetable. The child actor (Hugh O'Conor) is a fine matchup with Day-Lewis and does wonderful work, but the small Christy might affect us as a Tiny Tim if we didn't have the image of the adult blending with him. Lying on the floor under the staircase like part of the furniture, Christy watches the crowded family life dominated by the violent, heavy-drinking bricklayer father (Ray McAnally), and bound together by the large, reassuring mother (Brenda Fricker). Despite what the doctors say and what the neighbors think, Christy's mother persists in believing that he has a mind. One day when he's alone in the house with her, he hears her fall; pregnant and near term, she's unconscious at the bottom of the stairs, lying near the front door. He squirms and writhes, flinging his body downstairs, and then banging his foot against the door until a neighbor hears the commotion, comes to the house, and sends her off in an ambulance. But when the neighbors gather they don't praise the boy: they don't realize that he summoned them. Seeing him there, they think his mother fell while carrying this moron downstairs. I don't know that any movie has ever given us so strong a feeling of an intelligence struggling to come out, to be recognized.

Finally one day, the boy, seeing a piece of chalk on the floor and desperate for some means of asserting himself, sticks out his left foot (he later described it as "the only key to the door of the prison I was in"), works the chalk between his toes, and makes a mark on his sister's slate with it. The family, awed, watches. After that, his mother teaches him the alphabet, and his brothers push him around outside in a broken-down old go-cart—it's like a wheelbarrow—so he can play with them. He speaks only in strangled grunts, but some members of the family understand him (his mother always does), and his father, who calls Christy's cart his "chariot," boasts of his accomplishments. It's a great day for all of them when this pale, gnarled kid takes chalk in his toes and, with a gruelling effort at control, writes "MOTHER" on the floor. (Astonishingly, even at that moment you don't feel manipulated; the directing is too plain, too fierce for sentimentality.)

Day-Lewis takes over when Christy is seventeen and, lying flat in the streets, is an accepted participant in his brothers' fast, roughneck games. As goalkeeper for a soccer match, he stops the ball with his head. The whack gives you a jolt. It gives him a savage satisfaction; it buoys him up. Out with his brothers, Christy's a hardheaded working-class cripple. At home, he paints watercolors. And though he can't feed himself or take care of his excretory functions or wash or dress himself, his life is one romantic infatuation after another—he courts the girls with pictures and poems. (In some ways, his story is a whirling satire of the Irishman as impetuous carnal dreamer.)

This is Jim Sheridan's first feature film, but he's an experienced man of the theatre, with a moviemaker's vision and a grownup's sense of integrity. There's no overacting and none of the wordiness that crept into Christy Brown's later books. His autobiography, *My Left Foot,* published when he was twenty-two, is a simple account (with perhaps a surfeit of creditable emotions). His best-known work, the semi-autobiographical novel *Down All the Days,* published when he was thirty-seven (and smitten with Thomas Wolfe), is the kind of prose-poetry that's generally described as roistering and irrepressible. It's a chore to get through. But what a life he lived! Sheridan and Connaughton know that their story is not the making of an artistic genius: it's the release of an imprisoned comic spirit. What makes Christy Brown such a zesty subject for a movie is that, with all his physical handicaps, he became a traveller, a pub crawler, a husband, a joker. He became a literary lion and made a pile of money; *Down All the Days,* a best-seller, was published in fifteen countries. The movie may tear you apart, but it's the story of a triumphantly tough guy who lived it up.

In a section of the film called "Hell," the father is laid off work, the family has nothing to eat but porridge, and Christy can't paint, because there's no money for coal—he has to go to bed. (The boys sleep four to a bed, sardine style.) It isn't until Christy is nineteen that his mother is able to buy him the wheelchair that she's been saving for. She's tough, too: she won't touch the money even during the porridge days. (She has her own hell: nine of her children didn't survive infancy.) There's nothing frail about these people; they're strong, and they're uncannily intuitive. The mother, who has always understood what is going on in Christy, is aware of the danger that the woman doctor (Fiona Shaw) represents; the mother worries that the doctor has brought too much hope to Christy's voice.

The cinematographer (Jack Conroy) brings the family close to you, and the images of flesh—the broad-faced Juno-like mother, the sculptural pink jowliness of the father, the girls

in their first experiments with makeup, the raw-faced boys—
come at you the way they do in a Dreyer film. In one scene,
a bulging vein divides Christy's bony forehead right down
the middle; sometimes when he tries to talk, he drools spit-
tle. There isn't a wasted shot in the movie. A Halloween
fresco is instantly stored as something not to be forgotten.
And there is a moment that is simply peerless when Mr.
Brown, the head of the house, is laid low; he falls to the
floor—to Christy's province—and Christy is face to face
with his dead father. It's a mythic image. But it doesn't go
on a second too long. Neither does the wake—a real Irish
wake that ends in a brawl. A man there offends Christy, who
uses his talented left foot to kick the glass smack out of the
guy's hand. (Christy loves to drink so he can misbehave.)

Everything goes right with the movie—which probably
means that Sheridan and Connaughton hit the right subject
for them and surrounded Day-Lewis with just the right players. But probably none of it would have worked without
him and his demonic eyes. (At times, Day-Lewis's Christy
uses his eyes to speak wicked thoughts for him, as Olivier's
Richard III did. They're flirts, these characters. As for the
actors, when they're deformed they're free to be more
themselves than ever.) Something central in Day-Lewis con-
nects with what's central in Christy. You could say that they
share a bawdy vitality, and they do, but it's much more than
that. It's in the passion that Day-Lewis has for acting: he
goes in to find (i.e., create) the spirit of the character so that
he can release it. That's how he asserts himself. So he responds to Christy's need for self-assertion and his refusal to
see himself as a victim. Christy Brown died, at forty-nine,
in 1981; he choked on food at Sunday dinner. This great,
exhilarating movie—a comedy about suffering—gives him
new life as a legendary Irish hero.

Penn & Teller Get Killed

In the darkness at the start of *Penn & Teller Get Killed,*
voice-overs are heard—smart, brassy backstage talk. Then
the screen fills with hoopla and a blaze of graphics. The pair
of prankster magicians are on a live late-night talk show; we
see them hanging upside down on camera and standing right
side up on several monitors at the same time. Penn the big
bluffer—six foot six and with brass lungs—yells at the studio audience, "Are we live? Yeah!" He demands of the people that they yell along with him, and they do, repeatedly;
they enter into the lunacy of the screwed-up call-and-
response that he insists on, and the joke builds. It's as if
some new kind of bludgeoning, hip comedy were being invented—as if the Three Stooges had taken over "Saturday
Night Live." But as soon as the loud, bright TV show is
finished, and the studio audience is no longer there, the
film's layer of carny crudeness and excitement—the shoot-
the-works electricity—thins out.

The script that Penn and Teller wrote for their first appearance as screen stars is meant to take off from Penn's
remark on the talk show that it would be fun if a killer were
stalking him. Basically, the two magicians play murderous
practical jokes on each other, and, the way the material has
been directed, by Arthur Penn (no relation), it seems mechanical and surprisingly blunt. When the movie goes into
a film-noir mode, it isn't sleep-inducing, like the comedy it
calls to mind, the Carl Reiner–Steve Martin *Dead Men Don't
Wear Plaid,* but it has some of that film's laboriousness. It's
often on the verge of being funny or of being something;
you can weary of your own expectancy.

Teller resembles a number of wide-eyed clowns (Stan Laurel, the young Alec Guinness, Tim Conway, Henry Gibson),
but he doesn't light up anything in our imagination. This

silent, withdrawn, business-suited mime keeps what's funny to himself; it might be said that his art is in not giving you much. Penn gives you more than you crave; he means to be grating and obnoxious, but this is supposed to be a put-on. It feels like the real thing.

Possibly the two might be more welcome screen presences if they had given their tricks a fanciful context (comparable to the one created in *Pee-wee's Big Adventure*). But Penn and Teller's specialty is hipster magic—that is, anti-magic; they demonstrate that by practice they can duplicate the supernatural revelations produced at séances, and can even effect medical miracles. It would go against the grain of their act for them to carry the audience along into a fantasy. The pitfall here is that they seem to have lost touch with the fun in magic—the sheer joy the audience can feel at sleek trickery. Teller doesn't do the tiny, implausible tricks that have made their stage shows famous. And they don't give us jokes; they give us a course outline in sadistic comedy. When the bullets fly and the bodies pile up we want it to be funny and macabre, but it's only an intellectual idea of funny and macabre.

A Dry White Season

Marlon Brando is airily light as Ian McKenzie, the sardonic anti-apartheid barrister in *A Dry White Season*. A naïve white schoolmaster (Donald Sutherland) who's had his eyes opened to the police brutality involved in the death of his black gardener imagines that he can obtain justice for the man's family in the courts, and asks McKenzie to take the case. After many years of fighting for human rights, McKenzie knows that he can't get anywhere with the rigged

Johannesburg court, but he goes through the motions anyway. Directed by Euzhan Palcy, the young black woman from Martinique who made *Sugar Cane Alley* there in 1983, this new film is much more heavy-handed, and it has the disadvantage of an earnest, didactic script (by Colin Welland and the director, from a novel by André Brink). Performers such as Susan Sarandon, Jurgen Prochnow, Winston Ntshona, Janet Suzman, Michael Gambon, and Zakes Mokae sink into the obviousness of their roles and leave no trace. (Poor, uninspired, virtuous Sutherland is out of it; his characterization is one long whimper.)

Brando hasn't acted for years, but he's masterly, easy. There's no rust on him. The role is one of those humane, avuncular, Clarence Darrow knockoffs—the kind that Spencer Tracy and Orson Welles got to play—and his Indian-chief profile looks magnificent in court. He's even got specs pushed up high on his forehead; they give him a Dickensian air. He performs with such wry, smiling wit that he saves the picture (at least for the brief time he's onscreen).

The romantic in Brando must have responded to the old rebel lawyer's romantic gesture. McKenzie is showing everyone that no matter how strong a case he makes, the judge will rule against him. He's demonstrating the futility of trying to find justice in a corrupt, unjust system. But the audience is meant to see that his labor isn't really futile, that is serves to put pressure on the government and to wake people up—it's inspiriting. This applies to Brando's work as an actor, too. He may think it's futile, but he's wrong—it's also inspiriting. When he's on the screen, he's king of the hill and big is beautiful.

OCTOBER 2, 1989

WHOOPEE

The Fabulous Baker Boys

In *The Fabulous Baker Boys* the twenty-nine-year-old
writer-director Steve Kloves glides you through a romantic
fantasy that has a forties-movie sultriness and an eighties
movie-struck melancholy. Put them together and you have
a movie in which eighties glamour is being defined. Kloves
gets you to reminisce in a special way: you have your stored-
up forties fantasies, and now you see morose people in bars
and night clubs that look left over from those days, and
everybody's shrug about things being run-down is part of
the glamour. If this film has a specific progenitor, it might
be *Shoot the Piano Player,* Truffaut's comedy about mel-
ancholia, in which the piano-player hero wants not to care
anymore—to be out of it. (The heroine says, "Even when
he's with somebody, he walks alone.") Kloves has a new
New Wave vision. He trips you off, inviting you to laugh if
you want to. You feel the heat even if you're laughing.

Kloves has written quick, slang dialogue; most of what's
being said is unspoken. Beau and Jeff Bridges are Frank and
Jack, the Baker brothers of Seattle—a team of pianists who

have been working together for thirty-one years, the last fifteen in cocktail lounges. (Jack was a child prodigy when they got their start.) For round-faced Frank, the older brother (Beau), playing the piano is a livelihood—nothing more. A settled suburban family man in his early forties, he handles the business side, picks the music, does the patter onstage, and worries about his bald spot and Jack's longish hair and lack of grooming. (As Beau plays him, Frank is the human center of the movie.) Jack, who's in his late thirties and lives in a crummy tenderloin apartment, is so fed up with everything that he can barely stay awake during the performances. He seems depressed, surly, as if he might wander off at any moment, but he sits there and goes through the motions.

Their arrangements—pop classics, standards, and show tunes—sound dead, and they've been getting fewer dates, and those in tackier rooms, when Frank proposes that they take on a girl vocalist. They audition thirty-seven songbirds who can't carry a tune before Michelle Pfeiffer turns up, as Susie Diamond, a tough, honest floozy. Asked what kind of experience she's had, Susie answers that for the last couple of years she's been "on call for the Triple-A Escort Service." But when she sings (Pfeiffer does her own singing) she's a sexy dream—tender, nostalgic, just what's wanted of a lounge performer. Her interpretations of the standards are simple and natural in a way that cuts through the thick over-lay of pop banality. Once she's part of the act and she and the Baker boys are on their way up, she says she doesn't want to sing "Feelings" or "Bali Ha'i" again, but Frank insists, and when we hear her on "Feelings" she cleans away the psychodrama, and it actually sounds relatively fresh.

Susie loves to perform, and she has a low-down impudence—she gives the picture its kick. She's a funny girl, not as innocent or farcical as the lovelorn pixie that Pfeiffer played in *Married to the Mob* but with something of that free personality. Susie has a fast, profane way of saying what she thinks, and it's disruptive. Without especially meaning to, she challenges the brothers' relationship. She challenges it more directly after she discovers that Jack plays jazz piano when he's playing for himself. (The picture calls what he plays jazz, but it's not different enough from his bland team-work—just a little harsher and a lot showier. His jazz is dubbed by Dave Grusin; the runs sound like colored lights on waterfalls.) Seeing Jack in his secret jazz world, Susie knows that this is a different man from the almost patholog-ically laid-back pianist she's been working with—that he loves music the way she does—and she's drawn to him.

Frank senses what's going on and becomes more of a fuss-budget, nitpicking about Jack's hair and his smoking. The three of them are beginning to make real money, but Frank keeps crabbing—nobody's neat enough for him. When they're at an expensively tasteful resort hotel, booked for the Christmas holidays, Frank is indignant because Susie is keeping him up by listening to Ellington at two in the morn-ing.

While the pressures build, you're free-associating with old movies and smiling in recognition. Pfeiffer's good-bad Susie recalls the grinning infectiousness of Carole Lombard, the radiance of the very young Lauren Bacall, and Pfeiffer her-self in other movies (and in her eager, fluid performance in John O'Hara's *Natica Jackson* on PBS). Mostly, it's the emo-tional states of romantic melodramas that are recalled—the moments when the hero, hollowing his cheeks, looks like a god but, for reasons he can't explain, leaves the heroine out on a limb. Jeff Bridges has never been as glamorously be-yond reach as he is here. As Jack, he can show affection only to a dejected child and an old, sick dog. In the first scene, Jack has risen from the bed of a woman who asks if she'll see him again, and she's told "No." As he's closing the door behind him, she says, "You've got great hands." Jack is tall, quiet, sensual—a love object who spreads his long fingers and caresses the keys of a piano. Even when he plays alone at a jazz joint his face seems sad, blurred, as if he were remembering what music used to mean to him.

(That's the eighties side of the movie: this Sleeping Beauty may never fully wake up.)

Everyone has bluesy, narcissistic feelings, and that's what Steve Kloves is into. The movie is all fake blues, but the fakeness isn't offensive because it's recognized for what it is, and respected for the longings it calls up. Dennis Potter got it right when, in an interview, the critic Michael Sragow asked him, "Why do popular songs have so much power in your work?" He answered:

> Because I don't make the mistake that high-culture mongers do of assuming that because people like cheap art, their feelings are cheap, too. When people say, "Oh listen, they're playing our song," they don't mean "Our song, this little cheap, tinkling, syncopated piece of rubbish, is what we felt when we met." What they're saying is, "That song reminds us of that tremendous feeling we had when we met."

Essentially, at *The Fabulous Baker Boys* we're laughing together at the magnetism of popular music and the magnetism of commercial-movie emotions; they overlap so much they're practically the same thing. (The story line blends them.)

And we're laughing at the dazzling happiness that radiates from Michelle Pfeiffer as she sings eight songs, including "More Than You Know" and two by Rodgers and Hart—"Ten Cents a Dance" and "My Funny Valentine." We laugh the hardest when she writhes and thrashes about on top of Jack's grand piano in the ballroom of the resort hotel on New Year's Eve. Frank has been called away, and Susie finally has her shot at seducing Jack. She goes all out, while singing "Makin' Whoopee." Kloves and Dave Grusin blow the opportunity to make the song more of a communication between the piano and the vocalist, but with Pfeiffer in deep-red velvet crawling on the piano like a long-legged kitty-cat and sliding down to be closer to the pianist, something new has been achieved in torrid comedy. Pfeiffer's dress is red the way Rita Hayworth's dress in *Gilda* was black—as a statement. Hayworth hit a peak of comic voluptuousness in that gown, doing striptease movements to "Put the Blame on Mame," with Anita Ellis's voice coming out of her. Pfeiffer in red doesn't displace Hayworth; making love to Jack through her song, she matches her.

Kloves previously had a script produced that he wrote when he was twenty-two—*Racing with the Moon*. That movie was actually set in the forties, and it, too, had a moody, low-keyed texture and the kind of dialogue that allows the actors to find their way. But it was too much like a sensitive first novel. It didn't have Michelle Pfeiffer or anything like the swooniness that this demi-musical has. Kloves hasn't devised subplots that will pay off late in the story; he works with melodramatic atmosphere but not with melodrama, and he doesn't give the movie the boost that might be expected toward the end. It may seem to drift for a bit. Yet it has a look; the cinematographer, Michael Ballhaus, has given it a funky languor. By ordinary-movie standards, the pacing here could be snappier at times—more decisive—but it's of a piece with the bluesiness. The relaxed, nowhere-to-go atmosphere holds the film in a memory vise. The choice of songs, their placement, and the sound mix itself are extraordinary—so subtle they make fun of any fears of kitschy emotions. And there's a thrill in watching the three actors, because they seem perfect at what they're doing—newly minted icons.

The Bridges brothers don't have to act brotherhood; it takes care of itself. At one point, Frank is doing his usual inane, ingratiating patter about himself and his brother, to yank applause from the audience. Suddenly, the near-catatonic Jack says, "I love you, Frank," in a low, muffled voice. Is he just being hostile? Or are these true feelings that he had to express to cauterize the show-biz lies? Frank is so rattled that he needs to recover himself before going on with his routine. Kloves lets the two underplay their scenes together. They don't reach out to us; we reach out to them.

Breaking In

John Sayles' script for the Bill Forsyth film *Breaking In* (the closing-night presentation of the New York Film Festival) is confident, off-beat, and shallow, all at the same time. Burt Reynolds, Casey Siemaszko, and the other actors go looking for stuff to play that Sayles just hasn't put there. It's my impression that almost all the Sayles scripts have this deficiency. They're thoughtfully constructed, with neatly placed shards of irony, but I almost always come out of a Sayles movie feeling: Is that all? He's the thinking man's shallow writer-director; he doesn't give us drama, he gives us notions. When he directs his scripts himself, the faults can be attributed to his clumsiness with the camera, but the Scots wonder Bill Forsyth does a beautiful, clean job on *Breaking In*; I think he's brought out everything that there is to be brought out, and it still isn't enough. The movie is moderately entertaining, yet it never gets rolling. It has no innards.

And the characters have no interior life. As the sixty-one-year-old Ernie, the old-pro safecracker from New York who's operating now in Portland, Oregon, Burt Reynolds shows his polish in a somewhat impersonal role. (The film has youth's idea of maturity—i.e., that people become sane and dispassionate.) Siemaszko is Mike, the nosy, amiable kid that Ernie takes on as his lookout and apprentice. The level-headed Ernie is content to live in a tract home on the fringe of the city and not call attention to himself, but the kid can't resist flashing his new wealth. Forsyth has always been partial to fluky adolescents, and Siemaszko (he was Jonathan, the cartoonist hero of Spielberg's hour-long "Amazing Stories" film *The Mission*) gives Mike a wide-eyed furtiveness; he resembles Michael J. Pollard in *Bonnie and Clyde*. Mike keeps bopping around and catching your eye.

He's Ernie's opposite; he's so unstable you don't know what he's up to, and he doesn't know, either.

Everything is worked out in symmetrical pairs. Ernie maintains a steady, paying relationship with a prostitute, Delphine (Lorraine Toussaint), who fixes Mike up with *her* apprentice, Carrie (Sheila Kelley), but Mike is smitten with Carrie and insists that she quit dating other guys and let him take care of her. She's offended. The irony is less than supple; it's like G. B. Shaw on a bad day. Siemaszko and Kelley are both very active performers, though; they move right into their characters, and that helps the movie. (As the fools, they seem to have more free will than the other characters.) The film also features a pair of retired crooks (Albert Salmi and Harry Carey), who are Ernie's card-playing pals, and a pair of adversarial lawyers (Maury Chaykin and Steve Tobolowsky), who have a satisfyingly cynical—if unconvincing—negotiating session. (Chaykin, a true eccentric actor, creates suspense by keeping you in doubt about whether his character is very smart or very dumb.) Ernie and Mike don't appear to have any strong larcenous impulses, and so they don't arouse our own. They don't seem meant to: the film views burglary as a morally neutral trade or skill. (This is like Nietzsche on a bad day.) At the end, we realize that we're intended to feel the buddyship of the pair—that somehow, because of the construction of the story, it's supposed to be self-evident.

All the contrasts and symmetry might be miraculous in a farce, but in a movie about how professional small-time criminals live and practice their trades, this formal patterning seems consciously quaint. Forsyth may have imagined that he could go around the margins of the quaintness and show us American life out of the mainstream—the stuff you don't usually see in movies, the life behind the billboards. But with a Sayles script you go behind the billboards and there's nobody there.

Johnny Handsome

I doubt if the acting in American movies has ever been as good as it is right now. It's not just that the general level is very high; it's that some performers shoot way up above that level. There are inspired performances in the sort of popular movies where you don't expect them. *Turner & Hooch* is no more than a well-made comic Rin-Tin-Tin movie, but its light, flexible star, Tom Hanks, transcends it. Dianne Wiest does high-style comedy in *Parenthood*—the kind of acting that won acclaim for Broadway stars in the thirties. And in the ludicrously feral new revenge melodrama *Johnny Handsome,* Morgan Freeman and Forest Whitaker, playing antagonists—a tough-minded veteran police detective and a warm, idealistic prison doctor—have a couple of scenes together that crackle. Whitaker is planning to perform plastic surgery on a young hoodlum (Mickey Rourke), grotesquely disfigured from birth, on the theory that the kid will go straight if he's made handsome. Freeman listens to Whitaker and grins in disbelief: how can anyone be this innocent? Whitaker, with his fine, serious presence, holds his ground. The antagonism between the two is credible, and it's tickling to see them together. The story is a tortuous reworking of Joan Crawford's 1941 vehicle *A Woman's Face* (which was a remake of a Swedish film with Ingrid Bergman); the big change is that the new film's slant is cruelly kinky. (It's as if *A Woman's Face* were redone, with the Crawford character once again surgically transformed and all—only now in the last scene somebody throws acid at her.) The movie is hardly worth talking about, except that, in addition to Freeman, with his sharp wit, and Whitaker, with his expressiveness, there's someone turning up every few minutes who goes way beyond competence: Scott Wilson as Rourke's only buddy, David Schramm as a

money-launderer, Raynor Scheine (a gimmick name?) as a
gun dealer. The director, Walter Hill, must love actors (despite his enthusiasm for having them punched and pistol-
whipped).

OCTOBER 16, 1989

FLOATING

Drugstore Cowboy

Nihilistic humor rarely bubbles up in a movie as freely as it does in *Drugstore Cowboy*. The jokes aren't fully formed, and they don't seem prepared for; they just occur, almost passively, as if they were a haphazard part of how the director, Gus Van Sant, looks at things. After trying Los Angeles and New York, Van Sant moved to Portland, Oregon, in 1983. This is the second feature he's made there. The first, the 1986 *Mala Noche* (Bad Night), is a story of romantic obsession, shot in 16 mm., mostly in black and white, and made for twenty-five thousand dollars; it's the story of Walt (Tim Streeter), a young clerk in a skid-row convenience store, who falls hopelessly in love with a Mexican boy, a tease who accepts handouts from him but derides him as a "stupid faggot." Based on a short novel by the Oregon poet Walt Curtis, *Mala Noche* has a wonderful fluid, grainy look—expressionist yet with an improvised feel. It has an authentic grungy beauty; at moments, it's reminiscent of Jean Genet's short film masterpiece *Un Chant d'Amour.*

Van Sant's new film is less affecting, but it has a distinctive drug rust. The screenplay, by the director and Daniel Yost, is based on an unpublished novel by James Fogle, who has

served time in several West Coast prisons for drug-related
robberies. He is now about ten years into a twenty-two-year
sentence in the state of Washington, and is scheduled after
that to do time for a drugstore holdup in Wisconsin. (He's
fifty-two.) Set in 1971, the movie is about two couples who
live together and travel around the Pacific Northwest rob-
bing hospitals and pharmacies, grabbing fistfuls of pills and
capsules. They're like a junkie version of Clyde Barrow's
gang. Woozed out as they are most of the time, and living
from high to high, they plan the robberies in knotty detail.
The group's twenty-six-year-old leader, Bob (Matt Dillon),
takes his duties very seriously; his planning is like a simulation of a working-man's job. But as soon as he's in the
getaway car, with his wife, Dianne (the talented Kelly
Lynch), behind the wheel, he gives himself a fix. The robberies themselves are thrills, but the moving around, the
anxieties, and all the strategy sessions are wearing Bob
down. He has been in prison a number of times, and he
lives in a maze of superstitious thinking: anything that has
ever been associated with trouble with the police becomes
an omen, a source of terror, and so a hat on a bed or the
mention of a puppy can freak him out. (Dillon brings the
role a mixture of macho presence and light self-mockery
that helps set the mood of the film.)

When Bob is high, something in him seems to float free.
His visions (we see them in simple, animated form) suggest
a child's image of the cow jumping over the moon (and the
music suggests lullabies). Yet we can also feel the weariness
in him. The couples are presented as a squabbling family,
and Van Sant keeps us aware of what babies they are, and
of how the drugs make them feel pleasantly unhinged and
give them the illusion that they're being taken care of. Bob
is a baby, but he's also the father; he's smarter than the
others, more responsible, and capable of thinking of the
future. Rick (James Le Gros) is still just a dumb kid, learning
the ropes, and his teen-age girlfriend, Nadine (Heather Graham), is a wide-eyed blond cutie—perhaps no more than

sixteen—who wants to be accepted and have fun. (She's like an infant Angie Dickinson.) The only one Bob is close to is levelheaded Dianne; they were childhood sweethearts and have been together ever since. But he's lost his sex drive (he may be taking drugs partly to avoid the demands of sex), and that vacancy in their lives is separating them. By now, much as drugs mean to him, they mean more to her.

As the strategist, Bob plots the group itinerary so they can always get high; the four travel by car and send their cache of drugs ahead by bus, parcelled out to a series of stops. These four petty thieves scrounging for pharmaceuticals are so inept that the police are always right on their tails—it's like a game of Keystone Thieves and Keystone Cops. Their skill isn't in their thefts; it's in how effectively they hide their stash. When they go on the road, they cut a hole in the car floor; if they have to dispose of what they're carrying, they know they'll be all right at the next bus station.

The movie takes us inside a lot of underground attitudes, and the director likes these attitudes—he enjoys them, even though he's grown beyond them. The druggies are mono-maniacal about leading an aimless existence; they're proud of wasting their lives. During their robberies (which are generally a shambles), and even during their scrapping, they see themselves as romantic figures. (They're comic, but they're not put down for being comic.) When Bob applies to enroll in a methadone program, he explains to the social worker (Beah Richards) why people use drugs. He says that they're trying to "relieve the pressures of their everyday life," and, speaking slowly, as if he had no idea what example he was going to come up with, he says, "like having to tie their shoes." Dillon delivers a line like this so that it sounds utterly natural. We grasp what he's saying while we sense the exhaustion behind it. But now it's the drug life that's exhausting Bob.

When Bob is trying to break free, he renews his acquaintance with Father Murphy, the defrocked priest who, years before, turned him on to drugs. He doesn't resent what the old man did to him; drugs have given him pleasures that he doesn't get from anything else. And seeing Bob's tenderness toward the scrawny, formally attired old father figure helps us understand Bob's nature. But the film errs, I think, in casting William S. Burroughs as the junkie priest. Dillon is acting, and Burroughs isn't, quite. He does have a performer's booming voice, and he stylizes his big line about narcotics' having been "systematically scapegoated and demonized." But elsewhere the movie undercuts its characters' bravado, even as we're amused by it; it doesn't undercut him, and his scenes are too much of a guest-hipster number. Someone like Roberts Blossom could have played the role and acted it, staying in tune with Dillon.

Drugstore Cowboy has a superficial resemblance to *Bonnie and Clyde,* and it may recall the detachment of *Repo Man* and something of Jim Jarmusch's comic minimalism. But Van Sant isn't just a fan of his characters' style; he partakes of it. This is a believable absurdism. Van Sant accepts the kids in the drug subculture (and in the skid row of *Mala Noche*) without glamorizing adolescent romanticism (the way *Rumble Fish* did). A speed freak named David (Max Perlich), a little guy with an overbite, suggests the ratty kid at school that everybody avoided—can he really be dealing drugs? You smile every time there's a cut to Nadine's junkie doll face. (When the actress has a scene where she has to act a little, she isn't up to it, but a soft face like that would compensate for a lot worse acting.) Van Sant's films are an antidote to wholesomeness; he's made a controlled style out of the random and the careless. He rings totally unexpected bells. Dianne complains to Bob, "You won't fuck me, and I always have to drive." *Drugstore Cowboy* keeps you laughing because it's so nonjudgmental. Van Sant is half in and half out of the desire of adolescents to remain kids forever.

Crimes and Misdemeanors

In *Crimes and Misdemeanors,* Martin Landau is an eminent ophthalmologist who's trying to get rid of his hysterical mistress (Anjelica Huston) in order to save his reputation and his marriage (to Claire Bloom). His course of action raises serious ethical issues, which he discusses with his rabbi friend (Sam Waterston), who's going blind. That going blind is quite a touch! No, it isn't meant to be a giggle. It's part of the film's controlling metaphor. When the doctor was a boy, he was instructed at home and at the synagogue that "the eyes of God are on us always." *Crimes and Misdemeanors,* written and directed by Woody Allen, is a sad, censuring look at the world-famous doctor and other crooks in high places who (in Allen's view) have convinced themselves that they can do anything, because they don't think God is watching.

Landau is at his best when the doctor, trying to calm down the tiresome woman, can't help showing a New Yorker's nervous impatience. He brushes aside her claims that she's made sacrifices for him and he hasn't kept his promises; you feel the intimacy behind the arguments, and you can see the signs that his blood pressure is rising. This is the preliminary bout—it's preparing the audience for the crime to come— and Landau's actor's instinct not to waste any time meshes perfectly with the doctor's need to get away from this accusing monster. (We aren't asked to have any feeling for her; we see the situation strictly in terms of her threats to break up his marriage and expose his financial manipulations.) The doctor's predicament is so stale that Landau's gestures of impatience are the only saving elements.

Convinced that he has been forced into it, the doctor takes action to save his hide. Then he agonizes over what he has done, and in his disordered thoughts he revisits his child-hood *shul* and attends a Seder at his childhood home; he listens to the old wisdom (If a man commits a crime, he will be punished), and he hears it crudely challenged. Now the impatience is ours. Woody Allen isn't a clone of Ingmar Bergman this time; he's a clone of Arthur Miller. Of course, there's a difference. In Miller's plays you can see the wheels grinding but what happens has some punch. Allen keeps a polite distance. The doctor's self-torture has been worn smooth by generations of playwrights—it's ponderously abstract. And there's a difference befitting the era. Mil-ler's guilty father in *All My Sons* (1947) killed himself. Allen's much admired doctor who cheats on the most basic human decencies is meant to be symptomatic of the Reagan eighties. He learns to live comfortably with his lack of conscience. (And we can feel morally superior to the "successful.")

The tediousness of Woody Allen's attempt to deal with weighty questions is that he poses them in conventional, sermonizing terms. He appears to be pinning contemporary greed and crime on man's loss of belief in God. The movie represents a peculiarly tony form of fundamentalism. The sets, the clothes, and Sven Nykvist's cinematography all take the color out of color; there's no vulgar vibrancy here. And the cutting is let-the-edges-show modern. But Woody Allen seems to be telling us that believing there's a God who's watching us is our only safeguard against committing mur-der. He opens another possibility by introducing a boring humanistic thinker—Professor Levy (Martin Bergmann), a survivor of the camps—who tells us that it's we, with our capacity for love, who give meaning to the indifferent uni-verse. But this possibility is given a flip finish: the profes-sor's philosophy doesn't sustain him. The picture is saying that God may not exist but man needs to believe in Him in order to find meaning in life. (The professor goes the way of Alain Cuny as the voice of reason in *La Dolce Vita.*) Meanwhile, the plot line shows us that the doctor isn't punished, so he stops fearing God. It was only fear that kept him "moral."

In a parallel story line, where the misdemeanors take place, Woody Allen himself appears as a grubbing-for-a-living documentary filmmaker—a man trying to be true to what his camera eye sees. His wife (Joanna Gleason) keeps denigrating his accomplishments, and can't even be bothered sleeping with him. She's a well-connected woman: her two brothers are the rabbi and a darling of the media, a celebrity TV producer, played by Alan Alda. This egomaniac who is taken for a creative genius is the movie's satirical villain: he's tall, he's facile—he's everything that the little-guy documentarian fears and despises. And at first the little guy's raging jealousy is quite funny; it's the comic rage of the harmless—he's so preoccupied with exposing the producer's phoniness that he can't get anything else done.

Alda plays the enemy with a smug, screwy abandon; it's almost like an Ernie Kovacs turn. At a party this genius gives, he's suddenly struck by the brilliance of something that has come into his head and, afraid of losing it, he pulls out his tape recorder to preserve it. Alda is the one actor in *Crimes and Misdemeanors* who doesn't seem to be on automatic pilot. His performance may remind you that he used to be a member of Second City (in New York), and that before his eleven years on "M*A*S*H" he took on challenges like Caryl Chessman in TV's *Kill Me If You Can.* (He may have become too professionally affable in "M*A*S*H," but he didn't really earn his bad name until he went overly earnest in movies like *Same Time, Next Year* and *California Suite,* and in the ones he directed, like *The Four Seasons.*) The other actors perform very proficiently, yet (except when I was watching Landau's nerves being rubbed raw and seeing how intently Jerry Orbach played the doctor's shady, subdued brother) I didn't feel caught up in anything they said or did. (That includes even what Claire Bloom said and did:

she has no more than a glorified walk-on.) Woody Allen's
once sharp powers of observation seem dulled here. But the
whirlwind TV genius is alive and making an ass of himself.
The character is cheaply satirized, but you like him for his
self-infatuation.

Did Woody Allen know that he was letting Alda steal the
picture? I think he must have. There's a wide streak of mas-
ochism running through this movie. The documentarian is
worse off than Zelig: he falls in love with a Public Television
associate producer (played by Mia Farrow), and they have a
rapport, but he can't compete with the pontificating genius.
The documentarian is the man with impossible ideals, the
total loser; it's the villains who win. Woody Allen is tweak-
ing his own high-mindedness, yet he also appears to be revealing himself more nakedly here than in his other movies;
he appears to be saying, "This is who I am." But it may be
a false nakedness—a giving in to the safety of weakness, to
the feeling that nobody wants an honest man. His bald mas-
ochism in the later part of the picture is a betrayal of his
jokester's personality.

The two halves of this movie don't fit together in a way
that sets off reverberations. You can intellectualize connections between them, but you don't feel a connection.
Woody Allen's abrupt changes of tone as he moves from
one set of characters to the other, and overlaps them, keep
you from getting restless; he has become a skillful director.
But he's making the film equivalent of a play of ideas, and
the ideas have no excitement. He's telling us not just what
we already know but what we've already rejected. And it's
awkward to see him playing the pathetic failure—standing
in his editing room against a Chaplin poster and trying to
make time with Mia by showing her footage of the wise,
aged professor who lived through the Holocaust. (When he
had a date with Annie Hall and took her to see *The Sorrow
and the Pity,* it was a better joke.)

If Woody Allen were interested in drama (rather than pi-
eties), he wouldn't make us reject the emotional plight of

the doctor's mistress. The camera loiters on her rear end, as if to dehumanize her; she's presented as hulking and insistent, like the knife-wielder in *Fatal Attraction*. So the doctor's final acceptance of his crime against her has no horror. The film's emphasis is confusing: the spectator has more anxiety about the doctor's possibly revealing his crime to the authorities than about what he does to her. And if you don't care about this woman—or about the little suffering documentarian—this is just one more of Woody Allen's class-act movies. It comes complete with reassuring words about how most human beings have the capacity "to find joy from simple things, like their family, their work, and from the hope that future generations might understand more."

There's no avoiding the recognition that Allen has been coming up more and more with praiseworthy themes. Sam Waterston, having played Oppenheimer and Lincoln and William L. Shirer on TV and Sydney Schanberg in *The Killing Fields,* is perfectly modulated as the blind rabbi, the good, moral man afflicted by fate. How can the funnyman who assembled *What's Up Tiger Lily?* resist putting dirty words in that exemplary mouth? The answer is that Waterston's performance here suggests a blue-blooded Woody Allen. And the documentarian, when he's lost everything and is humbled, looks more dignified than before. Allen himself is turning into a rabbi. The years that he's been railing against the universe without definitive answers must have worn him down, so now he's supplying them.

OCTOBER 30, 1989

BOMBS

Dad

In *Dad,* Jack Lemmon plays a quiet dreamer who supported his wife and kids by working faithfully at the blue-collar job he hated in an L.A. Lockheed plant. Now seventy-eight and retired, with a bald pate and the white fringe of a circus clown, he's dominated by his wife (Olympia Dukakis); she does everything for him, enfeebling him. Dad is so repressed he seems senile; he barely walks or talks. But when his wife has a heart attack and is hospitalized, his Wall Street investment-banker son (Ted Danson) arrives, moves in with him, and stirs him to action: the helpless old coot comes alive. Up to this point, about twenty minutes in, the movie, which was adapted from the William Wharton novel, and written and directed by Gary David Goldberg (the "creator" of the TV series "Family Ties"), has a quiet dramatic logic. But the only suspense is: How is this film going to be prolonged? The answer is: By one damn episode after another. It's a short TV series jammed together.

First, the tough, acerbic wife is discharged from the hospital and is upset to find that Dad has become active and independent. Then it's Dad who has to be hospitalized, and there's a section devoted to doctors' megalomania and incompetence, and how their blundering causes Dad to go into a comatose state. But the son won't give in to the hospital's bureaucratic policies; he picks his father up in his arms and carries him out of the place. Soon after, the son puts Dad in the care of a black doctor (Zakes Mokae), who has a new treatment for him, and it's discovered that for decades Dad has had a secret fantasy life—an idyll of living on a farm, where Mom is warm and supportive. Revived, Dad begins to integrate this other, joyous life with his ordinary existence: he wears gaudy tropical prints, and socializes with the neighbors. (One of the movie's many peculiarities is that the images of Dad's dream farm suggest a nostalgia for an imaginary earlier America; they don't jibe with his loud new clothes and his wanting to step out.)

Dad is a generic nice guy. He never gets to express any anger at bossy Mom or show any awareness that she's infantilizing him. He's above hostile feelings; presumably, in his head he switches over to the farm. What really sinks the movie is that when his fantasy life breaks through, it, too, is generic. The two halves of his split personality don't add up to anything baffling or crisscrossed. For all Lemmon's comic lightness and dexterity, there's not much he can do in a scene where Dad is lying in a hospital bed, frightened, and says to his middle-aged son, "We've never hugged." The son says, "Want to give it a try?" and Dad says, "I do." Still, Lemmon is so insufferably nice and boyish and obliging that you feel he deserves the puling lines that Goldberg gives him.

Lemmon's conception of professionalism is to disappear into a role; so when a character has no character he doesn't bring it anything—or anything fresh. At the start, Lemmon has vanished so completely into the role of the feeble old fellow that you almost blink your eyes. But when Dad enters his joyous phase he has a familiar Jack Lemmon personality: he's self-pitying, and asks to be loved for his perkiness and his corny sense of humor. Ted Danson shares in his vacuousness. Even the gifted Kathy Baker, who plays Dad's daughter, is just about stumped, although, as her husband,

Kevin Spacey (who two TV seasons back played the gorgeously demented Mel Profitt on "Wiseguy") does manage a little wry, observant humor.

Making his first movie, Goldberg has attempted to open his sitcom sensibility to real life; he's filled *Dad* with therapeutic lore about old age and hospital care, as if moviemaking were a form of community service. It's the most impersonal personal movie I've ever seen. What comes through is that Goldberg wants to link the father and the son in a near-mystical reconciliation. (Basically, it excludes the wife and the daughter.) This is a son-gives-life-to-his-father story, and it seems deeply self-serving. (It's as if the son were trying to prove he could be a better mother-wife to Dad than old Mom is.)

A few months ago, the *Times* reported that Goldberg had sixty million dollars "drifting" into his bank account from the syndication of "Family Ties," a show that began when a TV executive "suggested that Mr. Goldberg write a series based on his own life." Goldberg has also said that he bought the rights to the novel *Dad,* in 1983, because "the guy in the book was so like my father," and that it was only after five years and fifty drafts that he felt his script did justice to his father (a postal worker, who died in 1986). He may have done more than justice to himself. In the movie, Danson, the Wall Street smoothie, simply gives up the appurtenances of wealth and power to go live with his father in his (too expensive-looking) tract house. Yes, this movie is about a good-man father. But he's a simple, passive character. The active good man—the hero and role model—is the son who rescues the father he loves.

The movie keeps going through permutations until, finally, the hero's devotion to Dad helps him reach out to his own (estranged, college-age) son, played by Ethan Hawke. The film's big emotional moment—it yanks tears very discreetly—comes when Danson, with a catch in his voice, says to Hawke, "I'm your father." After that, it's O.K. for old Dad to pass on; he's ready to go, because Danson is lying right next to him on his bed, holding him, protecting him from fear. This is a saga: three (television) generations.

Fat Man and Little Boy

In Roland Joffé's *Fat Man and Little Boy,* Paul Newman is miscast as General Leslie R. Groves, a part that Brian Dennehy played with spectacular verve in the TV docudrama *Day One,* which was run earlier this year. Newman is, for one of the few times in his career, left in the shadows. Actually, the whole movie is rather indistinct. Joffé and his co-screenwriter, Bruce Robinson, have taken an inherently dramatic subject and got lost in it; the script is a shambles. Viewers of *Day One* could see how General Groves and J. Robert Oppenheimer (David Strathairn) used each other, and how, once the Manhattan Project was started, it developed its own momentum, so that dropping the atomic bombs on Japan was the culmination of all that effort and expense. Viewers could see that the Project was both a scientific triumph and a moral descent. Directed by Joseph Sargent, from a script by David W. Rintels, the TV film had genuine complexity and a drive that carried you along all the way to the horror of the flash and the mushroom cloud. *Fat Man and Little Boy* seems to diminish both Groves and Oppenheimer (Dwight Schultz); at times, you may feel you detect a lofty contempt in its bald presentation of their motives. What you can't detect is any new interpretative skills that add to the other versions of the material (which include the 1947 M-G-M film *The Beginning or the End* and the 1982 seven-hour TV series *Oppenheimer,* starring Sam Waterston). Newman's Groves is gruff and deceitful; the performance seems held in, yet it's too smooth to be matched by

Schultz—he isn't a forceful enough actor to suggest Oppenheimer's Joan of Arc presence, which kept the collection of
scientists together. In this version, Oppenheimer is just an
arrogant, ivory-tower idealist, and the Machiavellian Groves
seems to pick him for his weakness.

Asked by a nurse (Laura Dern) to dance for her, a young
physicist (John Cusack) does a nifty little number. (The
composite character Cusack plays seems designed to show
that junior scientists can be regular guys who play baseball,
and that Oppenheimer was idolized by the juniors—which
makes his being a false hero all the more reprehensible.)
Natasha Richardson brings her lovely intensity to a scene as
Oppenheimer's old, Communist flame, and Bonnie Bedelia
is provocative as the worldly Mrs. Oppenheimer. The re-
creation of the expanding Los Alamos complex circa 1943
is convincing. But when it comes to dramatizing the fateful
decisions Joffé just isn't there. He drags in dubious claims
(such as that the mentally ill were used in plutonium experiments), and has characters deliver priggish-sounding
speeches to get across moral points. These English moviemakers may have a target (disarmament?), but their aim is
all over the place. Even the title, which must be meant to
refer to Groves and Oppenheimer as well as to the two
bombs dropped on Japan, doesn't score.

The Bear

The Bear, based on James Oliver Curwood's 1916 novel
The Grizzly King, is a French-made version of the romantic-
wilderness pulp that Hollywood turned out in the silent era.
A whimpering orphaned bear cub is the most vocal character; two strong, silent hunters and their dog handler are the

only human beings in sight. The director, Jean-Jacques Annaud, and the screenwriter, Gérard Brach, use only six hundred and fifty-seven words of dialogue, and those are in
English. The setting is supposed to be British Columbia in
1885, but the movie doesn't feel North American. It isn't
meant to. Annaud brings the genre a new bloodiness and a
primitive, lyrical pathos that are intended to universalize the
picture and make it timeless. (The market for it is also expected to be universal and timeless.) When Annaud and
Brach collaborated on *Quest for Fire,* Brach explained that
the film transcended "languages and nationalities and speaks
to the deepest human experience." This one is supposed to
speak to the deepest animal experience as well, and show
us what animals have in common with us. The story is told—
more or less—from what the moviemakers regard as the
bears' point of view. The hunters see the light, are humbled,
and put down their guns. And so the movie, with its anti-
hunting message, is bound to have its adherents.

Early on, the lonely, frightened cub tries to attach himself
to a huge male Kodiak bear (nine feet two and weighing two
thousand pounds), who has been shot in the shoulder and
growls, rebuffing the infant. The plucky cub's feelings are
hurt, but he ignores the threat, and follows the big bear,
pleading for acceptance; he comes close enough to clean
the wound with his tongue, and soon the two are kissing
and licking. They have "bonded"; the music swells (our
hearts are supposed to be swelling, too), and the film—a
whopping piece of anthropomorphism—gets rolling. (In interviews, Annaud talks about "making a film that would be
honest to animal nature.") Sometimes, as when the cub
dreams of enormous frogs, or when he eats psychedelic
mushrooms, groggily collapses, and has visions of mushrooms turning into butterflies, Annaud seems to be trying
to fuse a live-action form of the Disney storytelling in *Bambi*
with Czech animation and Jim Henson's animatronic pup-
petry. All three are used, and you can't be sure exactly what
you're looking at; the real (trained) animals frequently look

like Teddy bears. When there's a spectacular shot of the tiny bear and the giant bear standing up simultaneously and looking out over the mountains, you may be charmed and amused, or you may not be sure how to react, because you've been listening to too many baby-bear moans and coos, and looking at too many suspiciously endearing baby-bear expressions. And you've been drowning in a Philippe Sarde score that's like Broadway show tunes turned into baby-bear lullabies. (Suggestions of songs like "Lover, Come Back to Me" keep starting up.)

The footage was shot in the national parks of the Austrian Tyrol and Northern Italy (with a closing view of the top edge of the Canadian Northwest Territories), and the cinematographer, Philippe Rousselot, has given the images the soft light of the Romantic nature artists. What it all comes down to is a nature fake—trained animals and mechanical copies of animals placed in landscapes that faintly suggest the paintings of Caspar David Friedrich. At times, I felt as if I were watching hippie Muppets toddle about in Friedrich's visionary crags and ravines.

This seems harmless. Why does the movie make me feel angry and disgusted? I think it's the "primal" sell in Annaud's storytelling, which has the big bear avenging himself on the hunters by clawing their tethered horses, and also protecting himself by fighting off their pack of ten Doberman pinschers (and destroying a harmless pet Airedale). This is mixed together with the sweetness of the cub's snuggling with the big bear. The picture is a combination of raw pulp and gooey kitsch. It's saying that we shouldn't kill bears, because they're so much like us—after it fakes the evidence that they are. And suppose they were different in every conceivable way—should we then gun them down?

Clearly, Annaud put an immense amount of effort into trying to get the animals to act out the parts of the story that couldn't be faked, yet nothing—literally nothing—really feels right. Not the birdcalls under the titles or the honeybees that dive at the cub or the rockslide that kills his mother, or his sniffles. The moments that work best use the little bear for a fairy-tale image (like the scene of him trying to catch the reflection of the moon which he sees in a puddle) or use him as a comedian. At his funniest, he chases a frog and goes hopping and galumphing along like a life-size Winnie-the-Pooh, but even this is spoiled by a musical accompaniment that keeps pointing up how toylike he is.

When the story grows more violent—when the Dobermans track the big bear, who climbs ever higher into the mountains, with the cub following, until the cub can't hang on to the steep rocks and the big bear comes back down to rescue him—what we see is only a rough approximation of what the story line tells us we're seeing. We don't want it to be a closer approximation: we wouldn't want to see the Dobermans actually being torn apart. But we can't help being aware that Annaud and Brach devised the plan for a gory, sentimental myth and then fell back on sleight-of-hand cutting that never quite covers up the gaps. The human grunts and groans of the cornered big bear and the cub's constant crying out in terror are usually as close to telling the story as the film gets. The movie doesn't exist except for its dubbed sound effects. When a puma stalks the cub, the little one seems to be saying, "Oh, oh, whatever should I do?" It all sounds like a prank by Buck Henry, the screenwriter for *The Day of the Dolphin,* who supplied the voices of the baby dolphins—they prattled plaintively, in English.

NOVEMBER 13, 1989

SECOND TAKES

Henry V

Shakespeare's *Henry V,* written in 1599, or thereabouts, is perhaps the greatest jingo play ever conceived. It celebrates the victory of the underdogs—the English. At Agincourt, King Henry's valiant archers, outnumbered five to one and exhausted and fighting on foreign soil, destroy the expensively armored French. When the tally is handed to Henry, he reads it aloud to his men: the French have lost ten thousand men, the English just twenty-nine. Then the modest, devout Henry cautions his soldiers not to boast of this victory, and he orders the singing of "Non nobis domine" ("Not unto us, O Lord, not unto us, but unto thy name give glory"). But the play itself is far from modest. Written for an English audience, it tells us what great fighters we English are. And we're yeomen, naturally democratic; the French are sleek courtiers—an army of nobles, and a Dauphin who jeers at us.

Shakespeare is a jingo showman but he's no jingo fool. Along with the crowd-pleasing heroism the play offers doubts and complicated feelings. It suggests that what has led the Englishmen to Agincourt is military adventurism. Henry has allowed himself to believe the councillors who have told him he has a legitimate claim to the throne of

France. Yet the arguments that convince him sound like monkeyshines; the English are out for conquest.

At the center of this ambivalent patriotic play is the twenty-seven-year-old king, who is steeling himself for the responsibilities of leadership, and has given up the disreputable pals of his carousing days. Our Henry isn't merely an ideal leader, a fair-minded, disciplined, man-to-man king; he's the ideal Englishman—honest, considerate, bluff—and so the ideal man. Yet can an audience be meant to love a man who "killed the heart" of Jack Falstaff with the words "I know thee not, old man," and orders the hanging of the petty thief Bardolph, his former drinking companion? King Henry is too judicious to be loved. But the role is a star turn: audiences can love an actor for bringing it off.

Laurence Olivier played the part on the screen forty-five years ago, in a *Henry V* that he directed, with the encouragement of the British government. Britain was under attack, and his film caught the mood of the moment. It was— and remains—a heart-lifting triumph; it has bright colors, trick perspectives, and the enormous charm of childhood tales of chivalry. Olivier (he was thirty-six) brings a playful, bashful glamour to the role. His voice rings out thrillingly; you carry the sound with you forever. The new version, adapted and directed by its star, the young Shakespearean actor Kenneth Branagh (pronounced with the "g" silent), in no way replaces that first *Henry,* but it finds a niche of its own. Branagh's *Henry V* isn't exultant. His approach doesn't make possible the kind of patriotic triumph joined to an artistic triumph that Olivier had; the times don't make it possible, either. This new film reflects (or seems to reflect) Vietnam, and the Thatcher Government's Falklands War. Henry's archers with their longbows don't leap about in a way that suggests Robin Hood's men. The new battle at Agincourt is a slow-motion dance of bloody horror, and the victory is shallow and mournful.

Branagh—he was the confused, infatuated young man in the moonlit water with Jacqueline Bisset in *High Season,*

and he was Mr. Tansley to Rosemary Harris's Mrs. Ramsay
in the TV *To the Lighthouse* and Guy Pringle in the series
Fortunes of War—was born into a Protestant working-class
family in Belfast, in 1960. As Henry, he has the flyaway hair
of a schoolboy, and, under his shiny dark-blond mop, his
face is not what used to be called nobly proportioned. The
burning blue eyes, the thin slash of a mouth, the big, determined chin, the trace of baby fat in the cheeks—none of
them match. Together, though, they convey a suggestion of
secret knowledge, and his head, overscaled for his short
frame, rivets attention. He has something of James Cagney's
confident Irishness; he's an intensely likable performer, with
a straightforwardness that drives the whole film ahead.

Each of Henry's scenes with the gallant, intelligent French
herald, Mountjoy (Christopher Ravenscroft), advances the
plot by showing Mountjoy taking ever-larger measure of the
king; their encounters are like signposts in a friendship.
Once Henry is away from the dark palace, where high officials lurk in the shadows, and is out-of-doors, he becomes
a different man—the brave, affable soldier king. (He'd rather
be on his white horse than on his throne.) Part of the fun is
in Henry's surprising everyone by his resourcefulness, and
Branagh plays the same game with the audience. Just after
Henry has learned that his troops—mud-soaked, ragged, and
sick—will have to fight the fresh, finely accoutred French,
he says, "We are in God's hand." Rain comes pouring down
on him, and he raises weary, distrustful eyes to Heaven.
(The touch of irony is Olivier-like, but not too much so.)
And, at Agincourt, just after Henry has learned of the slaugh-
ter of the noncombatant page boys he listens to the compulsive chatter of the Welshman Fluellen (Ian Holm), a
pedant on the subject of military discipline, and the man's
nuttiness suddenly gets to him: with tears and blood still
streaking his face, he breaks into laughter. (This daring release feels like pure, spontaneous Branagh.)

This actor's earthy, doughy presence is the wrapping for
his beautiful, expressive voice. Emotion pours out of it with

surprising ease; he's conversational without sacrificing the poetry. His readings are a source of true pleasure. Listening to him, you think, With an instrument like that, he can play anything.

Yet he puts a symphony orchestra under the great St. Crispin's Day speech (which Olivier delivered a cappella). The "Non nobis domine" is magnificent as a male chorus joins the soloist; we hear it over the last view of the carnage at Agincourt, as Henry walks across the field of corpses, carrying Falstaff's murdered boy (Christian Bale). But then Branagh thickens the emotion with the rising sound of the orchestra, and the effect is banalized. He's given to thickening other actors' emotions the same way.

Much of the film has been set at night, with fiery lighting. Flames and smoke from the siege of Harfleur outline Henry as he sits on his white horse and inspires his soldiers to "cry 'God for Harry, England, and Saint George!' " Campfires and torches illumine the bivouac on the night before battle. Flickering fires give a Rembrandt glow to the interior of the inn where Falstaff (Robbie Coltrane) lies on his deathbed. There's a little too much Rembrandt glow; it's like the lush underscoring—it's imitation art.

Branagh is not an overnight great moviemaker. His attempts at spectacular effects strain his inventiveness (and he doesn't come up with anything comparable to the first flight of the arrows in the Olivier film or to the battle in Welles' *Chimes at Midnight).* Olivier staged the play between brackets, moving from the stage of the Globe Theatre to a larger world of artifice; he used color and design antinaturalistically. Branagh opens the play in a movie-studio soundstage and attempts a more realistic approach. It's rather basic, and it's overintense: closeups as a way to achieve immediacy, with many too many meaningful looks exchanged. (You may begin to fixate on the actors' trendy haircuts.) The battle scenes are powerful; shown very close in, the images of fighting and its aftermath are like details of a large—unseen—painting. But Branagh, like a clever gifted student, prolongs them, overworking his cadavers. He's a flamboyant realist. He has an appetite for theatrical excesses, as he shows in the deranged, Darth Vader entrance he gives himself. (He does everything but waggle a false nose at the camera.) He shows it, too, in some of Derek Jacobi's carrying-on as the chorus-narrator: Jacobi slithers about from place to place, and at times he's like a radio announcer at the racetrack trying to crank up the listeners' excitement. When the scenes require a light, stylized touch—Katherine of France (Emma Thompson) being given an English lesson by her companion (Geraldine McEwan); Henry wooing Katherine—Branagh echoes the Olivier version, but he can't quite find a rhythm. Since this fast-paced, fire-and-smoke movie lacks the formality that would give the courtship scene a tone, we don't know how to take it when Henry, having just met Katherine, says, "I love you."

Branagh's interpretation of *Henry V* emphasizes the price paid for war: the bloodshed. He's trying to make it into an anti-war film, an epic noir. But he can't quite dampen the play's rush of excitement—not with Henry delivering all those rousing words to his soldiers, calling them "we few, we happy few, we band of brothers." (Shakespeare shows how the English language itself can be turned into a patriotic symbol.) In keeping with his generation's supposed disillusion with war, Branagh has minimized the play's glorification of the English fighting man. His conception of how to film the play is to look closely at the conniving, the misgivings, the ego wars. He doesn't indicate why the French lost at Agincourt. We hear the Constable of France (Richard Easton) smugly saying "I have the best armor in the world," but Branagh doesn't show that the French and their horses were fatally encumbered by their armor and chain mail and other trappings; when the arrows hit—and obviously most of them would have hit the horses, whose bodies were more exposed—the riders fell into the water and mud, and were too weighed down to get up. They were massacred while they struggled like beetles on their backs. As Branagh stages the battle, with the two sides engaged in hand-to-hand combat, there's no way to understand why the English rather than the French won (except that God is with them).

But, scene by scene, there's always more than enough to take in. It's a company of stars: Judi Dench as Mistress Quickly, calling "Adieu" to her husband, Ancient Pistol (Robert Stephens); Paul Scofield as the melancholy French king whose face foretells the doom of his army; Brian Blessed as Exeter; Richard Briers as cherry-nosed Bardolph; Alec McCowen as Ely; and on and on. Branagh seems to have a special gift for bringing out great reactive moments: Ravenscroft's herald registering the probable consequences of the mistake the Dauphin has made in insulting this English king; the fear in the eyes of the English as they behold the hugeness of the approaching French army; Henry himself pretending not to be watching everyone watch him. Best of all, perhaps, is Ian Holm's Fluellen, too obsessed to gauge other people's reactions, his bright eyes flashing while he talks for his own satisfaction. The film's point of view leaves you without elation, but the actors are so up that you feel their pride in working on true dramatic poetry.

Valmont

The practiced seducer who is at the center of the Choderlos de Laclos novel *Les Liaisons Dangereuses* provides the title for *Valmont,* the new movie version, directed by Miloš Forman, from the script he prepared with the writer Jean-Claude Carrière. But there is no Valmont: he's just the blandly handsome actor Colin Firth, strapping and healthy and rather harmless. He doesn't have the energy to be a lecher, or even to make contact with the audience. There's always the danger that period movies will become intoxicated with jesters and fire-eaters and village fairs. *Valmont* has its share, but it's really into candlelit interiors and pale-rose bodices and rose-and-gold furniture. The story disappears among the cushions.

Like the novel, the late 1988 film version, *Dangerous Liaisons,* directed by Stephen Frears, gave a tightly coiled account of how the Marquise de Merteuil and the Vicomte de Valmont, French aristocrats in the late seventeen-seventies, plan their sexual conquests with the cold calculation that might be given to war games. She wants to get even with a former lover who is about to marry a teen-age virgin, and she asks Valmont to debauch the girl, Cécile, before the wedding takes place; he obliges, and he also amuses himself by breaking down the resistance of the virtuous young Mme. de Tourvel. When the Marquise realizes that he has fallen in love with his prey, she destroys the woman, and Valmont, and, inadvertently, herself.

That's also the framework of the story that is told here, except that now it's so lightweight and offhand there's no sting to it. It's so light you're not really sure what, if anything, happens to Mme. de Tourvel. The nature of the relationship between the Marquise and Valmont isn't clear, and you can't tell why she turns against him. It's no longer a tale of the ruthless manipulations of two aristocrats, who turn innocent people into pawns. I don't know what the theme could be. The novel is told by an intricate series of letters; Forman has stated that he and Carrière agreed, "We would not try to follow what the letters told us had happened—we would try to figure out what really happened before the letters were written." Looney Tunes! It might be fun to fantasize from a novel that way, but Forman appears to think he's getting at some sort of truth. It's all still in his head. *Valmont* doesn't have the affected speech that has often been the curse of costume pictures; the dialogue is simple. But the scenes don't build to anything; they drift away.

Or, worse, they turn into operetta. That's what happens to the background material that Forman brings in. He shows us the virgin-obsessed lover, Gercourt (Jeffrey Jones), whom the Marquise arranges to make a fool of, and he makes a central character of the fifteen-year-old Cécile (Fairuza Balk), who is infatuated with her seventeen-year-old music teacher (Henry Thomas). As this material has been worked up, it has an obviousness that could be mistaken for exuberance. Luckily, Fairuza Balk (she was Dorothy in *Return to Oz)* does show a comic flair for dopey sweetness, and when Cécile sings, at her music lessons and at a social gathering, her mixture of innocence and naughtiness is amusing. (A Forman type, she's a ringer for the young wife in his *Amadeus.)*

A couple of the performers win out over the bewildering conception. Meg Tilly, of the Eurasian-princess eyes (you can't mistake her for anyone else), is a believably sensitive, modest Mme. de Tourvel. The only sensuality that Valmont ever shows is in his formal, reserved dance with Tourvel: the fear of his sexuality which she's trying to repress and the emotion he doesn't yet know he feels come together. And the veteran actress Fabia Drake is marvellously entertaining as Valmont's ancient but still worldly aunt; the role is a bit reminiscent of the wise, lovable dowagers in old Hollywood costumers, and there are a few too many cuts to Drake for a laugh, but she's a solid, witty performer.

The actress who suffers most from frequent closeups is Annette Bening, as the Marquise de Merteuil. She does very precise, skilled work, but she's shown over and over with the same flirtatious smiles. This Merteuil is so pretty that we never get past it to the ugliness in her, or to her strength. If I hadn't seen Bening do stunning, often harsh work in the theatre and on television, what she does here would have made me think her a performer of excruciatingly limited resources.

Nobody in the movie has any weight. Even the characters' crimes seem petulant, superficial, not really meant. In an interview one of the cast members said of Forman, "Miloš was not interested in having us behave like awful people. He was interested in the *humanity* of the people, or the *humanness.*" That may help to explain the general insipidity. In the novel, the characters are often most human at their most awful. It's their humanness that's scary.

NOVEMBER 27, 1989

BUSTY, TWISTY, FISHY

Blaze

The love story of that old raspy-voiced rooster Earl K. Long, three-time governor of Louisiana, and the young red-headed stripper Blaze Starr is bawdy and satirical—it's Rabelaisian. It's a rich subject for a movie, and Ron Shelton, who wrote and directed *Blaze,* responds to it. (At least, he responds intellectually.) Ol' Earl was on one of his regular visits to the Bourbon Street burlesque clubs when he walked into the Sho-Bar and saw Blaze Starr. Life was a banquet for Earl, and when he met Blaze he'd found the centerpiece. It was early in January, 1959, and she had been in New Orleans only three or four days, but she had been working in Baltimore and Philadelphia and other cities, and was already a headliner. As she said in the autobiography *(Blaze Starr: My Life As Told to Huey Perry)* that's part of the source material for this movie, she loved stripping as much as Ol' Earl loved politics. He was a white-haired sixty-three when they met; she was in her slim, rounded twenties—ripe and bouncy. Earl was a hungry man; she would be the woman he could never get enough of.

Shelton (who made *Bull Durham)* cherishes Blaze (Lolita Davidovich, in her first major screen role), and he adores Ol' Earl (Paul Newman), who used his swamp smarts to fight the white supremacists. A. J. Liebling, who covered the Long politicking of 1959 and 1960 for *The New Yorker,* adored him, too. (The articles came out in hardcover as *The Earl of Louisiana,* which was reprinted in the good, fat 1982 compendium *Liebling at Home.)* Liebling, who says that he'd left New York "thinking of Earl as a Peckerwood Caligula," came to regard him as "the only effective Civil Rights man in the South." Shelton doesn't quite engage with the political ideas, and doesn't quite capture the richness of the love story, either. For a long time, we don't get into the film. Newman's Earl doesn't have the natural exuberance that we expect, and we don't feel as if we're hurtling along dirt roads in a Cadillac with tail fins. We're watching Earl K. Long, yet we never get to see his real oratorical genius with poor voters. (Liebling—a man not easily impressed—describes his own response to an Earl Long speech: "He called for a show of hands by everybody who was going to vote for him, and I waved both of mine.")

Shelton skitters over things: we don't feel the full effect on Earl of that first view of bosomy, overscaled Blaze in the spotlight; we don't get a moment where it hits us that the two belong together. But if the movie is a little flat, it's never boring, and it offers a ribald view of Southern politics that contrasts with the stern, melodramatic portrait of Earl's older brother Huey as a fascistic demagogue—a Peckerwood Caligula—in the 1949 film *All the King's Men.* (An incident demonstrating Earl's foxiness—he gets jobs for black doctors and nurses in the state hospital system by pretending to be shocked to see white personnel taking care of black patients—is actually drawn from Huey Long's life.) What sustains the viewer's interest is the joke that Ol' Earl doesn't fit the liberal-left stereotypes of what a virtuous politician should be.

The center of the movie is the event in Earl Long's third

term which became a national scandal and defeated him in his 1959 gubernatorial campaign. Ol' Earl was fighting the voter-registration law that was being used to disenfranchise blacks, and, rattled, angry, and maybe a little drunk, he took the floor of the state legislature and shouted, "You got to recognize that niggers is human beings!" The legislators thought he'd gone crazy—not because of his choice of words but because of his views. And, with the enthusiastic help of his estranged wife (who was upset about his dalliance with Blaze), he was given injections of drugs, hauled off to a mental hospital, and locked up. His beliefs got him diagnosed as a paranoid schizophrenic. (It's startling to look at newspapers and news magazines of the period and see how scathingly they described his outburst as evidence of insanity.) Confused and incoherent, he was still able to use his authority as governor to fire the mental-health officials and appoint a new top man, who promptly released him. (Afterward, he referred to himself as "a tried and true man, half crazy and half intelligent.")

Paul Newman has trouble with his earthy, expansive role. He just isn't the kind of actor to play a spellbinder who knows how to work up a crowd. Yes, he's red-faced and choleric here, and he uses the low, hoarse voice of a lifelong stump speaker. But it sounds false coming out of him; Newman's Earl Long seems an eccentric husk of a man. Newman tries hard to play a man of instinct, a man who's dishevelled and larger than life. And you're aware of the effort. Newman doesn't transform. He belongs in trim, self-contained roles— that's what he's built for. (There's something essentially private about Paul Newman.) Yet when he acts what he doesn't really have in him something works in his favor. We in the audience are touched by Newman. (We love him the way Louisiana voters loved Ol' Earl.) Our affection for him begins to fill in the character, and his acting fills it in, too. You can feel Earl's gratitude for Blaze's availability and generosity; this is the woman who liked to call the men she performed for "you li'l ol' evil tomcats"—you can feel how happy she makes him.

Born circa 1935, the year Huey Long was assassinated, Blaze came from a family with eleven kids who lived in a two-room shack in a Dogpatch in West Virginia. She left home at fourteen and became a carhop, and a couple of years later she was working in a Mayflower Donut shop; soon she was an underage stripper. By the time she met Earl, she'd been through enough to appreciate a courtly big spender. Lolita Davidovich, a Canadian-born actress (of Yugoslav parentage), resembles the real Blaze Starr and handles the twang very deftly; she has a lovely, creamy-skinned figure (padded in her clothes) and a wide-faced sensuality, and she's been given mountainous flaming-red hair. Davidovich doesn't show the overblown personality of a burlesque star, but she moves triumphantly in her comic steamy routines. She touches the right chord: the way she plays the part, you never doubt that Blaze loves Earl. His being the governor is part of what she loves about him, but she doesn't stop loving him when he's out of office. Blaze Starr herself—she's in her mid-fifties now—appears in a scene backstage at the Sho-Bar. She's in the dressing room that Paul Newman's Earl comes into—he pays his respects to her with a kiss on her shoulder.

Shelton isn't a leering director; he's protective of both the actress and the woman she's playing. He mythologizes Blaze Starr, in a clearheaded way. Shelton has a lyrical sense of America (as he showed in *Bull Durham*). He isn't antagonistic toward his characters. He likes the fast-talking strip-bar manager (Robert Wuhl) who puts the make on the scared young Blaze, and he enjoys the Southern politicians: Thibodeaux (Jerry Hardin), La Grange (Gailard Sartain), Tuck (Jeffrey DeMunn), and old Doc Ferriday (Garland Bunting). He doesn't find it necessary to condemn the professional segregationist Willie Rainach (James Harper) or the hot-under-the-collar police captain (Stanley Tucci). They're all family, like members of Preston Sturges's stock companies.

By the end, when Ol' Earl is running for Congress in 1960, and drives himself so hard that he has a heart attack on Election Day, we understand his refusal to go to a hospital—or even to lie down—until after the polls are closed. (He's afraid his voters won't turn out if they hear he's in bad shape.) On the street, staggering between cronies who hold him, he greets passersby and calls out "Vote for Earl!" as he makes it to the hotel lobby, where he can be propped up. Newman has won us over; we've come to understand that politics is life to Earl, and it's full of surprises. (He won the election; it was just fifteen months since he'd been locked away as insane.)

Ron Shelton didn't have to do much mythologizing with crude, gallant Earl; almost all the political side of the film is factual. Shelton just does some juggling here and there, moving the incidents around. *Blaze* should be a better picture than it is; it's a lame, rhythmless piece of work. Still, it's about populism, corruption, and raw high spirits all working together. It's a last hurrah for a high-powered ol' tomcat. Paul Newman begins too far into the character; we have to catch up. By the end, we're with him.

Back to the Future Part II

Back to the Future Part II is all manic and wacky. It's all twists. The amiably mad inventor Doc Brown (Christopher Lloyd) rushes into the frame to tell teen-age Marty McFly (Michael J. Fox) about new emergencies in the year 2015 or 1955 or an alternate 1985 (brought about by their disrupting the space-time continuum), and they go hurtling off to set things right. I've never seen another movie in such a hurry or with so much shouting. Or maybe I have—*Who Framed Roger Rabbit,* which, like this one, was directed by Robert Zemeckis. But I found *Roger Rabbit* such a nightmare that I put it out of mind; it's in a horrible genre all its own. *Future II* isn't nightmarish; it's sort of fun. But there's no real zest in it. It's more like a board game—or a video game—than a movie.

Zemeckis and his frequent writing partner Bob Gale are themselves obsessed mad inventors; they devise screwball-comedy contraptions that rival Doc Brown's DeLorean time machine. Their script for Spielberg's *1941* and their scripts that Zemeckis has directed—*I Wanna Hold Your Hand, Used Cars,* and the two *Futures*—are all marked by mechanical ingeniousness, but usually there's a spark of boyish impetuousness, too. Their movies are jokes that get carried away with themselves and swallow the universe. You can feel the kinetic impulse to go too far that drives these pictures forward; you can share in it, and feel terrific. But *Future II*—which is the middle film of a trilogy—smacks of the assembly line. All our attention is focused on where Doc and Marty are in time, which of their multiple selves or their relatives they're going to run into, and what the bullies Biff and Griff (both played by Thomas F. Wilson) are up to. The inventiveness seems to be on a treadmill in a void.

When Doc rushes onscreen (in 1985) and tells Marty that they have to go to 2015, because something has gone wrong with Marty's children, it's just a gimmick to get the picture off the ground; we barely get a look at "the children" (both played by Fox). Characters interact with themselves at different ages; they're multiplied all over the place. But the only humor is in the special-effects multiplication processes (which probably account for the film's looking so dark); there's no ingenuity in the creation of the characters themselves. (Making the Marty of 2015 a business executive who's a cringing loser goes against the grain of everything we've seen Fox do as the young Marty, and the movie seems rather offhand about making Marty's son a wimpish twit.) There are no performances—except, maybe, in a nasty scene or two featuring Wilson's young Biff—because the continuum is too speedy for acting. Marty's girlfriend, Jennifer (Elizabeth Shue), is brought on board the time machine and then rendered unconscious and slung around like a sack of potatoes. Lea Thompson, who brought a dazed sexiness to the role of Marty's mother-to-be in the first film, is now split into three selves, all of them blanks. Christopher Lloyd has just one real moment; it comes at the end—he evinces surprise and promptly faints.

Future II got made because, as the Universal publicity material puts it, "in its initial release, *Back to the Future* earned over $350 million worldwide, and emerged as the top grossing film of 1985." Obviously, if Zemeckis and Gale had not agreed to make the sequels themselves their characters and conception would have been turned over to other hands. It's no wonder that the film seems more hectic and more drab than the first. It doesn't have anything like the first film's what-the-hell Oedipal humor; maybe so much is at stake here that Zemeckis and Gale don't feel the freedom to be funny—they're caught in a machine-driven hysteria. The inventiveness is fast and furious, but low in spirit. Inventiveness has become a formula. And yet the construction keeps you going—it's like a frenzied daydream that you don't want to break off.

The Little Mermaid

Hans Christian Andersen's tear-stained *The Little Mermaid* is peerlessly mythic. It's the closest thing women have to a feminine Faust story. The Little Mermaid gives up her lovely voice—her means of expression—in exchange for legs, so she'll be able to walk on land and attract the man she loves. If she can win him in marriage, she will gain an immortal soul; if she can't, she'll be foam on the sea.

I didn't expect the new Disney *The Little Mermaid* to be Faust, but after reading the reviews ("everything an animated feature should be," "reclaims the movie house as a dream palace," and so on) I expected to see something more than a bland reworking of old Disney fairy tales, featuring a teen-age tootsie in a flirty seashell bra. This is a technologically sophisticated cartoon with just about all the simpering old Disney values in place. (The Faust theme acquires a wholesome family sub-theme.) The film does have a cheerful calypso number ("Under the Sea"), and the color is bright—at least, until the mermaid goes on land, when everything seems to dull out.

Are we trying to put kids into some sort of moral-aesthetic safe house? Parents seem desperate for harmless family entertainment. Probably they don't mind this movie's being vapid, because the whole family can share it, and no one is offended. We're caught in a culture warp. Our children are flushed with pleasure when we read them *Where the Wild Things Are* or Roald Dahl's sinister stories. Kids are ecstatic watching videos of *The Secret of* NIMH and *The Dark Crystal*. Yet here comes the press telling us that *The Little Mermaid* is "due for immortality." People are made to feel that this stale pastry is what they should be taking their kids to, that it's art for children. And when they see the movie they may believe it, because this *Mermaid* is just a slightly updated version of what their parents took them to. They've been imprinted with Disney-style kitsch.

DECEMBER 11, 1989

PULLING THE
RUG OUT

Enemies, A Love Story

Isaac Bashevis Singer sold his novel *Enemies, A Love Story,* a movie was made of it, and he still possesses it—that's a novelist's dream. Singer constructed a post-Holocaust sex farce with three passionately jealous women in love with a stealthy, guilt-ridden man. It's about refugees who are lost, who go on living in New York and chasing each other into bed after they've vanished from their lives. The director, Paul Mazursky, has gathered a superbly balanced cast and kept the action so smooth that the viewer is carried along on a tide of mystical slyness. It's overwhelming.

Ron Silver is quiet, self-effacing Herman Broder, a middle-class Polish Jewish intellectual who survived the Holocaust by hiding in a hayloft for three years; Yadwiga (Margaret Sophie Stein), a Gentile peasant who had been a servant in his family, risked her life to take care of him. When the war was over and he learned that his wife and children were dead, he married the sweet goose Yadwiga out of gratitude (and maybe a little lust) and brought her to New York with him. Now it's 1949. Herman and his devoted slavey Yadwiga live in Brooklyn, with a window overlooking the Wonder Wheel at Coney Island. He works as a ghostwriter, turning out sermons and books for a celebrity-lecturer rabbi, but he tells his wife he's a book salesman; that gives him an excuse to be away from home. He keeps another residence, in the Bronx, with his hot-tempered mistress, Masha (Lena Olin), a survivor of the camps. Herman lives in fear; he's still in hiding. But when he makes love to Masha he forgets the terrors of the past. It's the only time he forgets.

Herman invents dangers, and not only because he's anxiously trying to cover up his double domestic arrangements. The guardedness, the secrecy, the guile are all necessary to him; they're his strategy for survival. He was furtive even before he was traumatized by the Holocaust. It's part of Herman's passive nature to lie, rather than to risk showdowns. He can't make decisions; they have to be forced on him. He doesn't even initiate the almost constant sexual activity he's involved in; women keep jumping his bones, and he acquiesces. He doesn't want to give up his shining-eyed, pugnosed Yadwiga, who looks after him as if he were a lord, and he certainly doesn't want to give up the wild, teasing Masha, whose sexy voice is enough to fog his senses. When she thinks she's pregnant and threatens to leave him if she has to have an abortion, he marries her, too. And when his first wife, Tamara (Anjelica Huston), who was shot and left in a pile of corpses but dragged herself to safety, and has been in a camp in Russia, arrives on Manhattan's Lower East Side, he doesn't want to give her up, either. He would like to remain a trigamist. Who can blame him? Ron Silver makes Herman's predicament understandable. And Herman is understandably terrified of hurting anybody.

Herman conceals basic information about himself from the rabbi who employs him; he conceals different things from each of the three women. Then, at a lavish party given by the rabbi, Herman's worlds collide, and he's confused about what he's hidden from whom. It's a situation out of a classic boudoir farce, but Herman and his three wives—Tamara, the witchlike, seductive mother figure, with black-dyed hair; Yadwiga, the natural-blond child; Masha, the lover, with thick, dark, reddish hair—are not the characters we're accustomed to seeing in Frenchy bedrooms.

It's a central joke of the material that Herman and his Jewish wives, Tamara and Masha, who all suffered as Jews, are intellectually sophisticated nonbelievers but are emotionally half-believers. (They abuse God the Sadist, who put them in the hands of the Nazis.) The only practicing Jew is the simple Yadwiga, who has become a convert in order to be a dutiful, pious wife to Herman and bear his child. Yadwiga and her efforts to be Jewish are a source of amusement to Tamara and Masha. (In a moment of stress, Yadwiga forgets herself, and makes the sign of the cross.) Tamara and Masha can't help being Jewish. For them, it's not a matter of religious faith; it's a matter of memories, and of being lost. In their nightmares, they're still in Poland. When they wake up, they're in limbo.

Anjelica Huston's Tamara feels dead because her children are dead (though they return in her dreams and that invigorates her); she's a strong, capable woman, with an erotic aura, an accented, Garboesque voice, and knowing, sidelong glances. She takes over a shop specializing in Judaica— books, ornaments, ritual artifacts—and she holds Herman's life together. Lena Olin's Masha, who lives with her hyperemotional mother (Judith Malina), quarrelling and making up, both of them constantly in a state of nerves, is diabolically willful. She lives on tea, cigarettes, and liquor, and keeps Herman in torment with her hysterical threats that she'll go away and he'll never see her again. Masha is educated and smart, but she works as a cashier in a cafeteria; she has no connection with her job, her environment. She barely notices what country she's in, yet she lives intensely in the present, and pulls Herman into it with her. She's all id; she's part Angel of Death.

Ron Silver's owl-faced Herman, with his wise, sneaky expressions, may seem an unlikely pivot for this sex comedy—

he doesn't quite have the spoiled-Jewish-prince narcissism to attract these women—but the more you see of him the funnier and more likely he becomes. Herman has fear and irony in his face, and you can read his thoughts, if you ever get around to noticing him. If you lift up the brim of his brown fedora, there it all is. This ghostwriter to a rabbi (he's also the ghost of the scholars he's descended from) may sometimes pray, but he only believes in lust and hiding. Singer puts it simply:

> At moments when Herman fantasized about a new meta-physic, or even a new religion, he based everything on the attraction of the sexes. In the beginning was lust.

And following close upon that is his obsessive, prurient hunt for evidence of sexual betrayal; he can't bear the possibility that any of his three wives has ever been unfaithful to him—he schemes and wheedles to find out.

There's no special pleading or self-pity in Mazursky's view of the characters—not even in his view of ghostly Herman. These refugees who go on living after they've died retain their petty follies in an exacerbated form. When Herman first sees Tamara after the gap of years in which their children have been slaughtered, he says, "I didn't know you were alive," and she complains, "You never knew." The movie is full of jokes, such as the moment in a subway station when Herman, who has been commuting to the rabbi's place and from one domicile to another, can't trust his instincts and has to pause before mounting the steps to Brooklyn, the Bronx, or Manhattan. Herman's love life is a map of poor-Jewish New York, and when he goes to the rabbi's apartment, on Central Park West, he climbs the social ladder. The loud, big-hearted rabbi (Alan King) is the picture of happy assimilation. He would like to help Herman make his way in the city; he doesn't understand that Herman is a Jewish Bartleby the Scrivener and can't be helped—he has to recede, fade away, flee.

The plot suggests a tragicomic opera, yet Mazursky's tone is even-tempered, restrained. There's nothing aseptic about this restraint—it has its own deeply crazy turmoil. But restraint is not what we've come to expect from Mazursky. He has always adored the show-biz tradition of turning your own emotionality into something brazenly entertaining. Here he's warm and sensual without being showy; he seems fulfilled. The characters go in circles, getting themselves into sex in order to forget other things and then waking up back where they were. Mazursky pulls the rug out from under us, and we drop through the farce.

The movie is richly satisfying; it's an act of homage to a world-class comedian with a dirty mind of genius. Singer himself is a ghost who writes: *Enemies,* which came out in English in 1972, was his first novel set in America, and was, of course, written in the ghost language Yiddish. The minor characters—Malina as Masha's mother, Mazursky as the husband Masha must get rid of in order to marry Herman, Phil Leeds as Pesheles, the gnomish blabbermouth who reveals Herman's secrets at the party—seem to have folk roots in Singer's world. And Lena Olin gives Masha a feverish urgency. Olin's Masha has lowdown prettiness and transcendent beauty. The performance is conceived with a different kind of verve from that of Olin's bowler-hatted Sabina in *The Unbearable Lightness of Being.* Masha gives in to her impulses like a Dostoyevski heroine. Singer sums her up:

> Masha was the best argument Herman knew for Schopenhauer's thesis that intelligence is nothing more than a servant of blind will.

That's exactly how Olin plays her. Masha, with her irrational intelligence, is heated and bold in a way that gives the movie the demonism it needs. She and Tamara are both glinting-eyed sirens, but Masha is Herman's chief sexual enemy. She justifies his need to hide. The soundtrack features klezmer—a band with a clarinet (played here by Giora Feidman), trumpets, a snare drum, a bass drum, and a guitar or balalaika, performing a type of medieval Jewish party music. The sound has a whirling, brassy plangency. It's plaintive yet pitiless—it goes with the Wonder Wheel and Masha's tarty walk.

Driving Miss Daisy

The surprise of the director Bruce Beresford's movie of Alfred Uhry's much honored play *Driving Miss Daisy* is that it's been "opened up" just enough to satisfy our curiosity and make things seem natural, without impairing the structure—which is still a series of two-character sketches. There are a few dead spots at the beginning, when the camera loiters in Miss Daisy's house and we seem to be asked to observe how quiet life was for the tasteful rich in Atlanta in 1948, but after ten minutes or so the film finds its rhythm, and the spacious house, with its fine woodwork and interior archways, becomes a character—it has a presence. (And it helps to make Miss Daisy's economic security palpable.) I prefer the movie to the stage version, which felt too mild and sincere and messagey; it's an ingratiating play about race relations—what the theatre had been waiting for. Uhry, who did the screen adaptation, seems to have pared away a little flab. And the movie, by bringing the characters close up, creates a stronger emotional involvement. The material is full of manipulative bits—it's virtually all manipulative bits— but Beresford understands how to work them while cutting down on their obviousness. He gives them a light, airy texture; he sets them in the sun.

Jessica Tandy is tightfisted, suspicious Daisy Werthan, a Jewish widow of seventy-two who's determined to do things her own way. She drives her own way, and wrecks her shiny new Chrysler. No insurance company will give her coverage, so her son, Boolie (Dan Aykroyd), who runs the cotton mill started by his father and grandfather, suggests she hire a chauffeur to drive her new Hudson. She has a black housekeeper (Esther Rolle), whom she's been pleased with for many years, but she's outraged at the idea of adding to her household: she doesn't want her privacy invaded, and she regards servants as probable thieves. Seeing her trapped in her house by her contrariness, Boolie disregards her wishes and hires a black chauffeur, Hoke Colburn (Morgan Freeman), a widower about a decade younger than she is. Boolie arranges to pay Hoke's salary (in order to block her claim that a chauffeur would be a waste of her money) and sends him over. But Boolie, a relaxed Jewish good-old-boy Southerner, plump and content, can't persuade his mother to accept the driver as part of her household. It's up to Hoke to win acceptance. And so we have the entertainment of watching the dignified, shrewd Hoke use all his wiles on this anxious, straight-backed old biddy, courting her day after day. At first, she ignores him; then she rebuffs him. She spurns his efforts to make himself useful about the house and the garden. He's deferent and patient, saying "Yes'm" when she puts him down. (He says other things under his breath.) And finally, after six days, his well-mannered persistence wins out. She lets him drive her to the Piggly Wiggly (and pecks at him every inch of the way). That's only the first step in her acceptance of his services; he goes on courting her for twenty-five years.

The movie is the story of the companionship that develops between these two: the thrifty former schoolteacher, who grew up poor and still sees herself as poor, and the illiterate, proud, handsome Hoke. Their story is touched by the changes in Southern life during the years they spend together; the movie ends in 1973, covering the time of the civil-rights movement, and that's more than incidental. But the two are not representative figures. The movie is essentially about how Hoke changes Miss Daisy. Their relationship becomes closer and deeper, and as she ages and becomes more vulnerable and fearful she comes to accept him as her best friend.

The movie is really built. Uhry knows how to make the developments comic: he's got this huffy, ornery woman to play everything off. As Jessica Tandy's Miss Daisy becomes older and more dependent on Hoke, she seems to undergo a spiritual transformation: her skin becomes translucent, she looks poetically frail. But she doesn't go soft: she's as sharp-tongued and bossy as ever. I've seen Jessica Tandy in many movies, going back to her American début, in 1944, in *The Seventh Cross,* and she has never been as lovely and varied as she is here, at eighty, playing Miss Daisy, from seventy-two to ninety-seven. She's more subtly comic now, and she risks more; the very old Miss Daisy has the grin of a gamine. The role (based on Uhry's grandmother, with a few great-aunts thrown in) gives her a chance to show glimpses of what she's learned in a lifetime of acting, and she has the simple assurance to hold us in her palm. It's a crowning performance; Miss Daisy is convincingly likable and impossible.

As Daisy's son, Dan Aykroyd sounds more Southern than she does, and this feels right. By temperament she's not a relaxed drawler, like Boolie; she speaks like the prim schoolmarm she was. Aykroyd's Boolie is a man of great forbearance: he has to be, to get along with his mother and with his social-climbing, fanny-twitching wife, Florine (Patti LuPone, in a vital, funny caricature). Boolie is an easygoing onlooker; he enjoys watching Hoke break down his mother's stubbornness. This may be the first time Aykroyd has stayed within the limits of a screen character that wasn't shaped for his crazy-galoot style of comedy, and, with the help of a first-rate aging specialist, who thickens him, he handles the twenty-five-year span like a veteran charmer. He's quite wonderful as the humorous, unheroic Boolie; maybe the company he was in inspired him.

Morgan Freeman is a master of irony. The role of Hoke isn't written with the fullness that went into Daisy; chances are that Uhry didn't get to observe as many sides of his grandmother's chauffeur (on whom the character is modelled). But the Memphis-born Freeman—the one Southerner of the three (Tandy is from London, Aykroyd from Canada)—fills in the character from what he knows of Southern blacks' verbal styles of accommodation and of self-amusement. Tandy partners him flawlessly; their performances achieve a beautiful equilibrium. But it's his movie. We identify with Hoke—with his carefulness, his reserve. We feel the slight tension in his not being able to express himself directly. The speed and power that Freeman has shown in other roles are kept out of sight here; instead we get the low, resonant voice (with high notes when he's harried), the inflections of his "Yes'm," and wit in every line of his body. He's playing the most courtly and dependable of black servants of an earlier era, yet he keeps us aware that this man is never servile; Hoke is always measuring the distance between white Southerners and himself.

When Hoke has his job interview with Boolie, he tells him that he likes working for Jewish people, and gradually we see why. Miss Daisy is stiffly defensive on race issues; she claims to be free of prejudice. But she frequently senses her own vulnerability to insult, and she feels a bond with Hoke. (She detests her daughter-in-law, who doesn't know how to treat servants—i.e., doesn't understand what's due them.) The movie is about the love between blacks and whites (Jewish division) at a time when a wealthy Southern Jewish matron plays mahjongg, is addressed by her servants as Miss Daisy, and eats alone in the dining room even after she has become an advocate of civil rights. It's a time when a man like Hoke goes on weighing his words to the end of his days.

The movie gives us an insight into the author's background that we didn't get from the play, but it's still a rigged view of the past. The black man is made upright, considerate, humane—he's made perfect—so that nothing will disturb our appreciation of the gentle, bittersweet reverie we're watching. Yet there's a memorable unstressed moment when the radio in the sunny house carries the sound of Gabriela Benackova singing the numinous "Song to the Moon," from Dvořák's opera *Rusalka,* and we get a sense of how lonely and empty Miss Daisy's life is. And after the housekeeper dies (at work in the kitchen) Miss Daisy, Boolie, and Hoke sit together on a bench at the funeral; they listen to Indra A. Thomas and the Little Friendship Missionary Baptist Church Choir (of Decatur, Georgia), and maybe they're thinking, like you, that it's worth dying to have singing like that. The bursting forth of sensuality in that church, while Miss Daisy sits pale and pinched, is part of the (blessedly) unspoken meaning of the movie. *Driving Miss Daisy* retains its coziness and its slightness, but it has been filmed eloquently.

DECEMBER 25, 1989

MELODRAMA/ CARTOON/MESS

Music Box

A few years ago, the TV news was dominated by images of the big, square head of John Demjanjuk, the Ukrainian immigrant who, after decades as a Cleveland autoworker, was accused of being Ivan the Terrible of Treblinka. We watched as aged victims swore that Demjanjuk was their torturer, and we listened as he protested that it was all a case of mistaken identity, with papers rigged against him by the Soviet bloc. The new Costa-Gavras movie, *Music Box*, presents us with a fictional case based on Demjanjuk, and it has that same kind of fascination. Can the witnesses who testify against the retired Chicago steelworker Mike Laszlo (Armin Mueller-Stahl) be mistaken, or was he, in his youth, the monster they describe? Jessica Lange plays Laszlo's daughter, Ann Talbot, who is a lawyer and is defending him at a hearing that could cost him his citizenship; if he loses, he'll be sent back to Hungary, where the Communist government is waiting to try him for war crimes. Ann believes that the case was instigated because her father had been active in demonstrations against Hungarian dignitaries who have

239

come on visits to the United States, and she may be right
about that. But is there another man hidden inside the kindly
father she has always known?

The emotional core of the movie is that during the trial,
as the Second World War victims give their accounts of what
the sadistic young police officer did to them, Ann begins to
lose faith in her father's innocence. She's a skilled attorney,
and she presses on, but everything she has believed about
the upright, honorable widower who raised her shifts and
crumbles.

When the cast and the script are right for Costa-Gavras—
as they are here—he has the knack of giving tempo and
urgency to courtroom scenes. Others try for it; he really
does it. This melodrama has the pull of a thriller. Shot in
and around Chicago and in Budapest, it has no flashbacks
and none of the usual shock apparatus of movies about wartime atrocities: the impact of *Music Box* comes from the
testimony (and behavior) of the elderly witnesses. We take
in what they're saying, and we watch Ann taking it in. Costa-
Gavras provides a low-key, controlled atmosphere, and Jessica Lange fills it with passion that's begging for release. In
a recent interview, she was quoted as saying, "I love the
sound of the cello." That's her emotional sound in this role:
intelligent, searching, womanly.

Everyone I know wishes we could see Lange in more
fluffy-blonde comedy roles. (We long for another *Tootsie.*)
But she has been developing a deeper range. Her character
here doesn't have the dimensions of her Frances Farmer,
but within the limits of a melodrama she verges on the
astounding. Lange is one of those star performers—Diane
Keaton is another—whose characters don't necessarily come
on as stars. Ann Talbot is a brunette in plain business suits,
and her being slightly worn makes her beauty more accessible. Her curly hair suggests a bad perm; it sticks out in
funny ways and has no shine, no highlights. (It's as if there
were no hairdresser on the set.) Ann is a busy woman with
other things to think about, and we get to see the workings

of her mind. The competitive smartness of the opposing lawyers is always part of the drama of good courtroom movies, and Ann, working against a rather surly government attorney (Frederic Forrest), springs traps with crisp efficiency.

Costa-Gavras is a remarkably lucid storyteller. He doesn't dawdle, and you have to pay close attention to the courtroom evidence: things are planted very fast, and if you're not on your toes you'll lose out when the payoffs come. There's an excitement in this tightly constructed narrative: it builds, and the complications draw it even tighter. But you're conscious of how the film is setting you up; the screenwriter, Joe Eszterhas (who's the son of Hungarian refugees), lays things out almost too professionally. His commercialism can be like cold water in the face, after you've watched a procession of wonderfully varied character actors putting a lifetime of training into a few minutes of testimony. (Two of the most moving are Sol Frieder, as Istvan Boday, a bald old man with a goatee, who describes the murder of his family on the banks of the Danube, and Elzbieta Czyzewska, as a precise, closed-faced woman who describes how she was raped.) Eszterhas uses historical crimes very astutely, but he forces them into an entertainment package alongside old-Hollywood devices. The final plot developments (after the music box makes its appearance) are over-extended, and they feel fake. The focus of the material goes wrong: what we're watching is suddenly too much about Ann's suffering—movie-star suffering.

Costa-Gavras seems to have little pockets of innocence about how Americans live. There is nothing here as far out of kilter as a lot of the stuff in *Betrayed* was, but a weirdly misconceived black character, Georgine (Cheryl Lynn Bruce), who's some sort of crack legal investigator, floats around and seems to function as Ann's all-purpose aide. (In one scene, she turns up in African robes; she out-dresses her boss.) But Costa-Gavras has his wits about him in the key relationships. The German actor Armin Mueller-Stahl keeps the father from becoming too easy for the audience to decipher: he's a formal, Old World father—you never feel you know him. (So you understand his daughter's not knowing him.) And the film balances the daughter's smart toughness in her cross-examinations with the father's hand-some, cold-blue-eyed righteousness. I expected Costa-Gavras and Eszterhas to show us some connection between the father's mental dexterity and the daughter's choice of career, but maybe we were meant to pick that up for our-selves. What counts is the Old World, New World texture that Jessica Lange brings to toughness. Her beautiful throat-iness counts. She has the will and the technique to take a role that's really no more than a function of melodrama and turn this movie into a cello concerto.

Roger & Me

I've heard it said that Michael Moore's muckraking docu-mentary *Roger & Me* is scathing and Voltairean. I've read that Michael Moore is "a satirist of the Reagan period equal in talent to Mencken and [Sinclair] Lewis," and "an irre-pressible new humorist in the tradition of Mark Twain and Artemus Ward." But the film I saw was shallow and face-tious, a piece of gonzo demagoguery that made me feel cheap for laughing.

Roger is Roger Smith, the chairman of General Motors, who, in Moore's account, closed eleven GM plants in Flint, Michigan, in 1986 (despite big profits), laid off thirty thou-sand workers, and set up plants in Mexico, where the wage rate was seventy cents an hour. In the film, he's directly responsible for bringing about the city's (unconvincingly speedy) deterioration. Flint, GM's birthplace, is also Michael Moore's home town, and Moore, a journalist, previously in-

experienced in film, set out, with a camera crew, ostensibly
to persuade Roger Smith to come to Flint and see the human
results of his policies. This mock mission is the peg that
Moore hangs the picture on: he pursues Roger Smith over a
span of two and a half years, from February, 1987, to August, 1989. Moore, who directed, produced, and wrote the
film, and is its star, has defined his approach: "I knew the
theme would be 'looking for Roger' and showing what was
happening in Flint during this time period."

What happens is that Moore, a big, shambling joker in
windbreaker and baseball cap, narrates his analysis of the
ironies and idiocies of what's going on, and deadpans his
way through interviews with an assortment of unlikely people, who are used as stooges, as filler. He asks them broad
questions about the high rate of unemployment and the
soaring crime rate, and their responses make them look like
phonies or stupes; those who try to block his path or duck
his queries appear to be flunkies. Low-level GM public-
relations people make squirmy, evasive statements; elderly
women on a golf course are confused as to what's wanted
of them; visiting entertainers are cheery and optimistic; Miss
Michigan, who is about to take part in the Miss America
Pageant, tries to look concerned and smiles her prettiest.
What does Moore expect? Why are these people being made
targets for the audience's laughter? The camera makes brutal
fun of a woman who's trying to earn money as an Amway
color consultant, and it stares blankly at a woman who's
supplementing her government checks by raising rabbits.
(For a minute or two, we seem to be watching an Errol
Morris movie.) Moore's final jab is at a woman with a Jewish
name, whose job promoting the attractions of the city has
been eliminated. He asks her what she's going to do next.
When she says she's going to Tel Aviv, Moore seems to be
drawing the conclusion that the rats are deserting the ship;
something distasteful hovers over the closing credits.

Moore is the only one the movie takes straight. (Almost
everybody else is a fun-house case.) This standup crusader

appears to be the only person in town who's awake to the destruction of what used to be a thriving community. And we in the audience are expected to identify with his puckish sanity. The way he tells it, the people who run the town are incompetent twerps. (That's always popular with movie audiences.) He reports that the civic leaders have been thinking about solutions for the decay of the city and have come up with lamebrained fantasy schemes to attract tourism: a Hyatt Regency hotel and convention center; AutoWorld, a theme park; the Water Street Pavilion, a mall. The three projects are actually built; roughly a hundred and fifty million dollars is poured in, and all three are fiascoes.

I had stopped believing what Moore was saying very early; he was just too glib. Later, when he told us about the tourist schemes, I began to feel I was watching a film version of the thirties best-seller *A Short Introduction to the History of Human Stupidity,* and I began to wonder how so much of what was being reported had actually taken place in the two and a half years of shooting the film. So I wasn't surprised when I read Harlan Jacobson's article in the November–December, 1989, *Film Comment* and learned that Moore had compressed the events of many years and fiddled with the time sequence. For example, the eleven plant closings announced in 1986 were in four states; the thirty thousand jobs were lost in Flint over a period of a dozen years; and the tourist attractions were constructed and failed well before the 1986 shutdowns that they are said to be a response to. Or let's take a smaller example of Moore at play. We're told that Ronald Reagan visited the devastated city, and we hear about what we assume is the President's response to the crisis. He had a pizza with twelve unemployed workers and advised them to move to Texas; we're told that during lunch the cash register was lifted from the pizza parlor. That's good for a few more laughs. But Reagan visited the city in 1980, when he wasn't yet President—he was a candidate. And the cash register had been taken two days earlier.

Whatever the reasons for the GM shutdowns, the company had a moral and financial responsibility to join with government agencies and the United Automobile Workers in arranging for the laid-off workers to reënter the labor force. Moore doesn't get into this—at least, not directly. Possibly he thought that he'd lose the audience's attention if he did. Maybe he thought that it was implicit in the gimmick of his wanting to show Roger the damage the company has done, but it's almost perverse of him to pretend that what's happened is all Roger Smith's fault, and to tell the story in cartoon form.

The movie is an aw-shucks, cracker-barrel pastiche. In Moore's jocular pursuit of Roger, he chases gags and improvises his own version of history. He comes on in a give-'em-hell style, but he breaks faith with the audience. The picture is like the work of a slick ad exec. It does something that is humanly very offensive: *Roger & Me* uses its leftism as a superior attitude. Members of the audience can laugh at ordinary working people and still feel that they're taking a politically correct position.

Always

Was there no one among Steven Spielberg's associates with the intellectual stature to convince him that his having cried at *A Guy Named Joe* when he was twelve was not a good enough reason for him to remake it? True, there are flukes, and his remake, *Always,* might have worked at the box office and been acclaimed. But it could have worked only as a piece of gloppy, down-home mysticism—something unworthy of Spielberg's talent—or as a comedy about what the movie had once meant to him. Actually, it may be a sign of his mental health that he couldn't put much conviction into it. The 1943 picture—a Second World War morale booster about a flier (Spencer Tracy) who returns from death to watch unseen over the woman he loves (Irene Dunne) and encourage her romance with a younger flier (Van Johnson)—has been transposed to the present-day wilderness-fire-fighting service. Spielberg has caught the surface mechanics of forties movies. But he seems to have no grasp of how they worked—of the simplicity that made them affecting. He starts out with too much danger in one episode after another, and he overcooks everything, in a fast, stressful style. All he seems to want to do in each scene is get an audience reaction.

Balanchine had a simple explanation for his choreographic genius with dancers: I give them what they do best. Spielberg gives his stars, Richard Dreyfuss and Holly Hunter, nothing of what they do best. Dreyfuss, a put-on artist, is just too light for his role as a daredevil hero; his transitions are too facile. He has been made creamy-skinned and is photographed romantically, but he has no heroic presence. And when he and Holly Hunter sit in the bar at the airbase (where the heroine works, too) looking into each other's eyes longingly, there's nothing happening. (Spielberg has piled modern movie conventions right onto earlier conventions. After the tender thirties-forties scenes, the two characters go back to her place and sleep together, as they've apparently been doing all along.) Holly Hunter is a quick and direct actress, who comes at us with an excess of personality. Spielberg puts her in endless closeups, and there's not enough going on underneath. Photographed unflatteringly, she has so little color in her anxious face and she's so twisted with emotion that she begins to seem like a brown twig. A bland, glassy-faced new actor, Brad Johnson, is the shy pilot who succeeds the Dreyfuss character in the heroine's affections. Commenting on how handsome he is, she says he's like something she won in a raffle. But what you win in a raffle is a turkey.

There is one sequence in the movie that works: Hunter dances alone, thinking of her dead lover, and his ghost dances with her—of course, without touching. Almost everything else seems grandiloquent, rushed, confusing. The very first shot is of two fishermen in a boat on a lake: a plane, swooping off, comes right at them, and they dive into the water. Was the pilot a lunatic? Did the fishermen drown? Basically, it's just a visual gag. Probably Spielberg wanted to see if he could do his own version of the crop-dusting scene from *North by Northwest.* Dreyfuss gives Hunter a white evening dress, and when she puts it on, the dirty-faced men in the airbase bar are awed by her "girl clothes"; crowds of men part for her, as if she were a miraculous vision, and the firefighters line up in the washroom to get the grease off their hands so they can take turns dancing with her, to "Smoke Gets in Your Eyes." It's a fantasy sequence in a wartime musical, except that it's rhythmless and all wrong. There are at least a battalion's worth of firefighters in the scene; we know that these men wouldn't be covered with grease when they sit drinking beer at night; and the white dress is a fright, though it hugs Hunter's breasts and can help to sell the movie. Everything seems off. One moment, Brad Johnson is the goofus who can't follow orders; the next, he's the top flying ace. There's nothing in between. (This guy is a real find: you look at him and you want to know, "Does he sing?")

Audrey Hepburn, who plays Dreyfuss's supervisory angel, delivers transcendental inanities in the cadences that have stoned audiences at the Academy Awards and other film-industry shebangs; people see her, rise to their feet, and applaud. She's become a ceremonial icon, ravishing and hollow. Where has the actress gone—the one who gave a magnificent performance in *The Nun's Story*? There's no hint of her in this self-parody. But then, what Spielberg wants is the glowing goddess. John Goodman appears as Dreyfuss's best friend, and is turned into a fat-jolly-buddy icon. He saves himself from darlingness, but just barely.

Now that Spielberg is no longer twelve, hasn't he noticed that there's a voyeuristic queasiness in the idea of playing Cupid to the girl you loved and lost, and fixing her up with the next guy? In 1943, it was the finality of death that was being repressed. What the New Age hell is being repressed now?

JANUARY 8, 1990

POTENCY

Born on the Fourth of July

Ron Kovic (Tom Cruise), the hero of *Born on the Fourth of July,* believes everything he hears at the Independence Day ceremonies in Massapequa, Long Island. Pure of heart and patriotic, he trusts in Mom, the Catholic Church, and the flag-waving values John Wayne stands for. Ron thinks war is glamorous; it's how he'll prove himself a man. And so he joins the Marine Corps, goes to Vietnam, and is shocked to discover brutality, dirt, and horror.

It's almost inconceivable that Ron Kovic was as innocent as the movie and the 1976 autobiography on which it's based make him out to be. Was this kid kept in a bubble? At some level, everybody knows about the ugliness of war. Didn't he ever read anything on the Civil War—not even *The Red Badge of Courage?* When he was growing up, kids were into black humor, sarcasm, and put-ons. If he was as vulnerable to media influences as the movie and the book indicate, wouldn't he have heard of *Catch-22* and *One Flew Over the Cuckoo's Nest?* Wouldn't he have looked at *Mad?* Ron seems to have blotted out everything that didn't conform to his priggish views. When

249

his younger brother is singing "The Times They Are A-Changin'," it doesn't mean anything to him.

Born on the Fourth of July, directed by Oliver Stone, who wrote the script with Kovic, is committed to the idea of Ron's total naïveté. He's presented as a credulous boy whose country lied to him. Wherever you look in this movie, people are representative figures rather than people, and the falseness starts during the opening credits, with the dusty, emotionally charged Fourth of July celebration in 1956—Ronnie's tenth birthday. Massapequa is less than an hour from New York City on the Long Island Rail Road, but this set (constructed in Texas) looks like Oliver Stone's vision of Midwestern America in the fifties—clapboard picturesque. He uses slow motion to mythologize the drum majorettes. Even the kids' baseball game is a slo-mo elegy. A lyrical glow fuses sports and kids playing soldier and civic boosterism and imperialism. And John Williams' music is like a tidal wave. It comes beating down on you while you're trying to duck Robert Richardson's frenzied camera angles. So much rapture, so soon. I was suffering from pastoral overload before the credits were finished.

Of course Ronnie's country lied to him. Part of growing up is developing a bullshit detector, and kids usually do a pretty fair job of wising each other up. Ron Kovic's Candide-like innocence matches that hazy archetypal parade: they're both fantasies. But they make it easier for him (and the movie) to blame everybody for not stopping him when he wanted to be a hero. To Ron, the Marine recruiter (Tom Berenger) who comes to the Massapequa high school is like a god. Ron's virginal high-mindedness makes him the perfect patsy for a before-and-after movie. What's in between is Vietnam and the rise of the antiwar movement.

On Ron Kovic's second tour of duty, in 1968, when he was a twenty-one-year-old sergeant, his spine was severed, and he was left paralyzed from the chest down. The movie is a scream of rage at how he was betrayed, mutilated, neglected; it's also an uplifting account of how he boozed, quarrelled with everyone, and despaired until he stopped being contemptuous of the war protesters and became active in Vietnam Veterans Against the War. Kovic's book is simple and explicit; he states his case in plain, angry words. Stone's movie yells at you for two hours and twenty-five minutes. Stone tells you and he shows you at the same time; everything is swollen with meaning. The movie is constructed as a series of blackout episodes that suggest the Stations of the Cross; rising strings alert you to the heavy stuff. Then the finale—Resurrection—takes Ron into white light, and John Williams lays on the trumpets.

The central question that's raised is "Why did you tell me lies about what war would be like?" It's not "Why did you tell me lies about what the Vietnam War was about?" —although it shifts into that at times. Stone's most celebrated film, *Platoon,* culminated in the young hero's shooting the man who represented evil, but *Born on the Fourth of July* appears to be a pacifist movie, an indictment of all war, along the lines of Dalton Trumbo's 1939 protest novel *Johnny Got His Gun.* You can't be sure, because there's never a sequence where Ron figures out the war is wrong; we simply see him go from personal bitterness to a new faith. The morality of taking up arms in Vietnam (or anywhere else) isn't really what the movie is about anyway. The audience is carried along by Tom Cruise's Ronnie yelling that his penis will never be hard again. The core of the movie is Ron's emotional need to make people acknowledge what he has lost. There's a shrill, demanding child inside the activist—a child whose claims we can't deny. And Stone's visual rant slips by because this kid's outrage at losing his potency is more graphic and real to us than anything else. It affects us in a cruder, deeper way than Ron's sloganeering and his political denunciations of the war.

What we hear when Ron causes a commotion at the 1972 Republican Convention and shouts at Nixon is a kid who knows he has lost something and who is going to make an unholy fuss about it. He's going to be heard. Yes, he's ex-

pressing the rage of other disabled veterans who feel betrayed—wasted in a war we shouldn't have got into. But
what really reaches us is that Ron finds his lost potency
when the Convention cameras are on him. He finds it in
forcing the country to recognize what it did to him and
others like him. He's saying, "You owe me this," or, "Ac-
tivism is all you've left me, and you can't take it away." And
he's saying, "I paid for what I did over there, and I go on
paying for it. You haven't paid—your shame is greater." He
doesn't really say that, but it's what filmgoers hear and
respond to. The movie, having presented him as the innocent Catholic boy going to war for the glory of God, now
reaps the reward: the audience—some of the audience—
experiences a breast-beating catharsis.

Almost everything else in this antiwar Fourth of July parade that spans twenty years is chaotic sensationalism. When
Ron, in an argument with his mother, drunkenly pulls out
his catheter and says, "It's what I've got instead of a penis,"
and she shrieks, "Don't say 'penis' in this house!" she becomes a comic-strip uptight mom. And when he gets back
at her by yelling "Penis! Penis!" at the top of his lungs, so
the whole neighborhood can hear him, it's a phony, easy
scene. We're supposed to see that his mother denies the
realities of war and every other kind of reality—that this
repressive mom who told him the Communists had to be
stopped was part of the system that deluded him. We're
invited to jeer at her villainy.

A scraping-bottom scene that takes place on a roadside in
the Mexican desert has a druggy, *El Topo* flavor. The
burned-out, drunken Kovic brawls with another burned-out,
drunken paraplegic (Willem Dafoe), and they spit in each
other's faces, knock each other out of their wheelchairs, and
go on wrestling. The two men, fighting over which one
takes the prize for committing the worse atrocities in Vietnam, are like bugs screaming in the sand; they're right out
of the theatre of the absurd—they've even got dry, rattle-
snake sounds for accompaniment—and you have to laugh.

But it's too showy, too style-conscious; it makes you aware of how overblown the whole movie is.

In Vietnam, Ron's platoon, thinking they're attacking Vietcong, massacre a group of village women and children. Then, during the confusion of a skirmish, Ron kills a nineteen-year-old soldier from Georgia, but can't fully accept it—it happened so fast. He tells his major about it, and the major doesn't want to hear it; he doesn't know how to handle Ron's confession, so Ron is stuck with the sickening guilt. After Ron is paralyzed and in a wheelchair, he makes a trip to Georgia to confess to the soldier's parents and young widow. That may relieve Ron's pain, but what about the pain he causes the others? (The father had been proud of the honor guard that came with the body.) The scene might be affecting if it were staged to show that Ron's need is so overpowering he can't consider the family's grief. Instead, it suggests that Stone thinks even blind self-expression is good. (In the book, there's no visit to Georgia. Maybe the trip took place, and Kovic left it out. But I remember the scene from an earlier movie, where after the war the protagonist went to the dead soldier's family and asked forgiveness; there, though, the dead soldier was part of the enemy forces, and the protagonist was offering the family solace.)

Oliver Stone has an instinct for the symbolism that stirs the public. He clung to the Ron Kovic story that he first worked on as a screenwriter more than ten years ago. But he must never have been able to think the material through. *Born on the Fourth of July* seems to ride on its own surface, as if moviemaking were a form of surfing. Kovic doesn't turn against the Vietnam War until long after he gets home, expecting to be welcomed as a hero, and is put in the rat-infested Bronx Veterans Hospital. What would have happened if people had been considerate and kind to Ron, and talked up his bravery? Would he have gone on being a war-mongering patriot? I didn't expect the movie to answer this kind of question, but I expected it to show enough about

Ron's character for us to make some guesses for ourselves. We come out knowing nothing about him except that his self-righteousness—his will to complain and make a ruckus—is rather glorious. I don't think I've ever seen another epic about a bad loser; I wish Stone had recognized what he was on to, and shaped the conception. (In essence, *Born* is satire played straight. The impotent Ron Kovic holds the nation hostage.)

How is Tom Cruise? I forgot he was there. Cruise is on magazine covers. Of course he is—he's a cute kid and his face sells magazines. And magazine editors may justify their cover stories by claiming he's turning into a terrific actor. They may believe it, and moviegoers may assent. Moviegoers like to believe that those they have made stars are great actors. People used to say that Gary Cooper was a fine actor—probably because when they looked in his face they were ready to give him their power of attorney. Cruise has the right All-American-boy look for his role here, but you wait for something to emerge, and realize the look goes all the way through. He has a little-boy voice and no depth of emotion. (In Vietnam, when Ron barks orders to his squad there's no authority in his tone; he still has no authority when he goes in to speak, by invitation, at the Democratic Convention in 1976.) Cruise does have a manic streak, and Stone uses it for hysteria. (He might be a tennis pro falling to his knees and throwing his fists up in the air.) Cruise gets through Stone's noisy Stations of the Cross without disgracing himself, but he's negligible. Nothing he does is unexpected. He's likable in his boyish, quieter moments, but when those are over he disappears inside Ron Kovic's receding hairline, Fu Manchu mustache, and long, matted hair.

Oliver Stone has a taste for blood and fire, and for the anguish and disillusionment that follow. Everything is in capital letters. He flatters the audience with the myth that we believed in the war and then we woke up; like Ron Kovic, we're turned into generic Eagle Scouts. The counterculture is presented in a nostalgic, aesthetically reactionary way; it's made part of our certified popular memories. *Born on the Fourth of July* is like one of those commemorative issues of *Life*—this one covers 1956 to 1976. Stone plays bumper cars with the camera and uses cutting to jam you into the action, and you can't even enjoy his uncouthness, because it's put at the service of sanctimony.

JANUARY 22, 1990

THE 54TH

Glory

The Civil War epic *Glory* is based on fiery, spirit-stirring
material that has never before been tapped for the movies.
On January 1, 1863, the Emancipation Proclamation became
law, and a few weeks later the first black fighting unit to be
formed in the North during the Civil War—the 54th Regiment of Massachusetts Volunteer Infantry—began assem-
bling. The visionary plan, conceived by the abolitionists,
with President Lincoln's blessing, was to prove that black
men had the discipline and valor to stand up against the
enemy. Roughly a thousand freedmen and escaped slaves
signed up. Two of Frederick Douglass's sons were among
the enlisted, and the white officers, who came from prominent anti-slavery families, included a brother of Henry and
William James. The twenty-five-year-old colonel in command of the regiment was the shy idealist Robert Gould
Shaw, the son and grandson of abolitionists; he had left Harvard to enlist, at twenty-one, and had been wounded in the
battle at Antietam Creek. The nobility of the men of the
54th has been celebrated in bronze (in Augustus Saint-
Gaudens' elegiac bas-relief sculpture on Boston Common)
and in poetry (most notably, perhaps, in Robert Lowell's
harrowed *For the Union Dead*).

Glory, directed by Edward Zwick, from a screenplay by Kevin Jarre that's based partly on Shaw's letters, is affecting from start to finish, emotionally moving even when the scenes falter. Visually, it's formal yet lyrical and fluid. The cinematographer, Freddie Francis, doesn't try for a shocking immediacy. He uses colors delicately to suggest the vernal freshness of the land that the soldiers pass through, and he distances us slightly in the combat scenes. They're like something purified by memory. They're being poeticized, elegized as we see them, but this doesn't strike a false note. Rather, it seems a way to honor the pastness of the past. *Glory* is not as assured in dealing with the infighting that Colonel Shaw has to put himself through when he recognizes that the high command has no intention of arming the 54th—that the generals mean to use the men only in the rear area, for manual labor. The Colonel has to outmaneuver the Army to get his troops into combat.

As the small, sad-faced Shaw, who saw Hell at Antietam and is determined to prepare his men for what's ahead, Matthew Broderick shows us the misery of a softhearted commanding officer. His Shaw is not a natural hero; he has to work at it. Even Broderick's drawbacks (the flat tone of his voice, his relative inexpressiveness) seem to help here. Shaw is decent, uncertain of himself—a worrier. It's a lovely performance, as remote and touching as a daguerreotype. Broderick keeps a sense of proportion; his presence never dominates the black actors.

Denzel Washington, Morgan Freeman, and Andre Braugher, a low-voiced young dynamo from the stage, are performers of such skill that they're vivid, and almost persuasive, in hand-me-down roles. Except for Colonel Shaw, the principal characters are fictional, and you know it instantly, because they're the usual representative group of recruits who bicker and quarrel before they shape up and become fine soldiers. As Trip, a runaway slave with flogging scars on his back, Denzel Washington is the high-tension Bogart-Brando figure—sullen, cynical, smart. As a former gravedigger, a

calm older man who steadies everyone's nerves, Morgan
Freeman is a towering version of the Spencer Tracy figure.
Andre Braugher is a smiling, educated black in specs, a
childhood companion of the Colonel's—they were raised
together. Now he has to learn to live without the urban
amenities; he has to develop his body to match his mind.
(Franchot Tone used to play this part.) The conceptions are
based on white icons, but the actors perform these roles as
if they'd never been played before.

We get to know the three characters in the tent that they
share with a back-country man (the quietly impressive Jihmi
Kennedy), who has a slight stutter and a pure, radiant faith
in God, and with a mute drummer boy. Denzel Washington's ornery, troublemaking Trip jeers at Braugher's ill-at-
ease intellectual for being "a nigger who talks like a white
man"; Trip calls him Snowflake. The putdown recalls the
taunts in black exploitation pictures, and Trip's snarling
manner recalls a whole raft of angry young men strutting
their stuff. His style of defiance is modern; so is Washington's acting style. When he's about to be whipped, he pulls
open his shirt and flips his hands in the air in a gesture that
spells out "Method Actor." He has a modern charge of fe-
rocity; you're aware that it's anachronistic, yet it lifts you
up. The three black powerhouse actors get to play something besides dignity. Their collisions may be based on
scenes worn to the bone, but they have new undercurrents,
a new friction, and, of course, a new face. Braugher, the book-
ish soldier, with his volume of essays by the Transcendental-
ists, can no longer talk to his old friend Shaw or the other
white officers he used to be on equal terms with—that
would be "fraternizing"—and he's a freak to his fellow-
enlistees. His attempts to defend himself when Trip humil-
iates him are gallant and discombobulated; he seems on the
verge of a nervous breakdown. The way Braugher plays the
role, we don't dissociate ourselves from his physical weakness. We respect his coming apart.

It takes Morgan Freeman to moderate Trip's rage. We first

meet his character at Antietam: there's a lyrical moment when the wounded Shaw, lying on the ground, feels a boot testing whether he's dead, and looks up at the tall gravedigger, his head backlighted by the blazing sun, who asks, "You all right there, Captain?" Now, when Trip, who has picked a fight with Union soldiers from another regiment, expresses his hatred of the whites, the tall man speaks to him. As he sees it, whites have been fighting for *them*—for *their* freedom. And whites have been giving their lives; he knows, because he was digging their graves. With all the moral authority this superb actor can muster, he raises questions in Trip's head. Freeman's character is saying that not all whites are their enemies, that some whites (such as Colonel Shaw) are even willing to die fighting for the end of slavery. Trip's cynicism about white men has an inflammatory, rabble-rousing appeal for movie audiences. But when the gravedigger speaks for the facts, for sanity and justice, he carries the day. (Of course, the Civil War, which freed four million slaves, was not initially a war to abolish slavery; it turned into that through the actions of Lincoln and, some say, of the slaves themselves—they fled to Union Army posts. But the gravedigger isn't wrong.)

In the worst of the film's didactic set pieces, Trip refuses the honor of carrying the regimental colors into battle. He tells Colonel Shaw that he doesn't want to carry Shaw's flag, that even if the war ends slavery it won't end racial oppression. But when the flag-bearer falls during the climactic charge, at Fort Wagner, on July 18, 1863, Trip picks up the colors. *Glory* gives Trip present-day disaffected attitudes. Then it says that he became disaffected because his parents were sold off—he was orphaned and mistreated. Now that he's found a home in the regiment, he's straightened out. Disillusionment is used to give the antihero glamour and hipness, but then the movie wants him to be a foursquare hero with heart. It's a painfully used-up plot idea, and it makes *Glory* seem a bit of a cheat. Denzel Washington brings passionate conviction to his man-to-man talk about the flag with Colonel Shaw, but he can't rescue the scene; you half expect the prescient Trip to proclaim himself a man of the Third World.

The big Hollywood directors of the thirties and forties would have given dramatic flourishes like Trip's becoming the flag-bearer (and the film's final one, by which Trip and the Colonel are joined forever) a simplistic patriotic flash. Those directors would have yanked at our emotions. Zwick doesn't—and he's right not to—but he doesn't throw out the flourishes, either. He includes them halfheartedly. (He also includes a touch that's way off key: Colonel Shaw, on horseback, slashes a series of watermelons. Presumably, he's destroying stereotypes of blacks.)

The script is just a conventional melodrama. Zwick has made something more thoughtful than that. He uses James Horner's (sometimes intrusive) orchestral score and the Boys Choir of Harlem to compensate for the moviegoer's tendency to see battle scenes simply as exciting spectacle. And this musical equivalent to the righteousness of the men's cause can work on you even if you try to fight it. But Zwick can't always transcend the limitations of what's written: when the men sing around the campfire on the night before the battle at Fort Wagner, there's an emotionally perfect image of Morgan Freeman's huge, elongated hands clapping in syncopation, but there's also a flabby moment when Trip blurts out, "Y'all's the onliest family I got—and I love the 54th." A scene at an élite Boston party, and Colonel Shaw's meetings with his venal superior officers and other whites, could be out of any starchy historical picture, and, despite the effort to achieve authenticity, the dialogue is frequently tone-deaf for the period. (The Irish drill sergeant is a clean century off, and his use of female comparisons to insult the black soldiers seems witlessly gross.)

Some of the incidents aren't rounded. The movie shows what happens when the soldiers of the 54th are issued their pay vouchers and discover that they're to be paid ten dollars a month instead of the thirteen dollars that soldiers in other units receive. The angry Trip moves among the men, urging them not to accept, and they rip up their vouchers; pieces of vouchers flutter in the air, and, in a gesture of solidarity, the Colonel tears his in two. But the movie fails to tell us what happens next. Did the men get their equal pay, and how long did it take? (The historical fact is that many of the men died in battle before the thirteen-dollar payment came through.)

The Colonel volunteers his regiment for the foredoomed task of leading the assault on Fort Wagner, the Confederate stronghold that guards the entrance to Charleston Harbor. He and six hundred of his men advance over the sand dunes toward the fort. We're meant to feel that the soldiers' disciplined attack, with fire coming directly down at them—their willingness to be annihilated—establishes their right to be free men. (In the actual battle, forty-two per cent were killed.) Zwick may not want to put any stress on the Catch-22 irony that the black soldiers could prove themselves only by sacrificing themselves, or the irony that the Colonel's leading his troops to their death seems meant to represent the white man's redemption. We in the audience, with our inescapably modern attitudes, can't help wondering if Shaw, in volunteering his regiment for the honor of being massacred, wasn't doing just what his racist superior officers hoped for. But our suspiciousness is beside the point. The movie *Born on the Fourth of July* finds its meaning in seeing through the nation's call for sacrifice; *Glory* shows the high cost of war, and yet finds meaning in the sacrifice.

In the early scenes at Antietam, when body parts erupt and hover in the air, the randomness of the carnage seems appropriate. By the end, if the movie is to live up to the feelings it stirs in us, we need to see the bravery of the troops as they steadily move toward the concentrated firepower of Fort Wagner, the dead piling up on the slopes of the bastion and on its walls. This defeat (they couldn't take the fort) is meant to be experienced as a triumph. But the staging has a leapfrogging clumsiness. Zwick doesn't have the instinct for images that would burst the written framework. Like the inexperienced Colonel Shaw, he can take only measured steps. The movie is terribly literal-minded, with evenhanded pacing, and this fastidiousness mutes it emotionally. Still, Zwick's failure to inspire the awe that you feel in front of the Saint-Gaudens memorial or when you read Lowell's words about "man's lovely, peculiar power to choose life and die" doesn't make the movie a failure. *Glory* isn't a great film, but it's a good film on a great subject.

Internal Affairs

Mike Figgis's *Internal Affairs* is art-house sleaze. This label isn't meant to be totally pejorative: the picture has a creepy, rhythmic quality that sucks you in and keeps you amused. It's a sophisticated variant of other L.A. cops-and-coke-and-art-world thrillers, such as William Friedkin's *To Live and Die in L.A.* and Hal Ashby's *8 Million Ways to Die.* They were gaudy pulp, but this new one is swank pulp—smoother, better controlled, with expensive-looking couture and an ingeniously nasty subtext. The central character is a prosperous veteran cop, played by Richard Gere, who is everybody's friend. He's being investigated by two officers from the Police Department's internal-affairs division—a righteous, ramrod-straight Latino, played by Andy Garcia, and his sane, honest partner, Laurie Metcalf. As the team begins to close in on what makes the Gere character so popular, he contrives to meet the Latino's beautiful blond wife (Nancy Travis). More than that, he starts talking to the husband about the beautiful blond wife. And you realize you're seeing a dirty, sexy twist on the Iago-Othello relationship.

This Iago (Gere) has an advanced case of festering machismo. A womanizer who secretly makes out with his buddies' ravishing wives and is on good terms with his own wife (Annabella Sciorra) and his ex-wives, he's all sweetness and caresses with women. He feels no sexual tensions with them; he uses them like cuddly pets. He loves children, too; he's got eight, and another on the way. His tensions are in cuckolding men, or in just making them visualize him in flagrante delicto with their wives. He goads men to doubt their adequacy. This sniggering, vengeful interplay with husbands gives him more satisfaction than seducing their women. He torments the stiff-backed Othello (Garcia), boasting of his conquest, and Othello, in a jealous rage, tears off to confront his wife. When he finds her surrounded by her friends from the New Contemporary Museum, where she works, he grabs her and explodes in Spanish, whacking her. Eventually, the plot centers on a variant of Desdemona's handkerchief: a pair of panties. (They're white and so demure you feel *almost* certain the woman is innocent.)

Richard Gere looks better with a few years on him. His thick hair in a brush cut that's either graying or frosted, he slithers through the picture very dexterously, the smiling manipulator. You can see why women are drawn to him, and why men are taken in. He's heartlessly affable. Andy Garcia, though, gives a one-note, glaring-eyed performance. Maybe it's the humorlessness of his role that defeats him: except for his key, violent explosions (which are terrific), he's so rigid he's barely human. Laurie Metcalf makes more of an impression than the glamorous babes do. As a top-notch police officer, a lesbian who doesn't try to ingratiate herself with anybody, she shows a dry wit; it's a strong, contained performance, tough in just the right way.

Figgis, the English jazz musician and experimental-theatre man, who wrote, directed, and scored the 1988 *Stormy Monday,* worked this time from a very smart script (the first to be produced) by the American journalist and novelist Henry Bean. The movie is rather dreamy about the details of police corruption, and the construction goes wrong toward the end. (Bean and Figgis couldn't seem to think of a reason for Gere to go where they want him to be.) But this picture doesn't depend on solid construction or plot logistics. It depends on a sicko undertone and musical rhythms. Surprisingly, the score (Figgis shares the credit) is ponderous; it's generic psychopathology music—at one point, it's nothing more than a chic desiccated sound that the woman next to me suggested might be locusts. The movie represents commercialism that has gone so far into intensity for intensity's sake that it becomes a minority taste. You can't recommend *Internal Affairs* with a straight face—it casts a slimy-naughty spell. It's bad fun.

FEBRUARY 5, 1990

TUMESCENCE
AS STYLE

GoodFellas

Martin Scorsese's *GoodFellas* has a lift. It's like *Raging Bull,* except that it's not domineering. It's like *Raging Bull* made in a jolly, festive frame of mind. It's about being a guy and guys getting high on being a guy. In the Nicholas Pileggi book *Wiseguy,* which this movie is based on, the Mafia-led mobsters are moral runts—and that was the joke of how John Huston showed them, from the Don on down, in *Prizzi's Honor.* But Scorsese, a rap artist keeping up the heat, doesn't go in for ironic detachment. He loves the Brooklyn gang milieu, because it's where distortion, hyperbole, and exuberance all commingle. His mobsters are high on having a wad of cash in their pockets. The movie is about being cock of the walk, with banners flying and crowds cheering.

Is it a great movie? I don't think so. But it's a triumphant piece of filmmaking—journalism presented with the brio of drama. Every frame is active and vivid, and you can feel the director's passionate delight in making these pictures move. When Henry Hill (Ray Liotta), the central character, crosses a Long Island street to beat up the man who tried to put the make on his girl, the dogwood is in bloom, and all through this movie we're aware of the ultra-greenness of the suburbs that the gangsters live in; these thieves are always negotiating their way through shrubs and hedges. Or they're preparing food, ceremonially, gregariously—stirring vats of sauce, slicing garlic razor thin. We see them in bars and restaurants, where they take preferential treatment as their due, and in the tacky interiors of their noisy homes. We see them hijacking, fencing stolen goods, fixing horse races, shaking down restaurant owners, committing arson, preparing cargo thefts at the airport, burying murder victims. And the different aspects of their lives are like operatic motifs.

What's missing? Well, there are no great voices. The script, by Pileggi and Scorsese, isn't really dramatized; instead, Scorsese raises the volume on the music, and the guys work themselves up, get hard, erupt. This isn't the kind of mindless movie that offers up brutality as entertainment, with good guys versus bad guys. Scorsese offers up brutal racketeering and says this is all there is to these men. Scorsese's Jake La Motta could do one thing: fight. These guys can do one thing: steal.

The book is an account of the life of the actual Henry Hill, as he told it to Pileggi after he entered the Federal Witness Protection Program, and the movie picks up his story in 1955, with the obliging eleven-year-old kid, half-Irish, half-Sicilian, working as an errand boy at the cabstand hangout of the Brooklyn neighborhood gang headed by Paulie (Paul Sorvino). As the gang's pet, Henry gets the approval he wants and plenty of spending money; by the time he's fourteen, he's on the payroll of a construction company and knows the ins and outs of the rackets. In the years ahead, crime is a romp for him. He gets a real charge out of pulling scams side by side with his older pals, Jimmy (Robert De Niro) and Tommy (Joe Pesci), and when he takes his Jewish girlfriend, Karen (Lorraine Bracco), to flashy, expensive places he hands out big tips and is greeted as a celebrity. (He's twenty-one.) Karen, who's no bimbo (she has a sense of her worth), likes the danger that emanates from him. His life has the look of a Puerto Rican Day parade crossed with a rock concert; she's excited when she sees his gun (the gun he slugged his rival with). In *Raging Bull,* the young male tries to ram his way through a brick wall; in *GoodFellas,* the young male finds a welcoming warm spot, first with Paulie and the gang, and soon with Jimmy and Tommy, and then with his wife—Karen—and a couple of kids, and a mistress set up in an apartment.

It's a little off key when Henry reacts to Tommy and Jimmy's acts of violence with puzzled revulsion. During a card game, Joe Pesci's Tommy, clowning around, shoots a teenager who's slow to serve him a drink. Incidents like this—they're terrifically well framed—appear to be pointing toward an awakening sensibility in Henry, but nothing comes of them, so they seem perfunctory, a sop to conventionality. (De Niro has a scene where he goes berserk, and that doesn't develop into anything, either.)

The movie's underpinnings could have been linked together: they suggest that the Mafia and other organized-crime gangs are continually being destroyed from within by raw male lawlessness. De Niro's Jimmy brings off the theft of a lifetime—the six-million-dollar Lufthansa heist, until then the biggest cash robbery in United States history—but he can't control his troops; they're so undisciplined, such small-timers at heart, that they start spending ostentatiously, and paranoiac Jimmy, who wants to keep all the dough anyway, takes it as a regretful necessity that he has to whack them—i.e., bump them off. (There were at least ten murders after the successful robbery.) Paulie has strict rules against drugs, because drugs turn men into informers who destroy the "family." But the family doesn't have the decency (or forethought) to support the wives and children of the men who are sent to prison, so when Henry is sent up, Karen becomes his partner, smuggling him dope that he deals inside—it's like a regular franchise. And he begins snorting cocaine. (The movie is about how swindling makes you feel alive, and that's what cocaine can keep you feeling.) By the time Henry is out of prison and is running a dealership from his Long Island home, he's a manic wreck, ready to sell out his mentor, Paulie, and every hood he knows. And he feels justified, because his closest pal, Jimmy, is ready to whack him and his wife, too.

But Scorsese doesn't weight the incidents dramatically; he leaves the themes, and even the story, lying there inert. In a hurried, not very shapely concluding sequence he ties up some threads and tells us about a few of the characters in final titles—omitting, though, a high-comic piece of information: Hill was so determinedly crooked he used the new identity given him by the Witness Protection Program to start up a new life of thievery and was thrown out of the program. But then we've learned so little about him. It's startling to read the title telling us that Henry and Karen separated after twenty-five years, because we realize we don't have any knowledge of what kept them together so long. The picture has scope rather than depth. We see Henry Hill only from the outside, and he has been made to seem slightly cut off from the mob life. He has been turned into a retread of the anxious, dutiful Harvey Keitel character in *Mean Streets,* when he needs to be a rat and the motor of the movie. *GoodFellas* is like the Howard Hawks *Scarface* without Scarface.

Paul Sorvino's Paulie comes through; reluctant to move his bulk, he basks in his power quietly, and never calls attention to himself. Though Lorraine Bracco's Karen doesn't get much screen time, she has a hot, bright vitality; she seems more sexual, more full of go, than her husband. She's in love with him even when she pulls a gun on him. And some of the minor players give the movie a frenzied, funny texture. Tony Darrow is comically desperate as a restaurant owner who's so exhausted by the mob's harassment that he pleads with Paulie to accept a partnership in the business. Welker White brings a nip of assertiveness to her scenes as a Waspy drug courier who has to have her lucky hat to make a coke delivery. And all the mobsters and hangers-on and their women seem to belong to their settings. It's just the three major hoods, played by Liotta, De Niro, and Pesci, who don't have a strong enough presence.

Scorsese had a great critical success with *Raging Bull* (1980), selected by international polls of critics as the best film of the eighties—a picture in which he presented his central character as an icon of brutishness. This time, he wants the central characters to be realistically shallow. But what flattens the movie isn't that they're shallow sociopaths; it's that these sociopaths are conceived shallowly, the way they used to be in B pictures. (It wasn't just the low budgets that were evoked by the term "B picture"; it was also the unmemorable characters.) When Henry Hill is a child, he lives across the street from the Mafia cabstand and observes the sporty life of racketeers as they get in and out of limos; he wants to make it big like them. The life he watches is like the images on movie screens that Scorsese and the rest of us watched, but we're not invited to identify with his longings.

An actor can play a shallow hood and still be memorable if we're drawn in to understand the hood's motives and emotions. (Bogart used to take us pretty deeply into hoods.) But these actors seem too old for their parts, too settled in. They get to us only in isolated scary scenes: Pesci's Tommy demanding "What do you mean, I'm funny?," De Niro's Jimmy wearing an unnatural smile as he waves Karen into what might be a death trap.

Yet the moviemaking has such bravura that you respond as if you were at a live performance. It's Scorsese's performance. He came of age as a director in the early seventies, at a time when many film enthusiasts were caught up in the sixties idea that a good movie is always about its director. There's a streak of metaphoric truth in this, but here Scorsese puts the idea right up front.

The filmmaking process becomes the subject of the movie. All you want to talk about is the glorious whizzing camera, the freeze-frames and jump cuts. That may be why young film enthusiasts are so turned on by Scorsese's work: they don't just respond to his films, they want to be him. When Orson Welles made *Touch of Evil,* the filmmaking process just about took over—the movie was one flourish after another. But that was 1958, and making a thriller about your own wallowing love of the film medium was a thrilling stunt. And Welles didn't drain the characters; rather, he made them more baroque, to match his flourishes. He filled the screen with stars. In 1990, when a movie spans thirty years and runs to epic length, we may miss what big characters can do—what Nick Nolte's sly Lionel Dobie did for Scorsese's *Life Lessons,* in *New York Stories,* drawing everything together.

Scorsese the arousal junkie makes you feel you'd like to hang out with him and listen to him tell how he brought off the effects; he's a master. But this picture doesn't have the juice and richness that come with major performances. It has no arc, and doesn't climax; it just comes to a stop. Conceivably the abruptness could work, but I don't think it does. Will the lift of the moviemaking still carry some people aloft? Maybe, because watching the movie is like getting strung out on pure sensation. That's Scorsese's idea of a hood's life. It's also a young film enthusiast's dream of a director's life, and in Scorsese's case it's not too far from the truth.

The Tall Guy

In the English comedy *The Tall Guy,* Jeff Goldblum is used for his galumphing bigness—the huge features, the toothy grin, the sloppy, longish hair. He's used for his good-natured outlandishness and the fear that he's about to make a fool of himself which comes over him just before he does. As an American actor in London who has spent six years playing stooge to a detestably smug English comic (Rowan Atkinson), he has lost his confidence and most of his sex drive; if it weren't for his sneezes—he has hay fever—he'd hardly know he was among the living. This gangling wreck is paired with the precise Emma Thompson as the nurse who gives him his allergy shots. She wears neat, clipped hair and crisp white uniforms. There's nothing extra about her; she's stripped down to pure flakiness. At the opening night of an Andrew Lloyd Webber-style musical, she seems to be the one person at the Drury Lane who isn't overcome by all the artistry. It's not that she's sane, exactly; she's an original—her face registers tickled disbelief. Meanwhile, Goldblum's wild eyes are rolling inside the makeup that encases him: he's the lead in a new version of *The Elephant Man— Elephant!* the musical.

If the SCTV troupe at its peak, in the early eighties, had made a mild (for SCTV) movie satire of the life of the theatre, it might have had something like the inventive dottiness of *The Tall Guy*. This picture is the opposite of black comedy; it's friendly—one-liners spin about and skits seem to go leapfrogging. (As the stage doorman greets an actor with "Break a leg!" Goldblum, just coming in, falls on his face.) This is the first movie that Mel Smith (who's in his late thirties) has directed, but he's already a veteran stage director. He's also a comedy writer, and the plump half of Smith and Jones, the most popular comedy team in Britain. He turns up here in several bits: he's the blobby-faced fellow who looks like a pixie Alfred Hitchcock. Smith has a gift for keeping everything broad and loose, and as a director he has the kind of slapstick timing that some comics are blessed with: Goldblum's going to bed with Thompson in her tiny apartment turns into a classic destruction orgy.

Richard Curtis, whose first screenplay this is, seems a wizard at writing revue material that all fits together. Basically, the movie is a series of improvisations on autobiographical incidents: Curtis worked with Rowan Atkinson at Oxford, wrote for him for the BBC's "Not the Nine O'Clock News," and stooged for him on the stage; he also got hay-fever injections. But I doubt if the picture could have been so satisfyingly silly without an American—specifically, Jeff Goldblum. There's no pathos in his being banged about when he's a stooge; he's so big you figure he can take it. At the same time, his dopey, childlike quality sets off Rowan Atkinson's lethal genius at playing an articulate swine. (He doesn't even pretend to have a heart.) The whole cast seems to be acting in clover: Emil Wolk; Geraldine James; Hugh Thomas, as the diphead doctor whose hair sticks out like horns; Anna Massey, as Goldblum's gleaming smart agent; Kim Thomson, as a curly-haired singer; the insidious Peter Kelly, as the smarmy mountebank who stages *Elephant!* The show's mock-Lloyd Webber lyrics are too tenderly plaintive to quote; it would be stealing the movie's jokes. The screenwriter, Curtis, has said, in mitigation of his satirical pinpricks, "I love *Phantom of the Opera*—I regard it as one of the nine greatest musicals ever written." I count that as one of the thirty-two most forthright statements I've ever read.

SEPTEMBER 24, 1990

HITS?

Postcards from the Edge

Meryl Streep just about always seems miscast. (She makes a career out of seeming to overcome being miscast.) In *Postcards from the Edge,* she's witty and resourceful, yet every expression is eerily off, not quite human. When she sings in a country-and-Western style, she's note-perfect, but it's like a diva singing jazz—you don't believe it. Streep has a genius for mimicry: she's imitating a country-and-Western singer singing. These were my musings to a friend, who put it more simply: "She's an android." Yes, and it's Streep's android quality that gives *Postcards* whatever interest it has.

This tale of a sorrowful, wisecracking starlet whose brassy, boozing former-star mother (Shirley MacLaine) started her on sleeping pills when she was nine is camp without the zest of camp. It's camp played borderline straight—a druggy-Cinderella movie about an unformed girl who has to go past despair to find herself. The director, Mike Nichols, is a parodist who feigns sincerity, and his tone keeps slipping around. What's clear is that we're meant to adore the daughter, who is wounded by her mother's cheap competitiveness. Nichols wants us to be enthralled by the daughter's radiant face, her refinement, her honesty. He keeps the camera on Streep as if to prove that he can make her a popular big star—a new Crawford or Bette Davis. (She remains distant, emotionally atonal.)

When the novel that the movie is based on—Carrie Fisher's semi-autobiographical account of her life as drug-addicted Hollywood royalty—was published, in 1987, Fisher told the *Times* that she hadn't wanted to write the kind of book about star parents (hers are Debbie Reynolds and Eddie Fisher) that makes the child a victim. And she didn't play that game. But it's the game the movie plays. The script (which Carrie Fisher wrote, with Nichols' uncredited collaboration) has some funny, barbed lines, but, like everything else in the movie, they're shaped to show the daughter's self-deprecating courage and her superiority to the people she lives among. Streep's Suzanne Vale is a noble victim. She's also a talented singer, in contrast with her musical-comedy-star mother, who belts out Stephen Sondheim's "I'm Still Here" Vegas style, without a trace of musicality. Nichols directs Shirley MacLaine to overdo the mother's self-preoccupation; it's a blast-off performance—she's playing the stale essence of old show biz. Yet MacLaine has a reality that Streep doesn't have. The cartoon mother is meant to make a gut connection with the audience.

The tacky, bright-colored movie is watchable in the same way that Nichols' last film, *Working Girl,* was. Once again, there are a lot of people to look at. Dennis Quaid, who plays the predatory lech that Suzanne falls for, is photographed in profile, so that he seems to be nothing but a big nose. He gives a forced, overwrought performance, and his core speech, in which he reveals what a pig he is, is played off Streep's sensitive face. The virtuous characters are just as extreme: Richard Dreyfuss is pure niceness as the doctor who courts Suzanne, and Gene Hackman is a stern but fair movie director—a man of weight and authority who serves as a father figure to her. Hackman manages to give his lines a personal rhythm—he makes his scenes halfway credible.

Two women in the cast draw the audience to them: Robin Bartlett, as Suzanne's roommate in a drug-rehab program, and the striking Annette Bening, in the role of an actress who has been cast as a lowdown hooker. (For a few seconds, Bening is so alive she seems to run off with *Postcards.*) Streep does well with the ballad made famous by Ray Charles, "You Don't Know Me," and she does one tiny thing that gives you pleasure: in a slapstick routine, she hangs on to a ledge at the top of a tall building and lifts her hands in a lovely shrug.

The camp intensity that Nichols gives this newfangled, near-plotless version of a woman's picture is what makes it play. (It's this confident showiness that made *Working Girl* play better than his earlier *Heartburn.*) You see how many obstacles Suzanne faces, and you watch her (like the Working Girl) overcoming them. Nichols loads the scenes with banal revelations—"insights." The mother is seen as competing with the daughter, but the daughter is never seen as competing with the mother. *Postcards* is like *Mildred Pierce* told from Ann Blyth's point of view. It's also a variation of *Now, Voyager*: Suzanne Vale is first cousin to Bette Davis's Charlotte Vale, who escapes her repressive mother by going to a rest home. In the new therapeutic terrain, the ditzy mother and the smart-ass daughter get to know themselves (and each other) better. They're both troupers, and when the detoxified daughter hits the comeback trail the mother cheers for her. The movie reneges on everything it has said it was about, and it even provides the heroine with a fine, upstanding man waiting in the wings. Nichols doesn't go all the way with camp except in a hospital scene where the mother is shorn of her wig and photographed mercilessly without makeup; for a minute, Nichols tops the humiliation scene in *Mr. Skeffington* (when pieces of Bette Davis's curly coiffure fall on the dance floor). Even here Nichols is slippery. The scene is presented as sympathy for the shrivelled old lady, and admiration of her tough spirit.

There's a deep jadedness in this picture (and in *Working Girl*) that can pass for sophistication. Nichols appeals to the narcissism of show-biz insiders and to the would-be insider in the rest of us. The assumption of *Postcards* is the assumption of the tabloids: that all any of us really want is to be movie stars, and we despise the ordinary Joes who aren't rich. The movie brings out the part of us that feels bitchily superior to our own lives. If Nichols were up front about what he was doing, we might enjoy his pissing on the rnings of squares, but *Postcards* is jadedness pretending warm good will. There's an element of the gracious host in Nichols: he keeps retreating into taste.

The key scene is the Hollywood party where Shirley MacLaine's hairless old trouper in her red wig barks "I'm Still Here" and flashes her undies. The party guests love her style, and even the daughter, watching her, marvels. Nichols is saying, "You may be appalled, but the whole culture loves this stuff, and maybe I do, too." At the end, he's got Streep belting. Glamour and contempt are all mixed up in Nichols' work. He's acclaimed for being hip to the Zeitgeist.

Pacific Heights

Those of us who have had years of being pestered by stickler landlords or gouged by self-righteous ones may not work up much sympathy for the San Francisco lovers played by Melanie Griffith and Matthew Modine in *Pacific Heights*. Their attempt to join the propertied class is thwarted by a sicko scam artist (Michael Keaton), who takes over one of the two rental units in their Victorian house and calls the police when they try to evict him. This situation might have been sly fun if the director, John Schlesinger, and the scriptwriter, Daniel Pyne, had tempted us to root for the tenant with the perverted legalistic mind and the fiendish cupid's-bow smile. It's a drag that we're expected to identify with the dull young couple, who are meant to be idealized versions of ordinary people like ourselves. I don't know why the invader tenant hauls around a big collection of telephone books, or why he twiddles with razor blades, though I suppose that could be a character point—to indicate a streak of sadism. But then I don't even understand why he wants to sue the couple and "take over" their newly acquired house, since it's mortgaged to the hilt, and their equity in it can't be a staggering amount. (The plot is loonier than the tenant.)

What we see isn't really a thriller—it's more like an executive decision to make a thriller. That appears to be how Schlesinger approached the material. He has his professionalism—it shows in the clean, efficient staging. And he gives the film an expensive look; he puts money on the screen. But he scares you only by making you nervous. He might have come closer to the traditional fun of thrillers if he'd developed some momentum and given us more of Keaton, whose knotted forehead suggests a tense, screwed-up little boy. The movie picks up a gleam of interest when we learn about the tenant's wealthy background, and we get a bit of a kick when he plugs Modine. Keaton has a way of being blandly still when the character is at his deadliest; he's pretty silky, but with a little help from the writer and the director he could have been a memorable creep, like Robert Walker in *Strangers on a Train*.

For most of the film, Schlesinger tries to get us to care whether the young landlords are going to stay alive to make their mortgage payments. Modine's short-tempered frustration may be believable, but it's not amusing; there's nothing smoldering in this guy—he's just a virile stupe. Griffith seems meant to be a smart, loving professional woman, right out of the pages of an up-to-the-minute women's magazine. Her funky-little-girl voice was a tease in films such as *Body Double, Stormy Monday,* and *Something Wild*; here it's wearying. (If it's her only voice, she ought to be damn careful how she's cast.)

The film's pleasures are few: the most energetic scene is a quick, happily irrelevant satire of the Home Shopping Network on TV, and you may find yourself grateful for the vistas from the top of Potrero Hill (not Pacific Heights), where the 1886 house is located. A promising cast—it includes the uncredited Beverly D'Angelo, and Laurie Metcalf, Dorian Harewood, Carl Lumbly, Mako, Tracey Walter, Luca Bercovici, Guy Boyd, and Tippi Hedren as rich Florence—is all but thrown away. And Schlesinger has some puzzling lapses: for example, the camera circles dizzyingly during a conversation between lawyer and client. So it's rather shocking that he's willing to lay claim to *Pacific Heights* by doing a Hitchcock turn: in an elevator scene, he appears as the menace who turns out not to be the menace. Actually, he is the menace. He's foisting his boredom on us.

Avalon

When Barry Levinson writes and directs autobiographical material, he catches the rhythms of grouchiness, of irritation, of preening in the commonplace remarks that people make all the time. He's especially virtuosic at catching the sound of people who know each other too well: they've bored each other and picked at each other for years, but they always stop just short of drawing blood. Levinson has a gift for turning this everyday small talk into comedy routines. He makes familiarity funny, and when his work really clicks, as it did almost all the time in *Diner* (1982) and now and then in *Tin Men* (1987), it delights audiences in a true-to-life way. But, because of the homely nature of his comedy, when it doesn't click it reverts to tiresomeness. His new film, *Avalon,* a multigeneration epic, limps back and forth.

In legend, Avalon is an earthly paradise. Levinson uses the name as his Rosebud: it's carved into the façade of the Baltimore apartment house where the five Krichinsky brothers, Jews who immigrated from Eastern Europe before the First World War, make their first American home. From there the four surviving brothers move into brick row houses, where they live side by side and raise their children. During the week, they work as wallpaper hangers, and on the weekends they play waltz music at neighborhood parties. To Levinson, Avalon seems to represent his family's participation in the American dream, with cousins, uncles and aunts, grandparents and parents mingling in a convivial, quarrelsome atmosphere. It's what Levinson looks back on as a golden age: twenty-six relatives would sit down for Thanksgiving dinner, and at family-circle meetings the Krichinsky brothers would agree to chip in and put up the money to bring over destitute kinsmen. The film is set mostly during Levinson's childhood, in the late forties, which he sees as the period when the golden age begins to crumble—when his parents move to the suburbs, and TV breaks up the clan's social patterns, and the brothers have divided into feuding factions.

Avalon begins as a lulling reverie about the relationship of the boy Michael (Elijah Wood), who will grow up to be Levinson, with his paperhanger grandfather, Sam Krichinsky (Armin Mueller-Stahl). I don't find Sam as endearing as we're meant to. He's one of those life-spirit, storyteller characters, and he has too much Old World soul for me. It's Sam who makes the points that Levinson wants to put across; he's full of canny wisdom. And Sam's sweetness to the boy throws the movie into a wilted dreamland. There's a moment when old Sam, playing a melancholy piano étude, says that the boy should take lessons, and I thought, Good, why don't you try to teach him, so there can be a bone of contention here—some of the friction of the real world.

It's a relief to have an immigration story that isn't all pain and hardship; *Avalon* is unabashedly about people who prosper. But Levinson has honeyed the past (and made it look like his film *The Natural*). Early on, there's a comic tinge to Sam's feeling that the time of his arrival in Baltimore, in 1914, during the Fourth of July fireworks, was the high point of his life and of the nation's history, too. After a while, we seem expected to believe that it really was a high point of innocent expectations. Then we're shown the post-Second World War period and the subsequent decades of desecration. There's a wide streak of fuddy-duddyism in Levinson's notion that the family used to be the bulwark of the nation's value system. It may seem unfair to say this, but at times the movie seems like a product of the cultural wing of the Republican Party—a lament for those bygone days when mothers stayed home and watched over their children, and children obeyed their parents, and so on.

There's one character, as played by Elizabeth Perkins, who never buys into Levinson's vision of how great that past was: Ann, his mother, who lives with her in-laws, Sam and Eva (Joan Plowright), during the early years of her marriage and can't stand their ritual bickering. Listening to the perpetual spats and complaints at family-circle sessions, she's so bored she's a bundle of tiny frazzled nerves. The conception gives Perkins the chance to sustain her whole performance as a precise, marionettelike turn; the stylization becomes Ann's ticky personality, and Ann embodies more truth than the film's thesis. She wants to be with her husband, Jules (Aidan Quinn), and her son Michael; she wants some freedom from the immigrant generation that's been running her household. Living in an extended family, Ann is practically stiff from repressed annoyance, but she's too decent and too timid to explode. She walks around dumbfounded by her mother-in-law's interference with the smallest details of her life; at times, she might be shaking water out of her ears. Plowright plays the abrasive mother-in-law as a woman who's impervious and well satisfied with herself. She imagines she's jovial. (Plowright isn't allowed enough range, and her performance is a shade too realistic to be funny, but her shiny shoe-button eyes suggest the tenacity of the woman. She's formidable.)

Aidan Quinn's voice has an emotional timbre that's effective when Jules talks to his wife, Ann, or their son Michael. It's so emotional I never believed he was the glib, natural salesman we're told he is, but he's persuasive as an affable, responsible family man. When Ann—really harried—blows off some steam and pleads for help, Jules is evasive; he's not going to get caught between his wife and his mother. His specialty is keeping the peace. Quinn's Jules also matches up convincingly with his business partner and opposite number—his careless, risk-taking cousin Izzy, who is played by the West Coast standup comic Kevin Pollak. This comic has the inflections to pep up his lines; he's a true Levinson actor—he's like a slightly older version of the boys in *Diner*.

The movie tries to get by with a catchall construction, and it includes such elements as the arrival of Eva's brother Simka from Nazi Europe. It's easy to see why Levinson thought he needed to darken the texture of the story, but it's already overlong. There's also a likable but out-of-the-blue episode: the cousins Jules and Izzy have a double wedding, which is celebrated at a little night club Sam runs—a hot-jazz night club with black entertainers. This interlude isn't related to anything else in Sam's character, not even his love of music. If he had this jazz-loving side, wouldn't it have spilled over into his grandfatherly scenes with Michael or his arguments with his wife? The Sam we've been watching is a European moldy fig.

There are scattered fine moments. When the old brothers sit on a bench together, they themselves are like row houses. The image of Aidan Quinn working his way down a row block selling out of a suitcase recalls an earlier time effortlessly, and every time Elizabeth Perkins twists in discomfort she gets to us; she's in the tradition of Jean Arthur. Levinson shows skill in his handling of Elijah Wood as the alert little

Michael and Alvin Myerovich as the minuscule patriarch. And Lou Jacobi is frighteningly forceful as touchy Gabriel Krichinsky, who never forgives his younger brother Sam for ordering the Thanksgiving turkey cut before he arrives. But overwhelming financial success (of the kind Levinson has had with *Good Morning, Vietnam,* of 1987, and *Rain Man,* of 1988) often turns people into pundits, and Levinson is preaching his own brand of bourgeois fundamentalism. He embraces the family as a cure for social ills. I think he got caught up in a fantasy about rise and fall and began forcing his material to fit an epic pattern. (Has his family declined? I bet it's thriving.)

At Levinson's worst, he's as insistent as the Plowright character. He doesn't play fair with Ann: her desire to be free is linked with being brainwashed by TV. The scene of the Thanksgiving with twenty-six relatives spilling from the dining room into the living room has its rhyming contrast: a few years later, Jules and Ann and young Michael have Thanksgiving dinner on three tray tables while they watch "The Aldrich Family." We're expected to cluck with horror, but the film's attack on TV is so righteous it can make you want to defend TV: the show that the three were watching may have been more entertaining than *Avalon.*

This movie is an elegy to a mythical past. That's probably why people emerge from the theatre sniffling. They've been told they're suffering from soul-sickness—the loss of unity, harmony, family music. Under the closing titles, Sam plays the piano sadly, reflectively. And if you close your eyes you can see Levinson airlifting himself onto Mt. Rushmore.

OCTOBER 22, 1990

MOTHER, HUSBAND, BROTHER

The Grifters

Anjelica Huston has a mysterious presence. You can't tell what its sources are, but it seems related to the economy of her acting. In *Prizzi's Honor,* she used her Brooklyn accent to open up the character; in *Enemies, A Love Story,* the suggestion of pain gave force to each thing she did, especially when she made the pain comic. Huston is already past the age at which Garbo retired, and there's nothing youthful about her—but then there never was. (There wasn't much that was youthful about Garbo, either; being considered ageless often means looking older than you are.) Huston doesn't flaunt her androgyny or seem ashamed of it. Agelessness and androgyny are simply among her attributes. She's overpoweringly sexual; young men might find her frightening.

That makes casting her as Lilly Dillon in *The Grifters* an intuitive sneaky-right decision, because the core of the story

is the refusal of Lilly's son, Roy (John Cusack), to have anything to do with her. He's paying her back. In his childhood, she was cold and miserly; she withheld any kindness.
Now that he's twenty-five and has been on his own since
he was seventeen, she shows up. Lilly is tough and she's
seductive; she's the dominatrix as mother, and he's afraid
of her getting her hooks in him.

The Grifters is based on one of the punchier pulp novels
by Jim Thompson—a bitter, somewhat repellent book with
a misanthropic integrity. Published in 1963, it's about three
scam artists (Lilly, Roy, and Roy's bubbly bedmate Moira,
played by Annette Bening)—people who never got a break
and don't give anybody else a break. Each of these chisellers
has his or her own methods and agenda; there's no yielding
by any of them (and no redemption). The film retains
Thompson's hardboiled pitilessness, and a tension is created
by placing these fifties or early sixties characters in nineties
L.A. locations; we feel piqued, jazzed up. Toying with L.A.
film noir, the director, Stephen Frears, and the scriptwriter,
Donald E. Westlake, do twisted, anomalous things. The El-
mer Bernstein score tries for a tart, sour Kurt Weill effect,
and doesn't quite bring it off, but Westlake keeps some of
Thompson's slangy, compact dialogue and adds his own,
which has a madcap edge. The movie starts with comic cap-
ers, then uses Thompson's class resentment and grim hope-
lessness to smack us with discord. We're watching a form
of cabaret.

This criminal subculture doesn't come equipped with a
detective as moral explorer. It's a void, where Roy, who
holds a salesman's job as a cover, lives alone by rules he has
devised for himself. A cautious, hard-eyed practitioner of
the "short con"—fleecing cashiers by getting change for a
twenty and slipping them a ten, or playing craps with trick
dice—he doesn't have to worry about doing time in prison.
Roy has repressed any signs of an identifiable personality,
and he does nothing to attract attention; he won't let himself have friends—that's being a sucker. He makes himself

colorless, and socks his money away. It's a horrible, grubby life—a mole's life—and he's an intelligent, handsome kid, who could have gone to college, who could have lived among people. It's his angry touchiness about his young mother (she was only fourteen when she had him) that keeps him in his miserable isolation. He's getting even with her by throwing his life away.

Frears introduces the three characters (in the sections of a vertically divided triple screen) as they arrive at the places where they're about to do their grifts. Each of the three is putting on the face that he or she presents to the world. We're formally meeting three false fronts. It's Lilly's dream that her son will go straight and be a loving comfort to her, but she herself works for the Baltimore syndicate: she travels, placing bets at the tracks. Annette Bening's Moira* is a sex fantasy come to luscious life. She's irrepressible—a real tootsie—and it takes a while for her adorable, kittenish perversity to make you apprehensive. Moira the smiler has been trained in big cons—scams that rake in bundles of money but can also land you in prison—and she's out to make Roy her partner. Roy likes Moira in his bed, but he was jerked around by his mother and he's not about to get jerked around again. He hates feeling that people might want to make something of him; he's not interested in becoming anything. Cusack suggests that Roy is cocky enough to think that he's something already, that he's living on his own terms.

Roy turns both women down, but he's an innocent compared with these two blondes—the killer mom and the tease—who are close to the same age. (It's perfect that Cusack gives his most memorable line reading to the word "Mom.") The two women battle over Roy's essence—the money that's hidden in the clown paintings in his apartment. In the structure of the film, it's Roy who's the clown.

There's nothing to fill out in a Jim Thompson novel;

---

*In the movie, it's pronounced Myra.

there's no room for characterization. It's socially conscious thin stuff. The three are stuck. You grasp the limits of what's available to them and how hard their dreams hit those limits, and you see them try to break through by using each other. Frears and Westlake are smart enough not to attempt to make a big thing of it. They keep it snappy, and heighten the sexual electricity.

Bening's two-faced little-girl quality is dazzling—just what film noir thrives on. When Moira blames Lilly for Roy's rejecting her proposition and turns treacherous, Bening makes the shift convincing; she's a stunning actress and a superb wiggler. And film noir is enriched by two competing femmes fatales. Huston's power as Lilly is astounding. This actress generally plays tightly controlled characters. (Her Gretta Conroy in *The Dead* was an exception.) Lilly is usually peremptory, displaying the authority of a woman who has worked for big-time mobsters for years; her whole existence is based on manipulation and control. She's a thief trying to outwit the thieves she works for. When she isn't sure she's succeeding, we can read the terror under the control. She's like a trapped animal when her boss (Pat Hingle), who thinks she has tricked him, shows up to punish her. Hingle, sucking on a big cigar, is chilling; as the power m.c. pulling the strings, he gives what's probably his best performance ever, and Huston matches him. The scene has a jangle; it's *Cabaret* moved from Berlin to L.A.

Actors are con artists, and our entertainment is in watching them get away with things. When Lilly, at the close, comes down in the elevator at Roy's apartment hotel, you may be reminded of Mary Astor in the elevator at the close of John Huston's *The Maltese Falcon,* and when, a little before that, Lilly pulls a maneuver on her son that's just about the ultimate con, you may recall John Huston in *Chinatown* saying, "Most people never have to face that at the right time and right place, they're capable of anything."

The leading characters' acceptance of brutality in Martin Scorsese's *GoodFellas* fails to scare us, and it doesn't haunt

us afterward—perhaps it isn't meant to. But by the end of
The Grifters (which Scorsese produced) Lilly's ruthless amo-
rality is shocking—it has weight—and I think that's because
Anjelica Huston is willing to be taken as monstrous; she contains this possibility as part of what she is. And when Lilly
shows her willingness to do anything to survive she's a great
character. At the end of John Huston's *The Treasure of the
Sierra Madre,* the fortune is dispersed to the winds; here
it's gathered up. Anjelica Huston's Lilly bites right through
the film-noir pulp; the scene is paralyzing, and it won't go
away.

Reversal of Fortune

Reversal of Fortune comes to sophisticated hammy life
when Jeremy Irons, as Claus von Bülow, talks to the Harvard law professor Alan Dershowitz (Ron Silver) about rep-
resenting him. The deep, mellow drawl that comes out of
Irons' von Bülow is a triumph of comic affectation; it's the
voice of self-satisfaction—of a man who likes his vowel
sounds so much he lingers over them. Irons is naturally desiccated; he isn't outgoing, and he doesn't have the bullying
physique that, say, Rutger Hauer might have brought to the
role. He doesn't inspire dread. But with Hauer the material
might not have lent itself to light comedy. Scene by scene,
Irons' glassy aloofness is very funny. What he does is a
mock performance. It's a masterly conceit, and, as such,
it's bizarrely witty. It's what theatre critics used to call "de-
licious."

Irons' von Bülow is a pop conception of a decadent aris-
tocrat—a creep so polished and courtly and cynical that he
finds the accusation of murder too banal to be seriously

addressed. The director, Barbet Schroeder, is onto something: an actor playing an actor. At the time of the trial, von Bülow himself did seem to be mocking the public interest in him. The movie is a sick-joke docudrama about how his conviction for trying to kill his super-rich wife was overturned on appeal through the brainpower of Dershowitz and his team of students and former students. The crowd-pleasing satirical subtext is that our super-rich—the heirs and heiresses of the great fortunes—are useless, bored, unloving, and unloved. They adore titles (even fake ones, like von Bülow's von), and their adoration puts them at the mercy of wellborn fortune hunters.

Sunny von Bülow (Glenn Close), who lives on in an irreversible coma, serves, amusingly, as narrator, and the movie gives the strong impression that she was brain-dead before she was brain-dead. It also gives the strong impression that, whether or not von Bülow gave her toxic injections, he passively collaborated in destroying her by politely catering to her self-destructive wishes. (He says, "Sunny got what Sunny wanted," as if that explained why he handed more liquor to his already besotted wife.) So we need feel no sympathy for Sunny and no active involvement in Claus's fate. The staging is often amateurish (it's especially disappointing in the scenes where von Bülow gets together with Dershowitz's team), and Sunny's supposedly lavish décor looks tired, like the furnishings of an ostentatious seedy hotel, but it's an entertainingly trashy movie—a happy debauch.

Probably most of us would be even happier if it weren't for the time consumed by Ron Silver as Dershowitz. The script, by Nicholas Kazan, is skillfully constructed, but it's based on Dershowitz's book about the case, and he's the protagonist—the crusading lawyer searching for evidence of innocence. There's an idea here: the strapping Teutonic knight, in all his smug, anti-Semitic grandeur, is saved by the little loudmouth Jew. It turns out to be a bad idea. The lawyer-client relationship begins with a nifty double take:

Dershowitz (in his Groucho mustache) smarts at von Bü-low's patrician condescension. And we look forward to hooting at the lawyer's sanctimoniousness. But soon Ron Silver is playing healthy, feisty Jewishness. That this is a positive stereotype makes it no less a stereotype. Dersho-witz's life-enhancing scenes are flatulent, and they're dis-honest: the movie seems to be putting us down for enjoying the scandal satire it's dishing up. And, with Dershowitz's son Elon as one of the producers (and played as a warm, laughing son by Stephen Mailer), the film's emphasis on the lawyer's moral qualms and high principles is blatant grand-standing.

Clearly, Schroeder knows it: he directs Jeremy Irons and, in the flashbacks, Glenn Close with some flair, but he hasn't the stomach for lionizing the professor. You get no sense of intellectual capacity from Ron Silver's performance, and the scenes in which he works to keep his crew of assistants steamed up are standard, impersonal TV—emptily ener-getic. The fun here is that Irons' von Bülow is a depraved cuckoo. He simply can't resist playing ghoulish comedian and making Dershowitz his stooge.

Vincent & Theo

In *Vincent & Theo,* Vincent (Tim Roth) is slight, and has carrot-colored hair, jagged teeth, and workman's clothes smeared with paint; his tall, dark younger brother, the art dealer Theo (Paul Rhys), is turned out like a bourgeois aes-thete. But when they're together and flare up, their words burst out impatiently, spasmodically. They have similar tem-peraments and a helpless inability to be calm and rational with each other. The director, Robert Altman, and the screenwriter, Julian Mitchell, know that we have some understanding of the basic Vincent van Gogh life story—the loneliness, the self-mutilation, the early death. What they've given us is an interpretation of the bond between the brothers—the bond that helps to keep Vincent alive while it tears Theo apart.

Vincent is obsessive about his painting; Theo is obsessive about Vincent and about his own inability to sell Vincent's work and help him—he can give him only a pittance. When Theo gets the telegram from Arles telling him that Vincent has cut off his earlobe, he takes a minute to be sick and then goes to him. In Arles, he touches the words that Vincent has written on the wall of his house: "I am the holy spirit. I am whole in spirit." Theo fits his hand flat against the handprint Vincent has left on the wall, and we know that Theo will never be whole in spirit.

At the hospital, Theo takes Vincent's hand. As he sits there bowed down, Vincent cops a look at him, and there's a suggestion that Vincent is checking to gauge the depth of Theo's agony. When Theo returns to Paris, his wife, meaning to comfort him, reaches for his hand; he pulls it away, refusing solace. Ill with syphilis, he has some of Vincent's reckless urgency; it's at war with his efforts to make an elegant conventional life for himself and his wife.

The two brothers' names hand-printed on top of swirls of thick ochre paint form the opening title, and then there's a flash-forward to the auction at Christie's where "Sunflowers" is sold for forty million dollars. This is the movie's taking-off place: an irony too obvious to be satirical and too obvious to be ignored. The film looks at it straight on. The auction is a union of the worlds the brothers are trapped in, a culmination of their yearnings and frustrations. Throughout the picture, Altman crosscuts between Theo's attempt to function as a businessman dealer and Vincent's plunging further into sun and light and crying out for the companionship he needs to stabilize him.

It has become standard practice to disparage Vincente

Minnelli's 1956 *Lust for Life,* with Kirk Douglas as Vincent—principally, maybe, because it's a big Hollywood production. But it's an honorable big production, and Douglas and, in the relatively small part of Theo, James Donald are far from contemptible. What dates it is that Minnelli, following the dramatic conventions of his period, lays everything out for us, and, desperate not to be cheap or overblown, he's somewhat pedestrian. The Altman film is emotionally direct. When we first see Tim Roth's Vincent, he's lying on top of his bedcovers. The scene might be a still-life until he blinks and makes sudden, jerky movements with his pipe, moving it from his mouth to his hand and back again; Theo is in the room talking to him (about money, as always), and Vincent's reactions to him are so lightninglike they're almost subliminal. The brothers are inside each other's heads, and we have an extreme degree of empathy with Vincent. Without any overt "acting," Roth's Vincent simply gets to us, and we understand how he gets to Theo. Roth's acting is a form of kinetic discharge. It's 1879, and this is Vincent van Gogh taunting Theo with the announcement "I'm going to be a painter. What do you think of that?" Yet it's as if he were someone we'd grown up with—a self-amused, deracinated boy whose crooked, toothy smile drew us to him though he'd always alarmed us a little.

In the years that the movie spans—van Gogh's life as a painter, from 1879 to 1890—Vincent studies draftsmanship and tries to make the art scene, but he begins to be detached from the life going on around him. He takes part in it politely, but he's not there emotionally—he's only in his work. Vincent is a zealot about ways of seeing; then, as he becomes more isolated, his art becomes all about what he feels. And the film seems to pass beyond conventional sophistication and to see things from Vincent's point of view. Altman doesn't simply reproduce the scenes that van Gogh painted; rather, he brings out responses similar to the responses you have when you look at the paintings. He heads right for the sensuality, the intensity.

You feel that especially after Vincent has quarrelled with Paul Gauguin (Wladimir Yordanoff): a field of sunflowers in the wind is like a sulfur storm overpowering the artist. The orchestral score, by Gabriel Yared, is soft and lyrical, but with an exciting overlay of electronic discord—of something deafening. Vincent smashes a canvas among the sunflowers—then uproots a few to take home. Whenever he's painting, he sticks his brushes in his mouth; now, carrying the storm back to his room, he licks the paint and muck off his table, finishes the last of his booze, and takes a swig of turpentine. He spits out a mouthful, cries out, and takes another swig. This time, he gets it down. His lifting a knife to his ear is just the next step. At the end of his life, you feel the way you do when someone you grew up with dies. You feel as you do coming out of O'Neill's *A Moon for the Misbegotten*: you know that the character couldn't go on any longer. Vincent ruptures the flesh; he ruptures the canvas.

Theo, who's all big, protruding eyes, can't go on much longer, either. Throughout, in the crosscut scenes, we've been steeped in his oppressive workplaces and cramped apartments. In one scene, he tiptoes among dozens of tiny, ornately framed pictures laid out on the floor. The walls, with patterned wallpapers (like Vuillard's) and paintings hung frame next to frame, always seem to be closing in. And when he rents a room to commemorate Vincent's paintings—an empty space where he's surrounded by them—and his wife, Jo (the remarkable young actress Johanna Ter Steege), and his brother-in-law (Hans Kesting) look at him as if he's lost his mind, he shuts the door on them. He has told them the truth—that this art is the most important thing in his life. With Vincent dead, it's clear that Vincent was what was pagan and alive in Theo. Alone, he crumples on the floor like a Schiele figure; he's got nothing left but his torment. The film moves from Theo in his shrine vanishing into Vincent's paintings to Theo naked in an institution vanishing into madness. (He survived Vincent by only six months.)

This double Passion-play movie is very different from the other Robert Altman movies (even allowing for how different they are from each other). The theme—the bitter entanglement of art and commerce—holds Altman in a vise of his choosing. He doesn't go at it glancingly here. This great theme is his lifelong theme, and, staying with it strictly in terms of the van Gogh brothers, he's able to release his own feelings about how an artist's frustrations lead him to acts of self-destructive fury—cutting off his ear to spite his face. It's a movie about two sensualists made by a sensualist, who understands that their bond of love of art is also a bond of shared rage at the world of commerce. Theo suddenly walks away from Vincent's funeral, where the glib, fatuous Dr. Gachet (Jean-Pierre Cassel)—a collector who keeps his paintings in a vault—is speaking; Theo can't listen to the pomposities an instant longer.

There isn't a high-flown minute in this movie. It has a simple, fluid tactility and a quick tempo. Julian Mitchell's dialogue is to the point, and the scenes aren't resolved; they're left just slightly askew. Near the beginning, Vincent's prostitute-model Sien (Jip Wjingaarden) blows up at him because he goes on sketching her when she's on her break—when she isn't modelling, when she's herself. It's partly an issue of privacy, but it's also an issue of commerce; the breaks are *her* time. Vincent stops and apologizes, though it's when she is herself that she's a great subject. Perhaps he's just being politic. (Altman, famed for his spontaneity, his caught moments, allows for a faint ambiguousness.) Vincent takes the pregnant Sien and her small daughter to an exhibition of a three-hundred-and-sixty-degree painting, a diorama of a seascape that's like an ancestor of motion pictures, except that it's the spectators who move; the child goes into the seascape to pee. And there's a high-strung variation on the usual joyous repasts in the French countryside: Theo, Jo, Vincent, and others are gathered at Dr. Gachet's table listening to this self-congratulatory fellow shoot the breeze about Vincent's being cured and as sane as anybody. (When the Doctor is afraid that his daughter Marguerite, played by Bernadette Giraud, is becoming fond of Vincent, he says that Vincent is a hopeless case.)

Gauguin has an arrogant self-sufficiency that makes it clear he could never be the admiring friend Vincent longed for; Vincent was deluded about him. Vincent, trudging along with his backpack, has only Theo, and he obstinately pressures him, believing that Theo could sell his pictures if he just tried harder; he wants to believe that things are simpler than they are. After his experience with Gauguin, he gives up on humanity. But he still has flickering hopes. Like his brother, he's drawn to the wholesome, redemptive physicality of creamy-cheeked bourgeois women. Dr. Gachet's words about his condition close off this possibility.

This daring movie works on its own relentless, celebratory terms. The production design, by Stephen Altman (the director's son), and the cinematography, by Jean Lepine, are freshly thought out. With their help, the director gets images—such as the ones of Sien at the beach, staggering into the surf as she goes into labor—that have something comparable to the power of the paintings. Something devastating is achieved when Vincent in the wheat field where the crows are cawing sets a canvas on his easel. He draws a line on it, looks toward what he's about to paint, but is too upset to make another mark, and enters the picture. The crows take wing.

The actors and the moviemakers have felt their way into the van Gogh passion and madness, and come out with an austere movie. It doesn't flinch from the blunt banality of saying that there's no place for the artist's singleminded intensity in this commercial world. Which is true yet not quite true. Altman finds a sliver of an audience.

NOVEMBER 19, 1990

NEW AGE
DAYDREAMS

Dances with Wolves

A friend of mine broke up with his woman friend after they went to see *Field of Dreams*: she liked it. As soon as I got home from *Dances with Wolves,* I ran to the phone and warned him not to go to it with his new woman friend. Set during the Civil War, this new big Indians-versus-Cavalry epic is about how the white men drove the Native Americans from their land. But Kevin Costner, who directed *Dances with Wolves* and stars in it, is not a man who lets himself be ripped apart by the violent cruelty of what happened. He's no extremist: it's a middle-of-the-road epic. Lieutenant Dunbar (Costner), a Union officer, sees that the Sioux have a superior culture—they're held up as models for the rest of us—and he changes sides. Costner must have heard Joseph Campbell on PBS advising people to "follow your bliss." This is a nature-boy movie, a kid's daydream of being an Indian. When Dunbar has become a Sioux named Dances with Wolves, he writes in his journal that he knows for the first time who he really is. Costner has feathers in his hair and feathers in his head.

Once our hero has become an Indian, we don't have to feel torn or divided. We can see that the white men are foulmouthed, dirty louts. The movie—Costner's début as a director—is childishly naïve. When Lieutenant Dunbar is alone with his pet wolf, he's like Robinson Crusoe on Mars. When he tries to get to know the Sioux, and he and they are feeling each other out, it's like a sci-fi film that has the hero trying to communicate with an alien race. But in this movie it's the white men who are the aliens: the smelly brutes are even killing each other, in the war between the North and the South. Luckily, we Indians are part of a harmonious community. Dances with Wolves has never seen people "so dedicated to their families." And he loves their humor.

At the beginning, there's a bizarre Civil War battle sequence with the wounded Lieutenant Dunbar riding on horseback between rows of Union and Confederate soldiers, his arms outstretched, welcoming bullets in a Christ-like embrace, and throughout the movie he is brutalized, seems dead, but rises again. (Does getting beaten give Costner a self-righteous feeling? Even when it's as unconvincingly staged as it is here?) There's nothing really campy or shamelessly flamboyant after the opening. There isn't even anything with narrative power or bite to it. This Western is like a New Age social-studies lesson. It isn't really revisionist; it's the old stuff toned down and sensitized.

Costner and his friend Michael Blake, who worked up the material with him in mind and then wrote the novel and the screenplay, are full of good will. They're trying to show the last years of the Sioux as an independent nation from the Sioux point of view. And it's that sympathy for the Indians that (I think) the audience is responding to. But Costner and Blake are moviemaking novices. Instead of helping us understand the Sioux, they simply make the Sioux like genial versions of us. The film provides the groovy wisdom of the Sioux on the subjects of peace and togetherness: you never fight among yourselves—you negotiate. Each of the Indian characters is given a trait or two; they all come across as simpleminded, but so does the hero. Even the villains are endearingly dumb, the way they are in stories children write.

There's nothing affected about Costner's acting or directing. You hear his laid-back, surfer accent; you see his deliberate goofy faints and falls, and all the closeups of his handsomeness. This epic was made by a bland megalomaniac. (The Indians should have named him Plays with Camera.) You look at that untroubled face and know he can make everything lightweight. How is he as a director? Well, he has moments of competence. And the movie has an authentic vastness. The wide-screen cinematography, by Dean Semler, features the ridges, horizons, and golden sunsets of South Dakota; it's pictorial rather than emotionally expressive, but it's spacious and open at times, and there are fine images of buffalo pounding by.

Mostly, the action is sluggish and the scenes are poorly shaped. Crowds of moviegoers love the movie, though— maybe partly because the issues have been made so simple. As soon as you see the Indians, amused, watch the hero frolicking with his wolf, you know that the white men will kill it. Maybe, also, crowds love this epic because it's so innocent: Costner shows us his bare ass like a kid at camp feeling one with the great outdoors. He's the boyish man of the hour: the Sioux onscreen revere him, because he's heroic and modest, too. TV interviewers acclaim him for the same qualities. He's the Orson Welles that everybody wants—Orson Welles with no belly.

Edward Scissorhands

In Tim Burton's *Edward Scissorhands,* the towers and spires of a medieval castle rise high in the air right out of the end of a bare, flat suburban street. The houses and cars in the suburbs are in a comically limited palette of pastels; the dark castle is extravagantly junky and macabre, like the setting of an old horror movie seen on a black-and-white TV. The amiable suburbanites, cozy in their little square rooms (with very small windows), see the castle whenever they look up the street—its tangled shrubs and statues and fallen stones are a gothic, Expressionist playground—but they hardly seem to notice it. They refer to it casually and without curiosity as "the mansion."

One day, Peg Boggs, the Avon lady (Dianne Wiest), in her swing-skirted lavender suit and pillbox hat, having exhausted the sales possibilities among her regular customers in the neighborhood, sees the castle in her car mirror and thinks she'll give it a try. She pokes about the deserted, tumbledown place and is about to leave when a voice says, "Don't go." It's an adolescent boy, white-faced Edward (Johnny Depp), who looks like a somnambulist in a German silent. He has a snarled mop of spiky black hair, melancholy circles around his eyes, and a tiny Cupid's-bow mouth. It takes a second to register that the welts on his face are self-inflicted accidental cuts. Edward was created in the castle's kitchen workshop by an aged inventor (Vincent Price, in flashbacks), who gave him a gigantic cookie-cutter heart but died before he could attach the hands he had prepared. Orphaned, Edward is left by himself with two collections of long, sharp shears dangling where his hands should be. Peg, ever the professional, dabs at his cuts with astringent from her sample case, as if he'd cut himself shaving, and she tries to put a little color on his cheeks. Worrying and motherly, she feels she can't go back down the street and leave this polite, forlorn teen-ager, who spends his time whacking away at the shrubbery, cutting out topiary animals. She invites him to come home with her.

Johnny Depp's Edward is a fairy-tale boy: he's like Harry Langdon playing Cesare in *The Cabinet of Dr. Caligari;* he's like Frankenstein's monster by way of L. Frank Baum. But the Boggs family accepts him as if he were an ordinary guest in the house. Peg's husband (Alan Arkin)—a real fifties-style dad—is the perfect host; he makes the boy feel wanted. And the assorted suburban matrons welcome him. Gratefully he transforms their hedges into mythical creatures, and when they see his skill at trimming a poodle he's turned loose on their hairdos. They treat him as a minor celebrity and prepare to set him up in a salon. Suburbia is a form of surreal entertainment here: the physical layouts have an element of surprise; the score, by Danny Elfman, has an antic sweep to it. And you develop an affection for the residents because they make you laugh. But Edward falls swooningly in love with Peg's daughter (Winona Ryder), whereupon her vengeful boyfriend (Anthony Michael Hall) tricks him into a robbery, and the suburbanites, thinking he's dangerous, turn against him. And everything sours. We don't want to see the conventional "dark side" of these people: it's a betrayal of the film's comic spirit—the material turns into cheesy plot-centered melodrama.

There's something deeper the matter with *Edward Scissorhands*: the central idea of a boy who cuts when he wants to touch. It has no mystery: it's pre-interpreted. And Tim Burton is being too personal, too tenderly self-serving. Edward is the pure creative artist, who can't be around people, because he can't help hurting them. He's the person who can't reach out, can't communicate, can't express his love. He's the woeful misunderstood kid.

A draftsman director, Burton (he's thirty-two) is the most original of the younger moviemakers. His comic-book films—*Pee-wee's Big Adventure, Beetlejuice, Batman*—are all conceived graphically, and their hipster, exploding-cigar funkiness isn't fully explicable. *Scissorhands* is conceived graphically, too, but it's plaintive, and it doesn't seem to want to be more than that. Burton shows us the pale, lonely kid who feels there's no place for him. (*Scissorhands* suggests a picture he might have wanted to do when he was still a teen-age animator.) This representation of his interior life has to be only one part of it: where's the part that put the demon Beetlejuice on the screen and let loose the Joker? That's the interior Burton some of us want to see, not the droopy one who says, "I've always been a sweet guy." Johnny Depp's Edward is an emasculated Tim Burton. Edward isn't angry even when he's mistreated; his scissor hands have no relation to his mild, angelic nature.

A great script might have done something with the vision of Transylvania looming over suburbia. Burton has said that the gothic-movie world helped him get through childhood. Are the suburbanites completely cut off from it, as they seem to be? (Then what's it doing there?) The script, written by Caroline Thompson, based on Burton's sketches and the story the two of them devised, is undernourished. The movie is a tribute to the seventy-nine-year-old Vincent Price; it could have used more interaction between the inventor and Edward, and some suggestion of what the boy was intended for. (With those whirling, rhythmic shears, he should have become a film editor.)

There's one magical performance: Dianne Wiest's Peg pushes open the huge castle door, saying brightly, "Hello! Avon calling!"—Gracie Allen couldn't have done it with more radiant daffiness. As a comedienne, Wiest is like a more accessible Maggie Smith; you delight in her tidy gestures and wordplay. You *like* her being an Avon lady: Peg is daintily stylized—living kitsch.

But when the picture stops being comic it turns into a different kind of kitsch. *Scissorhands* is very Christmassy, and it's likely to be greeted by a congratulatory press—the kind that says, "At last, Tim Burton shows us what's in his heart.'' Well, the terms in which it will be praised should tell him what's wrong with it. Beetlejuice would have spit in this movie's eye.

The Sheltering Sky

It used to be said of the composer-writer Paul Bowles and his playwright-novelist wife, Jane, that he was afraid of nothing and she was afraid of everything. That was before he published his first novel, *The Sheltering Sky,* which seems an elaboration of the remark. The 1949 book was his semi-autobiographical account of their marriage—an account that fascinated readers by its Olympian closeted tone. Under the novel's vaporousness is a pop theme: what happens to a modern, dissatisfied woman—a New York artist-intellectual—if she's in the Sahara, her husband dies, and she's enslaved in a harem? She loves it and hates it; she goes mad. But this is not simply a male writer's version of a woman's harem-whore fantasy: the wife, Kit, seems to be fulfilling the nature and desires that the husband, Port, cannot fulfill for himself.

Bowles is so private he doesn't let you in on much. Reading the book, you can't tell who is who sexually; stonewalling is Bowles' literary art. But the novel attracted directors the way Malcolm Lowry's *Under the Volcano* did. Movie people talked about it with awe (Robert Aldrich, Nicolas Roeg, and Mick Jagger were among those who thought of filming it), and when Bernardo Bertolucci got caught up in it he must have been awed, too. His new *The Sheltering Sky* filters out the pop element that gives the book its bit of kicky horror.

Tall, blond Port (John Malkovich), powerfully built, has a

creamy voice, a soft pout, and slightly weaving hips. It's the postwar era, and Kit (Debra Winger), his wife of ten years, wears her dark curly hair cropped but piled high on her forehead—she looks like a fashionable illustrator's idea of a spunky lesbian. They're so close a couple they're almost a single person, yet they're unhappy, petulant, snagged. They're one person, but they're also isolated from each other. Even on the rare occasions when they have sex together, there's no passion in it. Most days, they can only quarrel. Port feels that they'll never be in synch, that he wants them to reach the country of the unconscious but Kit holds back. So they go on journeys from the decaying known to the scary unknown with a third person along as a buffer. On the 1947 trip that the film covers, it's rich, handsome, dull Tunner (Campbell Scott). His attentions to Kit give some sexual edge and jealousy to the married pair, and his presence binds them closer; he doesn't have their style, and they treat him as a clod. They're a nasty, brittle pair, strangling in their style.

Crossing boundless landscapes, the three go from Oran, in Algeria, to remote villages in the Sahara, because Port believes in testing himself; he likes rigors and danger, likes the idea of fearlessness. (It's his special arrogance; it's part of his narcissism to see himself as an adventurer.) He takes long night walks in unlighted alleyways and (rather risibly) lets a pimp steer him to a thieving Arab girl in a tent. Kit, hugging her hotel rooms and looking at her luggage for reassurance, lets herself be seduced by Tunner. Sneakily, Port contrives to get rid of him, and the couple, alone, go farther into the boredom of the desert. We wait and wait for all this trekking by train and car and bus to start paying off, but what Bertolucci and his cinematographer, Vittorio Storaro, give us is flies, squalor, and dunes. (*The Sheltering Sky* won't do a lot for North African tourism.) Eventually, with Kit watching over him but helpless to save him, Port succumbs to typhoid.

In Bowles' account (as I make it out), Port dies giving

birth to Kit's sexuality, and she becomes him. Fearlessly, fatalistically, she goes into the desert at night, joins a caravan of merchants, and is raped repeatedly by a crude, feudal old Tuareg tribesman and a younger Tuareg, who turns her into his chattel. Bowles' description appears to be his own fantasy of what the hypercivilized Kit—and Port—really want. Kit's (Port's) madness is a sexual version of the Heart of Darkness. The novel is a horror fantasy, like Bowles' most famous short story, the 1945 "A Distant Episode," about a French professor of linguistics who comes to North Africa to study desert dialects: nomads cut out his tongue, dress him in tin cans, and make him dance like a clown. In that story (which prefigures the novel), the professor goes mad—he becomes the nomads' clown. Bowles' *The Sheltering Sky* is high-toned sensationalism; by the end, it has turned into pulp exotica—the alienated intellectual's version of Valentino's *The Sheik*.

In the movie, all this is muffled. Bertolucci doesn't make any big alterations, but the attenuated story becomes even more attenuated, and after Port's death there's no suspense, no drama. When Kit goes farther into the desert, you may think the movie is about changing time zones, and, essentially, you're right. The older rapist is left out, and we don't feel the fullness of Kit's sexual release, or the fullness of her debasement when she's one of the women in the seraglio. She's never raped: the young Tuareg is a tender lover. What we get is too affectless to be a sex fantasy; affectlessness itself is the point.

In the novel, Kit becomes all about sex; the movie is about her giving over to another way of seeing. There may be nothing the matter with that, except as a viewing experience. The picture goes deep into monotony. Bertolucci has lost interest in pace and excitement and verve. He's up to something moral: he's looking outside Western culture, hoping for an erotic tranquillity—something abstract, like Islamic art, that will keep you fixated, not moving.

Would I like the movie better if Bertolucci had put in the

novel's cheap thrills? You bet I would. I might have laughed at the trashiness, but that's better than feeling apathetic. I don't respect his choice of this material, but, having chosen it, he might have tried to get at the high-risk desire to be overpowered, instead of filling the closet with sand and art. The whole thing has the impressively decadent look of an Armani ad. Storaro is Storaro. His cinematography is lovely but unsurprising—in truth, a little stale. (The graceful camels might be the same ones who posed for him in *Ishtar*.)

Port isn't simply a repressed homosexual; he's also a repressed heterosexual. He's a furtive, skunky aesthete, a man of no generous impulses—our worst self-image of white civilization. Bertolucci and his co-scriptwriter, Mark Peploe, have given Port a gloating moment when, after his session with the Arab prostitute, he holds up the wallet that she thinks she has effectively made off with. He has been contentedly nuzzling her ripe melon breasts, but he has to show her he has outmaneuvered her, even though that gives her time to make the shrill, trilling cry that alerts her protectors. (Perhaps Port wants to be chased.) The ingenious Malkovich brings new character textures to the screen: Port is full of smug self-hatred.

Winger takes on a definite resemblance to the iconic photographs of Jane Bowles, but what's the point when the makeup and hairdo aren't attractive on her? (Most people will just think she's losing her looks.) Winger speaks as if she were reading; she never seems to get the hang of the character. (Maybe nobody could, or maybe it would take someone like the young Katharine Hepburn.) Except for a bit of derisive mimicry of Tunner, Winger seems to have nothing to play until Port is feverish and dying. Then she can show hysterical anxiety; it's as if she suddenly dipped into surplus emotions from earlier roles.

At the beginning of the picture, we see that Kit has packed *Nightwood* in her bag. That's about a woman who becomes a dog; here she becomes a zombie. When Kit joins the caravan, rides a camel, and is on her way to becoming a contented love slave, we gauge how long she's en route by the phases of the moon. Her movement into the desert night seems to be intended as a rebirth. (By the time the caravan reaches its destination, she looks like a winsome, dark-skinned Arab boy. Or is it Port who has come out as a homosexual?) The moon phases in the deep-blue desert sky are charmingly cartoonish, but probably the mocking tone isn't intended. (It may be something that happens when Bertolucci gets consciously poetic, as in his 1979 *Luna.*) Once Kit is part of the caravan, we're meant to feel that there has been a shift in her psyche. Bertolucci signals us that she has moved away from the verbal, from definitions and categories, by giving us a long, silent passage (though he keeps the trance music—the drums and flutes—going). She has achieved Port's goal: the country of the unconscious.

The picture never quickens your response to anything. Rather, it's a New Age way of viewing the desert and its inhabitants as primal. Rolling benignly on their camels' backs, the tribesmen are themselves New Agey. We're led to believe that they're not neurotic, like Port, or dull, like Tunner. (In this view, the nomads don't have to strive to be unconscious; it's their heritage.) The seventy-nine-year-old Bowles has been enlisted to play some sort of presiding expatriate sage; he's like the zombie master when he looks into Kit's gray-blue eyes and asks her, "Are you lost?" As I interpret the movie, the wandering Kit, thrown out of the seraglio, may be lost but she isn't mad: having been transmuted, she's drawn to anonymity and impersonality. You're left with the impression that she'd rather be a nameless whore in some Casbah than return to the New York heebie-jeebies.

Bertolucci thought about the Paul Bowles novel so much it disintegrated. If he had filmed "A Distant Episode," he might have presented the insane professor of linguistics (who remained in the desert) as having made a sound political choice. I'm pushing it, of course; I'm trying to indicate that the sensibilities of Bowles and Bertolucci simply don't fit together.

Just as Bertolucci and his co-writer Peploe suggested in *The Last Emperor* that forced reëducation—Communist brainwashing—had saved Pu Yi's soul, so now they propose that Kit's blanking out is a form of cultural cleansing, and that her being used for nothing but sex (like a trained pet: a dog?) is sexual liberation. I hope I'm wildly overinterpreting this movie, because if I'm not, Bertolucci has become a caricature of the Western intellectuals who reject Western values. And at the same time that he's telling us how decadent we are he's making this overscaled, sensuous, sumptuous fantasy that looks as if it's about Lawrence of Arabia's sex life.

Everybody Wins

I became ill last January, just as I was about to praise *Everybody Wins,* in which Debra Winger went further with the kind of liquid acting that made audiences at *An Officer and a Gentleman* stare at her and smile with pleasure. Practically no one saw her performance in *Everybody Wins,* or even heard of it, because the thriller, directed by Karel Reisz from a surprisingly cool, quirky Arthur Miller screenplay, was opened without press screenings and was generally taken for a dud. It disappeared almost instantly and hasn't returned, but it's available on tape, and I wouldn't want to let the year close without urging you to see it, and shouting that, despite *The Sheltering Sky,* Winger is one of the two or three finest (and most fearless) screen actresses we've got.

Everybody Wins is set in a (fictional) small, decaying in-

dustrial city in New England. (The exteriors were shot in
Norwich, Connecticut.) A prominent doctor has been murdered, and his young nephew has been convicted for the
crime. Winger plays a local girl, a seductive sometime
hooker named Angela Crispini, who persuades a private investigator, an outsider (played by Nick Nolte), to look into
the case. She claims that the youth is innocent and that "everybody" knows who the real killer is. The movie asks,
What's going on? Why have the town officials conspired to
convict the wrong man?

The mood-swinging Angela is the chief mystery: Can anything she says be believed? She's always acting things out
on a stage of her own creation. She's out of control, and
Winger makes her irrationality passionately real. Winger's
Angela is soft and boneless and appealingly whory, with an
automatic pretty smile. She wears slips and has breakdowns;
she's all femininity and formlessness—she can become anything at any time. (The director seems to let the actress set
the film's rhythms.) Winger warms up her voice: it's less
husky than usual—more maternal. Her sexuality is never
hyped; she doesn't have to prove it—it's just there. Angela's
switches of personality seem natural and defensive; she gets
haughty and temperamental whenever she's challenged.

You can see why the investigator—Tom O'Toole, a former Boston cop—becomes her lover and her patsy. He's the
literal-minded male who wants to know what's going on.
She's maddening: she behaves in contradictory ways, and
he can't pin her down. She keeps him off balance and in a
courting position. Nolte, playing a lapsed Catholic, wears a
trim beard and has the shaggy bangs of a Richard Burton
priest; Tom is tenderhearted and inexperienced—a lug.
Drawn into an erotically charged game, he always catches
on to Angela's emotional manipulations too late. Angela is
as anxious and deceitful and bewildering as Marilyn Monroe. Arthur Miller has lived in Connecticut a long time and
has carried Monroe in his head a long time. Writing this
script, he put together his exterior life and his interior life—

his *An Enemy of the People* consciousness and his Marilyn Monroe problem—and they fuse in a way that cures him of rectitude. This may be the least prosecutorial writing he's ever done. When Tom asks Angela what her interest in the case is and she rattles on, saying things like "Everything's just one step away from a dream," she's avoiding his question, but her likably odd cadences tell us that she's also answering it.

For a brief period in the late sixties and early seventies, moviegoers seemed willing to be guided through a movie by their intuition and imagination; if this slyly funny picture about the spread of corruption had been released then, it might have been considered a minor classic. It's satirical in an odd, hallucinatory way. There are fresh (often startling) scenes, with Frank Military as the kid who's falling apart in prison and becoming suicidal; with Kathleen Wilhoite as a stoned girl whose mentor (Will Patton) knuckles her on the head when she tries to join a conversation, and then comforts her; with Frank Converse as the State's Attorney; with Judith Ivey as Tom's sister; and with Jack Warden as a retired federal judge. (And Nolte, in his priestly mode, has a fine, tense scene in which he persuades the killer to confess.) Except for the innocent kid, practically every male character we meet has had carnal relations with Angela. By the end, we know why she has to save him: she's tormented by her sense of justice. It may be her only torment that she can do anything about. The picture is a classically constructed detective story, with a mysterious woman who lures the fact-oriented man into something that ramifies in every direction and is way over his head. (But he's dogged.) Maybe the only reason Winger's performance hasn't been hallowed is that it hasn't been seen.

DECEMBER 17, 1990

VANITY, VANITIES

The Godfather Part III

At the end of *The Godfather Part II* (1974), the story was complete—beautifully complete. Francis Ford Coppola knew it, and for over a decade he resisted Paramount's pleas for another sequel. But the studio's blandishments became more honeyed, his piggy bank was smashed, and late in 1988 he had an illumination: he discovered how the story should be continued. Michael Corleone would be in his King Lear phase, with his empire slipping from his hands. Michael, he announced openly, without shame, was going through what he himself had been going through. In Coppola's thinking, he had become his own tragic hero. (Mario Puzo, who wrote the 1969 novel on which the films were based, and collaborated with Coppola on the screenplays, held his tongue.)

Most of the emotional force went out of Coppola's moviemaking in the late nineteen-seventies, when he was working on *Apocalypse Now,* and it has never fully come back. Pictures such as *One from the Heart, The Outsiders, Rumble Fish, Tucker,* and *The Cotton Club* were preceded by so much buildup in the press that early audiences kept being stunned to find an empty shell of a movie. We've never had another director whose fall was so prolonged, or one who harangued the press so bitterly, blaming it for his burnout and his miscalculations. Coppola makes himself the issue. After each new film, he was so nakedly hurt and upset that you couldn't help becoming involved in his pain. (For a while, he was Tucker, the victim of the big car companies.) By now, you can't discuss his movies apart from discussing him—he's made it impossible. He blames the press for that, too.

Coppola has been licking his wounds publicly for over a decade. He's turned his exhaustion and wound-licking into the subject of *The Godfather Part III*. Its emblem is the sagging face of Michael Corleone (Al Pacino), the Godfather. In the first film, Michael became a killer for the sake of his family. (He treated it as his duty to kill his sister Connie's treacherous husband.) In *Godfather II* we saw that it wasn't family he cared about now—it was power. Predatory and vicious, he'd killed his poor weakling brother Fredo. He'd put himself beyond redemption, and at the end he had lost his wife Kay (Diane Keaton) and was alone with his two pampered children and Connie (Talia Shire). Yet in *III* we're supposed to believe in a remorseful, basically good Michael Corleone. Twenty years have passed, and now he's trying to give his family a good name and protect his daughter Mary's innocence. (That is, he's trying to keep her in ignorance of his murderous past.) He has moved the family wealth out of gambling and into banking and investments, but the other mobsters resent his climb toward respectability, and—here's the tricky element—the higher he moves in international banking circles, the crookeder the action, and the more he is victimized. *Godfather III* is about worldwide corruption.

Trying to put the Corleone family above reproach, Michael enters into negotiations with the Vatican; it has the standing to launder his money and his name. (That seems to be his way of expiating his crimes.) Michael, it turns out, is honorable compared with the big-time grandees who deal with the Vatican. It's Michael who tries—and fails—to save the life of Pope John Paul (Raf Vallone); he is poisoned by the consortium of European financiers. (Since the movie is set in 1979 and 1980, Michael was doomed to failure; John Paul actually died in 1978.)

The first two *Godfather* movies are peaks in our movie-going experience. In their combined seven and a half hours, they're our gangster epic, our immigration epic, our national passion. They belong to us. So we care about this huge, ambitious new project; watching the sequences, we pull for Coppola, worrying about whether he'll be able to bring them off. Lightning didn't strike three times; the movie is lumbering. Yet I was relieved—I felt he could get by with it. It resembles the first two pictures, and there's always something happening. I don't think it's going to be a public humiliation, and it's too amorphous to damage our feelings about the first two.

Godfather III feels as if it had been ripped from Coppola's hands before he could shape it and finish it. That's probably what happened; he may have needed two or three months longer, though chances are that if he had been given a year it would still be messy. This picture isn't just unpolished and weakly scored; it lacks coherence. The internal force has vanished from his work, but you still expect some narrative flow; instead, he reaches for awesomeness. Trying to make a masterpiece, he resorts to operatic pyrotechnics that don't come out of anything.

Coppola chose to make *The Outsiders* in the style of *Gone with the Wind;* he's made *Godfather III* in the style of the earlier *Godfather* movies. But there's no connection anymore between Coppola and this style. The sensibility is different; the quality of feeling—what gave the films their lyricism and made the public bond with them—is gone.

In the first two *Godfather* pictures Coppola took opportunistic, sensationalist material and turned it into drama. In *Godfather III* you catch glimpses of news stories. Joe Mantegna, as the smooth-faced hood Joey Zasa, is like Joey Gallo dressed in John Gotti's wardrobe, and the package deals with the Vatican recall the Sindona affair. But Coppola doesn't transform the sensationalist material; he just presents it, with an aura of solemnity.

Michael now lives in a New York penthouse and buys himself the Order of St. Sebastian by donating a hundred million dollars to the Vatican to distribute to the poor of Sicily. The amounts bandied about are trashily large: he agrees to hand the Vatican six hundred million dollars more, and is swindled. These transactions illustrate why Michael can't go on as Godfather. The point appears to be that he was meant for something better. He's grieving, and you get the sense that it's not for the brother and brother-in-law he killed, or his first wife and his brother Sonny, whom others killed, or his dead parents; it's for the lost possibilities in himself. The action doesn't seem attached to anything, because Michael's passions are spent and his thoughts are elsewhere. He wants out. Coppola might be saying, "I shouldn't have to be doing this. I've already made this picture."

Al Pacino gives a good morose performance, with deep pouches under his eyes. He plays the role with fine professionalism, but it's no longer a startling role, with hidden currents that suddenly come to the surface; it's limited and monochromatic. Robert Duvall's Tom Hagen isn't around, and he's missed; Pacino has no one to play off. Michael doesn't reveal himself with the old sneak of a don who pretends to be harmless (a too effusive performance by Eli Wallach) or with his lifelong henchman Al Neri (Richard Bright); he's a silent, solitary figure, his body hunched over, his face a mask of lethargy. It's a mistake, I think, to have given him no new sex partners and left him clinging nobly to his forlorn love for his ex-wife, Kay. It's great to see Diane Keaton, but she has always seemed wasted in this poorly written role; now eons have passed, and Kay is still dropping bland moral judgments. She and everybody else keep telling Michael that they love him and forgive him—how much reassurance does Coppola need?

After Michael's son, Anthony (Franc D'Ambrosio), refuses to study law and goes off to become an opera singer, Michael takes on the training of his nephew Vincent (Andy Garcia), his brother Sonny's illegitimate son (in *King Lear,* Edmund, the bastard). Sonny was a hothead; Vincent is a torpedo, a killer without guilt pangs. His speed in violence suggests a kinetic self-realization with a gun. Physically, Garcia is well cast. He has a widow's peak, and he flashes fire, or his liquid brown eyes twinkle, or he speaks with a sexy undertone. But the illusion never takes hold. Where are the scenes in which Michael would recognize that Vincent has the steel and cunning to hold power? Michael seems to turn his empire over to a loyal bodyguard. The movie appears to be saying that Michael recognizes that in this depraved world Vincent, with his killer instincts, is the man for the job—the man that Michael now thinks he never was. Maybe that's too self-serving for Coppola to make it more explicit.

The Irish actor Donal Donnelly—he was the drunken, stuttering Freddy in *The Dead*—is perfection as the mealy-mouthed Vatican banker Archbishop Gilday. And as a photojournalist whose casual bedroom date with Vincent puts her in the middle of an attempted hit, the frisky Bridget Fonda has comic electricity popping out all over. As Michael's financial adviser (a replacement for Duvall), George Hamilton, loitering in the background, looks as if he were born encased in a stretch limo; too bad he has nothing to do. Negative publicity about the movie has centered on Coppola's daughter Sofia, who plays Michael's adored daughter, Mary. It's obvious that this teen-age girl is not a trained actress; she seems uncomfortable at times, and her voice (or a dubber's voice) lacks expressiveness—which is a serious flaw in her last scene. But she has a lovely and unusual presence; she gives the film a breath of life, and I grew to like her. (What I didn't like was that Coppola makes you feel protective toward her. And there's one layer too many when she says "Dad" at the end.)

The strongest performance—in terms of sheer animal strength and suggestions of emotional reserves—is given by Talia Shire, whose Connie calls up dark plotting women like

Livia in *I, Claudius,* and Lady Macbeth, and Lucrezia Borgia;
she's tough. It's Connie who angles Vincent into the family;
when she's fed up listening to him talk about how he wants
to kill one of the Corleones' enemies, she says "Do it," and
her words have the kinetic charge of his actions. Part of
Connie's silent-movie witchiness is in her resemblance to
Pacino's ravaged Michael, and part is in her reflective,
knowing half smile. Connie acts like family: when she says,
"Come *on,* Michael," it's in a gutsy, impatient voice that
only she would dare to use.

Visually, *Godfather III* is disappointingly soft and dark;
it's so toned in to the earlier films that it seems to belong
to a brown past. (The processing must be at fault: the film
looks as if it were already on TV.) The core colors of the
three movies come through in the blood-red silks and vel-
vets, burnished dark wood, and gold details of the opera-
house scenes in Sicily, where Anthony makes his début as
the tenor in *Cavalleria Rusticana.* This Sicilian opera about
La Vendetta represents where the saga of the Corleones began, when young Vito's parents were murdered. And while
the music goes on, a series of assassinations is carried out—
an echo of the assassinations that ended the first film. The
picture might have had some fresh wit if we'd seen that now
that the Corleones were in the legitimate business world
they had lawyers do their dirty deeds. Instead, it's the same
old bang-bang, and this time there's no horror in the bloodshed—only grandiosity. (You may not even be quite sure
who's doing what, or why.) When Michael has his big scene
on the steps of the opera house, with a prolonged silent
scream and then an actual scream, we don't experience his
agony. His later, final moment seems just an addendum, a
mistake.

There's no conviction in Michael's atonement, and none
in Vincent's fire, either. *Godfather III* looks like a *Godfather* movie, but it's not about revenge and it's not about
passion and power and survival. It's about a battered moviemaker's king-size depression.

The Bonfire of the Vanities

Brian De Palma walked right off a cliff when he made his version of the Tom Wolfe novel *The Bonfire of the Vanities*. Other movies about the political circus surrounding a criminal trial (movies such as *His Girl Friday* and *Roxie Hart*) encouraged us to sympathize with the innocent defendant. In the Wolfe novel—a satirical exposé of how democracy works in New York in the eighties—the rich, seemingly secure Wasp Sherman McCoy is caught in the justice system. He and his mistress, in his Mercedes, hit a young black man; as a result, pressure groups, politicians, and newspapermen are out to get him, and they break him. But if the movie allowed us to feel a natural empathy with McCoy it would violate Wolfe's deliberately heartless, mocking tone. So De Palma tries for a rollicking impersonality. Intending to use the big city as a flamboyant comedy set, he comes up with an expressionist stylization of the Preston Sturges conniption-fit comedies: exaggeratedly large rooms, high and low perspectives, and people looming in the shots. At times, the décor suggests the super-artificial scene designs in *A Clockwork Orange*. It's ingenious; there's clever thinking behind it. And it's a fizzle. The movie has a shrill sprightliness; it's like a sci-fi version of a loud, over-bright screwball comedy.

Bonfire has a throwaway quality: bizarre, glittering things go by so quickly they don't take time to salute themselves. At the beginning, there's a splendiferous view looking down on Manhattan from the wing of a gargoyle on the Chrysler Building. And then, in a showpiece tracking, Steadicam shot that goes on for five minutes, elevator doors open and close at the instant required; the precision is the gag, but it misses being really funny because it's *too* precise. It's ahead of us. All through the movie, De Palma's timing is off, as if his instincts had gone on holiday. You feel a kind of fanaticism in his directing: he's planned everything—it's an exercise in wrong-headed style.

The picture grates on your nerves: you sit there listening to Melanie Griffith's metallic whine and you watch Bruce Willis fail at the simple task of playing a comic drunk. These are talented people—what's happened to them? Just about everybody in the cast seems keyed up too high. Tom Hanks (as Sherman McCoy), Morgan Freeman, F. Murray Abraham, Kim Cattrall, John Hancock—they all seem caught in a frenzied competition to overdo everything.

Hanks has his moments. When McCoy, at his brokerage firm, stands preening, with his chest flung out, he looks fit and invulnerable—a newly hatched fool. After his arrest, his face is frozen; he smiles inappropriately—a sickly, terrified smile. But the picture slights his being put behind bars and how he's affected; the scenes are fast and hysterical, without momentum. So the central episode of the story doesn't sink in, and there's no satirical fun in McCoy's terror. We don't really get to see that all the elements in the city which he, in his smugness, has ignored—the full range of people on the make—are using him to advance their careers.

The movie has two points of view, and they don't jibe. In the final courtroom scene, Freeman, as the judge, makes a speech that shames the political operators and agitators, and brings them to their senses. The movie descends to Capraesque sincerity at this point, so we have to assume that it's the message we're to take home. But Willis, as the tabloid journalist who exploits McCoy's predicament, is the cynical narrator, and he's the winner—he profiteers on a profiteering decade. Literary prizes are lavished on his book about the case, and we're supposed to find this swine's triumph ironic and hilarious. A subway scene where he gets to know McCoy and recognizes what he's done to him has no follow-through; effective scenes with Richard Libertini, Robert Stephens, André Gregory, and Alan King don't add up to enough. Whatever one's feelings about the Wolfe novel (I disliked it), it works. Michael Cristofer's thin script doesn't; it's as if he had been hired to make the worst adaptation that could be made. And the score, by Dave Grusin, never clues you in; totally distanced from the action, it's in some tinkling world of its own.

De Palma, who showed a genius for sophomoric comedy in his youth, had already made his *Bonfire of the Vanities*. It was the daring race-relations jamboree *Hi, Mom!* (1970). And he made a slapstick rock-musical *Bonfire* called *Phantom of the Paradise* (1974). You see that crazy-house bravura here in the swirling overhead shots and *Dr. Strangelove, Touch of Evil* camerawork, in the love of visual detail, in the intricate patterning of tiles and bricks. But the story is overwhelmed by a style that's meant to be dizzyingly aggressive. What's missing is the shock and offensiveness that could give the commotion some point. The picture keeps pulling back from the true outrageousness of borderline racist humor—the only thing that could save it. That was what gave the novel its hostile charge. Without that, not only does the movie miss the target, you don't know what the target is.

JANUARY 14, 1991

THE DOCTOR
AND THE
DIRECTOR

Awakenings

The neurologist Oliver Sacks is a supremely odd and complicated man. This bearded giant, a motorcyclist, a fern lover, and a weight lifter (who has been known to squat-press six hundred pounds), has a passionate curiosity about people. Born in London, in 1933, of physician parents who trained in neurology, and with two older brothers who became physicians, he grew up in a household where everybody swapped medical stories, and he has developed the clinical case study into an art form. Published as collections of essays, his narratives about his patients are speculative, exploratory, and maybe a little mad. He's drawn into his patients' aberrant states—he sees their abnormalities as brilliantly unique forms of consciousness to be charted—and, as he attempts to interpret them, he's drawn in further and further. He never closes off a subject; he goes on raising more possibilities, and his emotional essays sprout footnotes—excursions into ideas he's trying out. Reading him, you're absorbed in the play of his mind. (You may suspect that he is, too—that he's half bewildered by himself.) He probably makes more outré reaches of the imagination than any other essayist, and you might think you were reading freak-show detective stories if it weren't for the transforming power of his childlike sincerity and his tough-mindedness. Following him down a byway in a footnote, you think, This is loony, and then, as you read more of the tiny print, it doesn't seem so farfetched—it seems marvellously plausible. You entertain the idea, conscious that his interests are encyclopedic and he could go on footnoting forever.

A few months before the literary critic Anatole Broyard died last year, he wrote, "My ideal doctor . . . would resemble Oliver Sacks. . . . I can imagine Dr. Sacks *entering* my condition, looking around at it from the inside like a benevolent landlord with a tenant, trying to see how he could make the premises more livable for me. He would see the genius of my illness. He would mingle his daemon with mine; we would wrestle with my fate together."

Sacks is like a mythological physician: part philosopher, part medicine man—a specialist in illnesses so peculiar that they double as miracles. His 1983 essay *The Man Who Mistook His Wife for a Hat* (it came out in book form in 1985) was turned into an opera, and the opera was turned into a movie. His 1973 book, *Awakenings,* about administering a drug that woke up patients who had been frozen in apathy for decades, inspired poems and stories, and was the basis for a remarkable 1974 documentary by Yorkshire Television and for several radio and stage adaptations, including Harold Pinter's 1982 one-act play *A Kind of Alaska.*

The new, Hollywood *Awakenings,* directed by Penny Marshall, who made *Big,* is far from a terrible movie. Marshall is talented and persuasive; she understands tone and pace. But her talent is to work the audience. There's an underlying conflict between Marshall, who comes from a show-business family, and Sacks, the fabulist of illness. She exalts the normal, and she keeps zapping us to feel the humanistic, the obvious. (Her forte is to make blandness ring true.) The producers sent her the script before she'd read the book, and the scriptwriter, Steven Zaillian, had prepared the way for her approach by turning Sacks' tragicomedy of brainsickness into a do-gooding synthesis of three Academy Award winners: *Charly, One Flew Over the Cuckoo's Nest,* and *Rain Man.*

In the years between 1916 and 1927, during and after the flu epidemic that affected half the world's population, there was also an international epidemic of encephalitis lethargica—virus-borne sleeping sickness—which took or blighted the lives of about five million people. Some of the survivors recovered but later developed an advanced form of Parkinson's disease, with tremors and tics and twisted, bent-over bodies, and they relapsed into a vegetative state and remained nearly motionless and speechless for decades. In 1966, Oliver Sacks, who had trained in medicine at Oxford and in London, and had moved to this country in 1960, began working in a Bronx hospital for the chronically ill, where there were about eighty of these "living statues." In the spring and summer of 1969, he gave them L-dopa, which had previously been given only for ordinary, mild Parkinson's.

The book *Awakenings* is Sacks' account of how the individual patients—twenty in particular—responded. It's about their exuberance when they woke from their trances, and then their anguish when they recognized that they were in their fifties and sixties, and their lives had been used up, and it's about their confusion when each reacted to L-dopa differently and they ran into what Sacks calls "radical trouble." Some of them went quite mad, and in agitated ways. In an epilogue that appears in the expanded 1983 edition and in the further expanded 1990 edition, Sacks includes follow-up material on their subsequent ordeals. It's an unbelievably rich story. Sacks makes you feel how much is at stake for each one of them. You feel how trapped they are in their uncontrollable bodies.

In the movie, Sacks has turned into Dr. Sayer (Robin Williams)—kind but sweetly inept and distant from everyone. Sacks' eccentricities have been used as the homey, lovable foibles of a movie genius circa Paul Muni. (Dr. Sayer is always fumbling to make a note on his hand or his sleeve, because he doesn't remember to carry a pad of paper; he panics about where his glasses are when they're on his nose; his shirttails hang out; and so on.) You'd think you were going to get the story of a humble scientist who makes a great discovery; that's the model for much of the movie. Dr. Sayer's intuition tells him that the statues are "alive inside"—a possibility that other doctors reject—and he finds ways to prove it. When he sees a Ouija board at the hospital, he's struck by an idea: he gives one to a benumbed patient, Leonard (Robert De Niro), and Leonard taps out a reference to Rilke's lines about the caged panther.

The movie's Leonard is the test case—the first one to be given L-dopa. When he awakens, he seems to be a quiet, average sort of fellow—not the kind of man who'd quote Rilke, or anybody else. The poetic allusion is a tattered remnant from Sacks's case history, which tells us that though Leonard's post-encephalitic disease began when he was fifteen, he graduated from Harvard and was finishing his Ph.D. thesis when he became so incapacitated he couldn't go on. He was hospitalized in a nearly petrified state when he was thirty, but, with the help of his mother, he had gone on reading; he could make tiny voluntary movements with one hand, and he used an alphabet board to turn out book reviews for the hospital magazine. There was no mystery about whether he was "alive inside"—he'd been tapping out his side of literary conversations with Sacks for several years before he took L-dopa. (Sacks described Leonard's book reviews as showing "a vital, humorous, and at times Rabelaisian relish for the world.")

On being physically liberated, De Niro's Leonard doesn't

exhibit the hyperbolic joy of Sacks' Leonard, who speaks in "a loud and clear voice" and is suddenly "drunk on reality." De Niro's Leonard has a genteel romance with Paula (Penelope Ann Miller), a lovely young woman who comes to the hospital to visit her paralyzed father; this courtly Leonard is nothing like Sacks' Leonard, who within a few weeks of awakening had formed an image of himself as "a Dionysiac god packed with virility and power" and had "started to masturbate—fiercely, freely and with little concealment—for hours each day." In the movie, after a frenzied paranoid phase and the return of his tremors and tics, Leonard feels himself reverting to helplessness, and, eager to help others, he calls to the doctor to photograph what's happening, and exhorts him, "Learn from me! Learn. . . ." This bears some relation to a passage in a fifty-thousand-word autobiography that Sacks' Leonard had typed out during a three-week high. He'd written, "I am a living candle. I am consumed that you may learn. New things will be seen in the light of my suffering." But that was euphoria. In the later editions of *Awakenings* Sacks documents Leonard's last days, when he was ill and emaciated and, after twelve years of experiments with L-dopa and other drugs that failed, he was once again given L-dopa. Sacks writes, "I was in the clinic when the ward phoned to say that Leonard had 'come to.' Astounded, and fearful, I rushed to his bed. He had an enormous voice now, and he yelled his soul out: 'Hell and damnation! Fucking DOPA, fucking miracle. Look at me now—I'm falling apart. I'm dying, almost dead, and *now* you resurrect me with L-DOPA! This is a *stinking* miracle—obscene—a lot worse than Lazarus. . . . For Christ's sake stop it, and let me die in peace.' I stopped it, of course, and let him be."

The movie douses everything fiery. Everything is shaped for you to root for the resurrections, and then nothing much happens. Even the flapper salaciousness that a little old woman in the book had preserved from the twenties is gone. The humanism is so pallid that the awakened patients don't seem very different from the way they were in their coma-tose states. Though the movie medium would make it pos-sible for a series of awakenings over days and weeks to be edited together so that we could have a short spell alone with each of the film's roughly fifteen patients, and a chance to respond to the rhythmic variations of how they come to speak and move, the moviemakers chose to falsify what happened and have the whole troupe awakening at the same time. They're a blur, with famous performers, such as Anne Meara and Judith Malina and Dexter Gordon, turning up like special guest sleepers.

After raising the false question "Are they alive inside?," the movie doesn't really answer it—doesn't make it clear if, when they were thought to be braindead, they actually knew what was going on around them and were cognizant of rough treatment or neglect. (When awakened, did they recognize the people who'd been caring for them?) Paula, the woman whom Leonard develops the crush on, says that she doesn't know if her father (who's had a stroke) is con-scious of her visits; Leonard tells her, "He knows. Your fa-ther. He knows you visit him." But it seems as if Leonard is just reassuring her. (He's not an expert on strokes; we're being fobbed off.) In Sacks' account, the torpid patients are aware in dreamlike ways, and their symptoms reflect what's happening to them in the hospital. The movie is less inter-ested in the interior life of the "frozen" patients than in setting up a symmetrical plot pattern: the awakened patients may regress to a stuporous despair, but Dr. Sayer awakens—i.e., he loses his fear of human contact. Could anyone think there was an equivalence here?

This is another of Robin Williams' benevolent-eunuch roles. He's the good man here, as he was in *Good Morning, Vietnam* and *Dead Poets Society,* and he does a fine job of it: he shows the warmth and reticence and empathy that Dr. Sayer needs. Sayer needs something else, though, in order to be a real character: some ruthlessness, perhaps, or more ego-tism—something to keep him from being a noble fud. And

Williams shouldn't have to hold himself in like this. He'd better move on, before he turns into the movies' permanent winsome messiah. As the head nurse, who breaks through to Dr. Sayer, Julie Kavner has something of Peggy Ashcroft's transcendent plainness. She doesn't overdo her fluky inflections or her comedy timing; with almost no material, and with a role that's an embarrassment, she gives the best performance in the movie. Yet Penny Marshall can't help herself; she's a cajoler. Knowing that Kavner is the real thing, she still uses her to touch us and touch us and touch us.

As for De Niro—well, when you're playing a silent, somnolent person who wakes up and soon afterward erupts into madness, you certainly give the impression that you're acting. Twitching and shaking (impressively), De Niro is upping the ante on Dustin Hoffman's autistic savant in *Rain Man.* This is not a field of acting that commands respect. In *My Left Foot,* Daniel Day-Lewis played the arrogant sensualist inside the deformed body; that's not the kind of thing De Niro is doing. He's giving you an actor's idea of a decent guy who'll be appealing to people. There's the smile of happy complicity between Dr. Sayer and the awakened Leonard. There's Leonard, on his feet, opening his arms to greet his mother. (You may never be able to scrape off Randy Newman's syrupy "awakening" music.) When Leonard is coming apart and says goodbye to Paula—to his dream of a normal life—she dances with him in the cafeteria, without music, and her nearness to him keeps him peaceful. The scene is performed with great tact; we're being pressured by that tact. And when Leonard, writhing with jerks and tics, goes back to the ward and, from behind the grate on the window, watches Paula go down the street, his symbolic imprisonment—once again the caged panther—is simply more than we need. Mostly, the too-muchness is Marshall's, but sometimes it's clearly De Niro's. When he holds out his arms to his mother, he knows he's a poster boy.

Of course, we're affected by people coming to active life

after decades of stillness—how could we not be? But this forced banalizing of our emotions is show-business shtick. The patients don't exist except as fodder for pathos.

The movie is all about the doctor being a caring individual. Oliver Sacks, who's sensitized to prodigious kinds of experience, is turned into an absent-minded professor banging his head. The movie is at its most nakedly manipulative in another cafeteria scene where, just after Leonard has revived, Dr. Sayer pleads for the money to give L-dopa to the fifteen remaining post-encephalitic patients, and his supervisor (John Heard) says it would cost more than he's got. Overhearing this, the head nurse comes over to their table and hands the boss her personal check, and then the other nurses and the orderlies come over and hand him their personal and payroll checks. It's Dickensian, and Marshall, who values a warm huggy, pushes it further. The supervisor sets up a meeting with the hospital benefactors; they look at film of Leonard before and after, and when they (simultaneously) start writing checks Dr. Sayer's eyes fill. He's shilling for us to cry.

Sacks was technical adviser on the production, and in the latest edition of the book (it keeps growing, like a journal) he includes a description of the making of the movie. This piece of puffery mars the book, but it's invaluable as an example of the higher self-deception. Sacks wants to dissociate himself from the script's inventions without damning them. And so he writes, "There was a fine dramatic ending which moved me as I read it, even though, factually, it was completely untrue," and "While in some ways [the script] aimed at a very close reconstruction of how things had been, it also introduced a plot, several plots, which were entirely new. But I saw that this was necessary, and I liked many of the dramatic inventions (though I had reservations about the creation of a violent psychiatric ward . . .)." He writes about guiding the director and Robin Williams and De Niro to various hospitals where they could obseve the patients and talk to them, and he expresses his awe of De Niro for mastering the symptoms of Parkinson's. And then he writes, of watching the mass awakening being shot, "What was overwhelming for me was the *truth* of this scene. Steve Zaillian had invented it, but he had invented it right." Philosopher, ideal doctor, sucker.

Sleeping with the Enemy

In *Sleeping with the Enemy,* Julia Roberts doesn't have the vivid big grin that gave last year's *Pretty Woman* its spark. She has been turned into a blank goddess; she's touching, at moments, yet the way the camera fawns on her she could be posing for stills. She plays a frightened young wife who fakes her death and changes her identity to escape her rich husband (Patrick Bergin), a psychopathic perfectionist. Julia Roberts is an incredible object—you can at least see why a perfectionist would want to hang on to her. But, watching her as she innocently digs clams on Cape Cod, you may have premonitions of dullness. And when she escapes her posh, sterile beach house and takes on her new identity in Cedar Falls, Iowa, the wholesome town where she feels at home, she's happily caught up in a Fourth of July celebration, and then—our cup runneth over—she gets to go to a carnival. When she agrees to have dinner with a sincere young man (Kevin Anderson) who teaches drama at a local college, she arrives to find he's burned the roast. Do men in the movies always have to burn the dinner so we'll know they're straight?

You might expect the plot to have a few surprise twists, but the script, by Ronald Bass, out of a novel by Nancy Price, is one letdown after another. Joseph Ruben, who directed, has proved himself a smart tease and trickster; he's brought off three thrillers in a row—*Dreamscape* (1984), *The Stepfather* (1987), and *True Believer* (1989). And he does a smooth job here, with snappy editing every time there's a cut to the enraged husband on the wife's trail. But a lousy piece of music well conducted doesn't get you very far.

The whole movie is spent waiting for the husband to arrive. Meanwhile, we look at Julia trying on outfits in the college theatre's costume room. *Sleeping with the Enemy* is a glossy combination of secondhand showing-off-Julia scenes from *Pretty Woman* and secondhand scares from *The Stepfather*. A little tawdriness would have helped. I was reminded of Roy Blount's

> Blondes who don't go far enough,
> *Film* that isn't *noir* enough.

L.A. Story

The jokes in *L.A. Story* spin by as if choreographed by summer breezes. Carl Reiner has been heard to say of Steve Martin, "There's a mysterious man in there who comes out when he writes his own scripts." On the evidence of *L.A. Story,* which Martin wrote and stars in, it's a mysteriously happy man. Maybe Martin couldn't have written this autobiographical fantasy if Woody Allen hadn't made *Annie Hall* and *Manhattan,* but what he loves about L.A. is what Allen rejected it for: its pleasure-loving, materialistic irresponsibleness. Allen sees moral lightness as immorality, as evil; he didn't ever seem to get the humor of L.A.

Martin's movie is a take on *Annie Hall* that turns it inside out. His attitudes are close to the ones that Paul Mazursky developed, starting with the script of *I Love You, Alice B.*

Toklas! and running through his whole series of L.A. movies: *Bob & Carol & Ted & Alice, Alex in Wonderland, Blume in Love,* and *Down and Out in Beverly Hills.* Mazursky was a New Yorker, but he fell in love with the loop-the-loopiness of L.A.—he didn't fight the pleasure or crab at it. For Martin, who grew up in Southern California, superficiality is the norm. *L.A. Story* is totally inconsequential, and he accepts that—it doesn't bother him. He isn't afraid of silliness. And that's what makes the movie such a light-headed joyride for an audience.

As Harris K. Telemacher, a clowning TV weatherman, Martin is split between his wonder-struck obsession with a British journalist, played by Victoria Tennant (in an Annie Hall hat), and the carefree high of sex without love, represented by a bouncy nymph played by Sarah Jessica Parker. That's all there is, really—that and the jokes and the atmosphere and a batch of sharp performers (Rick Moranis uncredited, Marilu Henner as a tough dame with a cold stare, Susan Forristal as Martin's pal, M. C. Shan as a waiter-rapper, and Richard E. Grant, Kevin Pollak, and Patrick Stewart, among others). What keeps most of it airy and tingling is the artfulness of the director, the English TV ace Mick Jackson (who's best known here for his mini-series *A Very British Coup,* starring Ray McAnally), and the talents of the cinematographer, Andrew Dunn; the editor, Richard A. Harris; and Peter Melnick, who provided a funny, lilting score.

Sometimes the jokes aren't fresh: there's a particularly long, dull one about a painting. And things don't move fast enough toward the end. I think that's because Martin, an old-fashioned romantic at heart, doesn't see that Sarah Jessica Parker, twirling around him, her long, curly hair like eiderdown, is the natural heroine of an L.A. movie. She's the spirit of L.A.: she keeps saying yes.

FEBRUARY 11, 1991

Index

329